**Migration in
Post-War Europe**

D0293723

Migration in Post-War Europe

Geographical Essays

Edited by
JOHN SALT
and
HUGH CLOUT

OXFORD UNIVERSITY PRESS
1976

Oxford University Press, Ely House, London W.1

OXFORD LONDON GLASGOW NEW YORK
TORONTO MELBOURNE WELLINGTON CAPE TOWN
IBADAN NAIROBI DAR ES SALAAM LUSAKA ADDIS ABABA
KUALA LUMPUR SINGAPORE JAKARTA HONG KONG TOKYO
DELHI BOMBAY CALCUTTA MADRAS KARACHI

CASEBOUND ISBN 0 19 874027 1
PAPERBACK ISBN O 19 874028 x

*Set in Great Britain by Campbell Graphics
and printed by Whitstable Litho Ltd.*

Preface

This book originated from our conviction that the role of long-distance migration in changing the population map of Europe over the past thirty years was incompletely recorded and relatively little understood. Our interest in this aspect of the migration process coincided with a widening concern for European affairs, especially in view of the enlargement of the European Economic Community. Because of the diversity of the Continent—particularly the division between East and West—and the complexity of the migration process we chose to examine selected themes only and enlisted the co-operation of two other authors.

Many people have helped in the preparation of this book and we wish to express our thanks to each of them. The maps and diagrams were drawn by members of the Cartographic Unit in the Department of Geography at University College London under the supervision of the Chief Technician, Ken Wass. The majority were drawn by Tina Hill and Richard Bryant. Our thanks go to them especially, to Chris Cromarty and to members of the secretarial staff. However, the authors alone bear responsibility for the opinions expressed.

University College London
June 1975.

JOHN SALT
HUGH CLOUT

Contents

List of figures

List of tables

INTRODUCTION

Since 1945 Europe has undoubtedly been a continent on the move, its inhabitants probably experiencing a greater degree of spatial mobility than ever before. That mobility has taken on many forms; some have been in response to the general evolution of national economies and societies, others have acted as stimuli or contributory causes for fundamental social, economic, and political changes.

The movement of people from place to place in the peaceful years since 1945 has been of crucial importance in fashioning the human geography of Europe in the second half of the 1970s. Problems of backward rural regions, declining industrial zones, depopulating urban cores, and dynamic metropolitan areas are all associated, in one way or another, with human migration, as are the social and economic hardships experienced by members of the many 'newcomer' groups that have arrived in Western Europe in such great numbers since World War II.

It is clear that not only the volume but also the direction and composition of European migration streams have varied significantly with the passage of time, so that 'cycles' of flow and 'stages' in migratory evolution may be recognized. For example, at the close of World War II some countries, such as the United Kingdom, were already highly urbanized, but others, especially in eastern and southern Europe, were much less advanced along the 'ladder' of urbanization. Not surprisingly, regional trends in migration in recent decades have reflected the stages of economic and social development that had been reached in the various parts of the continent by 1945 as well as the speed and direction of change that have been accomplished since then.

The aim of this book is to elucidate the role of selected aspects of migration in regional change in Europe since 1945. In doing so the emphasis is placed on recording the spatial patterns of migration and understanding its nature rather than describing in detail the many changes in regional conditions to which migration has contributed. Thus it is with the migrants, moving within and between the nations of Europe (and indeed coming from nearby non-European countries), that the extended essays that make up this book are concerned. How many people are involved? Where do they come from? Where do they move to? Why do they migrate? What jobs do they take? How do they settle in? What effects does their migration have on the regions they leave behind and on those they move into? It is our intention that the chapters that follow, dealing with selected migration themes, should cast some light into the many dark corners of such questions. But it must be stressed that the survey attempted is a partial one. By no means all of the important problems posed by migration will be tackled let alone those of smaller consequence. There will be no attempt to provide a general synthesis.

Various approaches to the study of human migration have been developed

1

over the years. The main theoretical framework for analysis, at the macro-level, has been provided by the discipline of economics. Classical and neo-classical economists have traditionally adopted an equilibrium approach, although more recently various disequilibrium models have been put forward (Lind, 1969). For the most part economic theory has assumed homogeneity and perfect mobility among the potentially migrant population. As a result, attention has been focused primarily on differences between origin and destination areas in accounting for patterns of movement.

Such an approach assumes that all would-be migrants react in a similar fashion to stimuli that might encourage movement. Since World War II an increasing number of micro-scale studies by sociologists and other social scientists have adopted a behavioural approach. Instead of relying on broad areal differences to account for patterns of movement, attention has recently been directed to differences in the migration behaviour of groups in society. Migration has come to be appreciated as a social process, with individuals and families evaluating a range of criteria in making the decision to move or stay. It is true that a number of general reasons for moving emerge from many studies and these can reasonably be used to 'explain' patterns of movement, but it is necessary to disaggregate the migrant population into its constituent groups in order to achieve *really* satisfactory levels of explanation. Empirical studies have shown that decisions relating to moving may well reflect the norms and values of particular groups in society, rather than just the differences that exist between areas.

Much, of course, depends on the scale of inquiry that is adopted. In studying a large and complicated network of migration flows of varying types, as attempted in this book, it is necessary to simplify reality in order to reduce the problem to manageable proportions. Geographers have worked at various levels of generalization. These tend to be 'intermediate' in scale, concerned with groups of varying sizes rather than with individuals, and emphasize the spatial dimension of human migration. The essays in this book bear witness to such a preoccupation with space, as attempts are made to identify the specific origin and destination areas of migrants, to plot the channels and precise volumes of movement involved, and to trace how and why distinctive patterns of migration have become established since 1945 and have subsequently evolved. Attention is paid to the implications of migration for reception and departure regions, which in themselves not only display a great variety of conditions but are also experiencing a complicated, interrelated set of social and economic changes in which the precise role of migration is frequently uncertain. In conceptual terms it may be clear that migration can both initiate change in the human geography of an area and also respond to regional changes that have been caused by other factors; in practice it is often very difficult to disentangle cause from effect. In addition, attempts are made in the following essays to identify characteristics that not only differentiate 'movers' from 'stayers' but also distinguish one migrant group from another, and thus contribute to a wide range of distinctive patterns of movement. It should be noted that as well as involving shifts of population between areas, migration also encompasses the exchange of ideas between resident and migrant groups and between different migrant groups and may thus encourage a tendency towards greater uniformity in social norms and values over ever-widening areas. Many people feel that social life in Europe is losing some of its internal differentiation and it is our belief that migration has been a major contributory process in this respect.

The objectives of identifying and explaining migration flows are difficult to achieve for a number of reasons. Admittedly information has improved in recent years, but data sets relating to migration in many European countries are still very imprecise reflections of reality; they vary in quality, availability, and reliability, and relate to differing periods of time. As Fielding (1975) has shown, annual registers of internal migration are kept in some countries; in others precise questions on migration are asked in population censuses; in a final group of countries it is necessary to rely on the so-called 'residual method', whereby natural change (births minus deaths) is subtracted from total population change in order to identify net migration. Such problems are serious enough in studying migration within individual countries, but become particularly grave when attempts are made to examine flows between countries. However, it is to this growing international dimension in migration that at least some of the recent improvements in statistical inquiry must be attributed. Immigration and emigration are very much themes of public concern and as such now need to be recorded with a fair degree of accuracy.

In spite of deficiencies of data and other problems, one may appreciate that contemporary Europe displays a great variety of migration flows, which may be classified in a number of ways. These range from short-distance daily commuting movements (which in some parts of the continent may comprise flows across national frontiers), and weekly flows to second homes; through longer-distance seasonal movements to holiday areas, and short-distance residential moves out into suburbia; to relatively long-distance inter-regional and international flows of a permanent or quasi-permanent nature. When they undergo long-distance movements, which are usually associated with a change of employment as well as of home, migrants experience varying degrees of 'uprooting' from their home environment. It is this element of change in basic activity patterns of migrants, with important implications for regional economic and social well-being, that seems to distinguish long distance flows from all the other types of movement. Undoubtedly the other flows mentioned above and the departure of Europeans to distant destinations, such as Australia or the United States of America, are also of great significance to contemporary Europe. Certainly they have generated a large and distinctive amount of research literature. However, they lie beyond the scope of the present book, which concentrates exclusively on long-distance flows within the migration systems of Western and Eastern Europe.

These long-distance streams of migration in Europe have been subject to various types of encouragement and control, which differ from country to country and, of course, have changed with the passage of time. For example, in the face of growing shortages of labour, resulting from falling rates of natural increase and rising rates of economic growth, numerous contracts for international labour migration have been signed in recent years. In addition, attempts at international co-operation and economic integration in Europe have reduced the role of political frontiers as barriers to movement. Admittedly the descent of the Iron Curtain across the continent has effectively created two broad systems of migration, but, as will be seen in later chapters, these systems are no longer entirely separate. In addition, within countries, spatial variations in income and opportunities have led to various types of regional planning policies which in turn have had their influence on migration.

Long-distance movement primarily associated with employment thus forms the substance of this book. Individual chapters examine key themes in which the contributors have particular expertise. These themes are illustrated with reference to appropriate countries. Authors have not attempted to present a standardized, Europe-wide view. Indeed, data deficiencies render such a task impossible, no matter how desirable it might be. Instead, they have chosen to work within the confines of the broad migration systems that operate on either side of the Iron Curtain. Thus, after a brief examination of Europe's demographic changes in the twentieth century, four chapters are devoted to migration themes affecting the countries of Western Europe (plus territories that supply migrants to them). A final, lengthy chapter discusses aspects of migration in the less familiar context of Eastern Europe and its component countries. Our working definitions of 'Europe' and 'European migration systems' have in fact been drawn in such a way as to exclude the U.S.S.R. but to permit an examination of conditions in the Maghreb states and in Turkey which are important suppliers of migrant labour to continental north-west Europe.

Flows of population from the countryside to the town form the first theme for discussion. In the highly urbanized and mobile societies of north-west Europe, with their spatially dispersed forms of city living and their reverse flows of city people who choose to live in the countryside, such rural—urban movements are now much less significant than they were in the past. By contrast, migration from the countryside is still relatively clear cut and involves large numbers of people in the countries of southern and eastern Europe that occupy a number of less urbanized 'rungs' on the 'ladder' of economic development. The second theme is the migration that occurs between urban regions. Such flows are highly developed in the United Kingdom and are of growing importance in the countries of continental north-west Europe, yet they have been little studied. The urbanized, industrial nations have also attracted large numbers of international labour migrants from a very wide range of sources during the past quarter-century. As well as giving rise to political and cultural problems, which have been examined in various studies in recent years, such movements have had important economic and social implications for both reception and departure areas. The nature of and reasons for this movement combine to form the third major theme. Finally, a variety of recent migration trends are scrutinized in detail in the countries of Eastern Europe.

We hope that the essays in this collection may not only permit a better appreciation of selected aspects of Europe's migration systems but may also present information to elucidate some of the fundamental changes that have occurred in the continent's human geography since 1945.

References

Fielding, A. J. (1975) 'Internal migration in Western Europe', in Kosiński, L. A., and Prothero, R. M. (eds.), *People on the Move*, Methuen, London, pp. 237—54.
Lind, H. (1969) 'Internal migration in Britain', in Jackson, J. A., *Migration*, Cambridge University Press, pp. 74—98.

1. THE DEMOGRAPHIC BACKGROUND

HUGH CLOUT AND JOHN SALT

European overview

The twentieth century has been an important period of change in the population geography of Europe. Not only has growth in human numbers continued, albeit at a slowing rate, but marked redistributions of population have occurred. The incidence and repercussions of two major wars have had significant effects on population structure which persist in some areas to the present day. The progress of the 'demographic transition', moving broadly south- and eastwards across the continent, has been marked by varying rates of natural increase and by a changed relationship between population and resources. In particular, economic growth and the spread of industrialization, especially since World War II, have led to major shifts in population in response to the changing location of economic activity.

This chapter describes briefly the main demographic changes that have taken place in Europe during the twentieth century, and especially since World War II. The level of analysis is aggregated, although there is some discussion of regional variations within countries in selected aspects of population distribution and change. The aim of the chapter is to provide a general demographic context for the subsequent essays, and also to discuss briefly some aspects of international migration, especially those connected with wars and political changes, that are not taken up later in the book. In discussing the demographic situation at the national level, both Eastern and Western European countries will be reviewed. However, more attention will be paid to the latter, especially when regional situations are examined. The reason for this is twofold. Firstly, most of the book is concerned with non-Communist Europe and it is therefore appropriate to devote most attention to the West. Secondly, and more pragmatically, regional data comparable with those for Western Europe are difficult to obtain for Iron Curtain countries.

The pace and pattern of demographic change in modern Europe owe much to political realities. Some countries, particularly France and most countries in Eastern Europe, have followed vigorous pro-natalist policies. Elsewhere, especially in the United Kingdom, disquiet has been voiced about the implications of current rates of growth. As a consequence governments have introduced measures, usually in the form of family planning availability, to reduce rates of increase. Countries have also adopted measures designed to control or halt international migration, with the Iron Curtain being the extreme and most important example. Most Western European governments have also adopted regional policies, primarily geared to economic development and using a variety of policy tools, but all ultimately designed to influence internal distribution of population.

During the nineteenth century and the early part of the twentieth, population growth in Europe was rapid and especially so in the western countries. From early in the nineteenth century mortality rates declined steadily, the retreat of death gaining momentum in the face of advances in medicine and hygiene. Falls in fertility rate lagged and population increased at a rate hitherto unrecorded. Inevitably there was demographic pressure in some areas and migration overseas was a frequent response. Europe started the twentieth century with its demographic transition far from complete. In most of the north and west peak rates of natural increase had been passed but in the south and east falls in fertility still lagged way behind those in mortality. As the century progressed, Europe's population continued to grow, but especially since World War II its rate of increase has fallen behind that of much of the rest of the world. In 1900, Europe's 300,000,000 people (excluding Russia) represented about 18 per cent of the world's population; by 1972, numbers had risen to 474,000,000, but the continent's share of the world population had fallen to 12 per cent. Over the same period, Europe's rate of increase (63 per cent) was less than half of that of the world as a whole (135 per cent). This disparity between European and world growth rates has been particularly marked since World War II. Between 1950 and 1972 Europe's growth rate was 21 per cent compared with 54 per cent for the world. During the 1960s the number of Europeans increased by only 0·8 per cent per annum, but rates of over three times that were recorded for Africa (2·5 per cent) and South America (2·7 per cent), well ahead of the world average of 2 per cent per annum.

Inevitably, calculations of population increase at the aggregate European scale hide significant national and regional variations. Despite differing political ideologies and attitudes to economic development, both Eastern and Western Europe had similar increases in their over-all population—18 per cent—in the 1950s and 1960s. The range for individual countries was wide: of those increasing their population, Albania had the highest rate of growth (+78 per cent) and Austria the lowest (+7 per cent). In fact not all countries did increase their numbers and East Germany and the Republic of Ireland both experienced net losses. Growth well above the European average involved countries on either side of the Iron Curtain, namely Iceland (50 per cent), Switzerland (34 per cent), Poland (32 per cent), Netherlands (29 per cent), Yugoslavia (26 per cent), West Germany and Romania (24 per cent), and France (22 per cent). Most of these countries owed the bulk of their recent growth to natural increase, although immigration was of great importance in Switzerland and West Germany, as was repatriation in France and the Netherlands.

When regional rates of change are examined, it is apparent that during the 1960s high rates of increase in Western Europe occurred in the economic core zone from South-East England through the Rhinelands to Northern Italy (Biraben, Peron, and Nizard, 1964; Pressat, Biraben, and Duhourcau, 1973). However, the highest increases (over 30 per cent) were in the urbanized areas around Barcelona, Bilbao, Copenhagen, and Oslo (Fig. 1.1).[1] By contrast, population declined in peripheral and predominantly agricultural parts of Western Europe including sections of Southern Italy, Iberia, Ireland, the eastern frontier area of West Germany, Scotland, and the Norden countries, with the Massif Central and the Po Valley also standing out as 'islands' of loss.

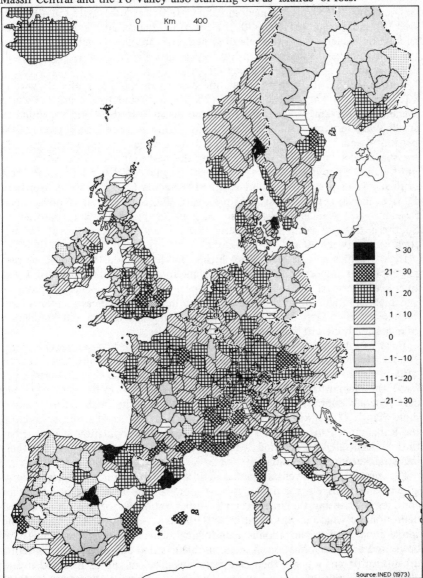

1.1 Western Europe: population change, 1961–1971 (after Pressat *et al.* 1973).

The slowing rate of increase in European population over all is reflected in the 'league table' of populous nations. By 1972, West Germany, with 59,600,000 inhabitants, was the only European representative in the 'top ten' most populous countries in the world, coming in eighth position. Three other European states were close behind: United Kingdom (55,800,000, eleventh), Italy (54,400,000, twelfth) and France (51,700,000, fourteenth). Whereas Europe may no longer be a world leader either in its rate of growth or in absolute population numbers, the continent is distinctive in other ways, especially in its very high over-all densities and its high degree of urbanization.

Europe still has the highest population density among the continents, with c. 120 persons per km^2, ahead of Asia (95 per km^2) and four times the world average (29 per km^2). The highest national densities in the world are found in small island territories such as Hong Kong (3,946 per km^2), Singapore (3,700 per km^2), and Taiwan (399 per km^2), although Bangladesh (424 per km^2) is in the same order as Taiwan. Within Europe, the Netherlands (397 per km^2) is the most densely populated state followed by Belgium (318 per km^2), and West Germany (248 per km^2), and the United Kingdom (228 per km^2). Northern Europe displays the lowest densities, with Finland, Iceland, Norway, and Sweden each averaging fewer than 20 persons per km^2. Six countries in Southern Europe, along with Austria, France, and the Republic of Ireland, supported between 20 and 100 per km^2.

High densities are maintained by highly developed industrialized economies relying on the import of raw materials, some foodstuffs, and animal feed. It has thus been a central plank of various European government policies to promote and maintain high rates of economic growth in order to increase trade. As will become apparent later, this has involved both tacit approval of and stimulation of migration both within and to individual countries.

These national population densities mask notable regional variations (Fig. 1.2). The greater part of Norden and the Scottish Highlands and Islands, together with parts of Spain, emerge as Europe's 'empty lands' with fewer than 20 persons per km^2. The main urban industrial zones that comprise Western Europe's economic core generally supported more than ten times that density, with figures rising to more than 1,000 per km^2 in heavily urbanized areas such as Lancashire, London, the Ruhr, inner Paris, and parts of northern Italy. The population of Europe has thus concentrated in selected localities, chosen for the most part for their industrial—economic potential.

The process of concentration has resulted in an advanced degree of city growth and Europe's population is now more 'urban' than that of any other continent. Assessing the true extent of urbanization is not easy, for national definitions of what constitute urban settlements vary considerably. Indeed, the whole concept of urbanization is open to great debate and several measures have been used in its qualification. A major problem is that different countries define urban in different ways in their censuses. This problem will be returned to and discussed in more detail in Chapters 2 and 6. If national statistics are taken at their face value, it is seen that twelve European countries had more than half of their population living in urban settlements in 1970 and in six of these the proportion rose to more than two-thirds (in ascending order, Belgium, France, West Germany, Sweden, United Kingdom, and Netherlands). If, instead of using national definitions of 'urban', the absolute size of cities is examined, Europe had only Paris (fifth) and London (seventh) in the 'top twenty' world cities.

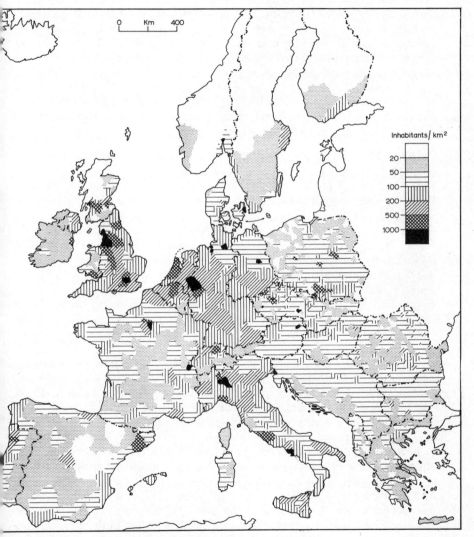

1.2 Europe: population density, 1971 (after Pressat *et al.* 1973).

However, with only 12·2 per cent of the world's population, Europe had 44 'urban agglomerations', each with more than 500,000 inhabitants, out of a world total of 168. If the urban threshold is lowered, Europe contained 365 cities with more than 100,000 inhabitants; and in eight countries more than 30 per cent of the national population lived in cities of more than 100,000 with the proportion reaching 53 per cent in the United Kingdom.

The over-all picture of European population that emerges is thus one of a slackening rate of increase, particularly in comparison with the rest of the world; of high densities relative to the land area; of population concentrated in urbanized zones in economic core areas, with a much less densely peopled rural periphery. This general scene, however, masks quite marked regional variations within both core and peripheral regions. This pattern of peopling is a result of the interaction of processes of natural change and migration. Whilst this book is primarily concerned with the latter, it is necessary to appreciate trends in birth and death rates and their current spatial patterns in order to understand the nature of the role of migration in post-war Europe.

Natural change

In 1970 most of Europe had low crude birth rates. Only Albania (35·6 per 1,000) and Turkey (40 per 1,000) had high rates by world standards, although Iceland, the Republic of Ireland, and Romania each had more than 20 per 1,000, with highly urbanized western states such as Belgium, West Germany, and Sweden at the lower end of the spectrum. When trends in crude birth rates over recent decades are examined, a marked convergence of experience is clear (Fig. 1.3). By 1970, the earlier demographic distinction between the 'developed' and 'less developed' nations of Europe had become less marked. In the 1920s the whole of Eastern Europe plus Italy, the Netherlands, Portugal, and Spain had recorded crude birth rates of over 25 per 1,000, with substantially lower rates in the more industrialized nations, such as France, Germany, Sweden, and the United Kingdom, which had a high proportion of their population in urban areas.

Although Europe has displayed an over-all tendency towards declining fertility rates during the twentieth century, since the last war particularly individual countries have experienced periodic fluctuations in birth rates which have had important economic and social repercussions. For example, fluctuations have led to variations in the number of people coming on to the labour market and these have not been easy to match to the demands of the economy. They have also led to fluctuations in the demand for social services, such as schools, and they have affected patterns of consumption. They have made it difficult to forecast with accuracy future levels of population and labour force. The major perturbations have been the two World Wars. The slaughter during World War I removed many males of fertile age. Partly owing to this and to the depression of the late 1920s and the 1930s, the inter-war years were times of falling birth rates, a trend caught up by and compounded by World War II. In England and Wales, for

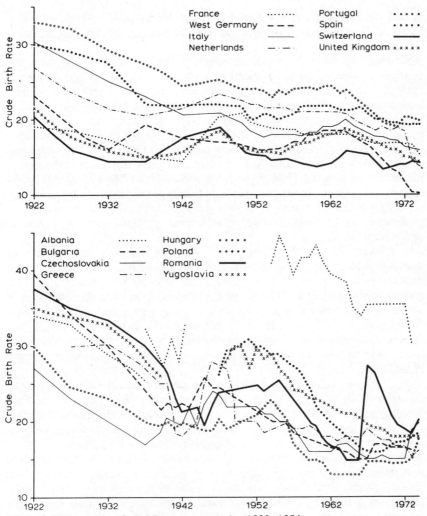

1.3 Crude birth rates in selected European countries, 1922–1974.

example, the outbreak of war in 1939 found the average number of children per family standing at little more than 2, with widespread prophecies of population decline. The fall in family size had occurred despite a fall in age at marriage.

In Western Europe the years after 1945 were characterized by 'baby booms' especially pronounced in France, but occurring more slowly in West Germany. During the 1950s birth rates tended to stabilize, then rose only to fall again in the mid-1960s, the plunge being dramatic in West Germany and Portugal, even though the Portuguese rate was still quite high by Western European standards. By 1970 West Germany averaged only 2 children per family, that is, below replacement rate.

National fluctuations varied considerably. In the United Kingdom, for example, number of births increased to a post-war peak in 1947 and fell steeply until 1951; in 1955 another major surge occurred, lasting until 1964, when a peak higher than 1947 was reached. Since then, birth rates have fallen steadily. The impact of such fluctuations can be seen in attempts to forecast future population levels for the United Kingdom. A 1955-based projection made when the birth rate was near its post-war low suggested a figure of a little more than 50,000,000 by the year 2,000 A.D.; in contrast, a projection made at the time of the birth rate peak of 1964 suggested a population of 75–80,000,000 by the end of the century. Bearing in mind that such projections form an important part of government planning strategies for economic and social development, the importance of seemingly minor fluctuations in birth rate must not be underestimated.

In Eastern Europe, the demographic situation has been less consistently recorded than in the West. Over-all birth rates have gone down steadily, and since 1945 have generally been below those of non-Communist Europe. The decline in Poland since 1950 is most pronounced and the recent change in direction in Romania is in response to a reversal of policy which had favoured abortion until 1967 (Bodrova, 1972; Pressat, 1967). Indeed, in several Eastern European countries, more strongly pro-natalist policies have been adopted in recent years in an effort to bolster population increases and, ultimately, growth in the labour force.

By 1970, virtually all countries in Europe had passed through the truly transitional stages of the demographic transition and entered the final 'low-fluctuating' phase. The reasons for the accompanying reductions in fertility are diverse, highly complex, and inappropriate to discuss in detail here. In general terms, falls in fertility have been due to changing attitudes in society. As death rates fell, survival of the species required fewer children, who came to be seen as a deterrent to the acquisition of material possessions produced by consumer economies. More particularly, reasons for fertility decline include greater acceptance and availability of family planning and abortion, linked with improved technology of birth control. The changing status of women in society has often meant that child-bearing has become just one of several functions, instead of the principal one. The transition from predominantly rural to predominantly urban societies, especially in many of the 'less developed' southern and eastern parts of the continent, has induced a gamut of social changes which include a preference for smaller families.

The crude death rates of European countries have also tended to converge over the past half-century, allowing for the very disturbed period of World War II (Fig. 1.4). This trend is in response to two main processes. The first is the improvement of medical care in the less urbanized, less developed countries of southern and eastern Europe which has reduced death rates. The second is the result of earlier improvements in health conditions, which have produced a marked ageing of population in the urbanized countries, especially of north-west Europe. Now the lowest death rates in Europe are in Iceland (7·0 per

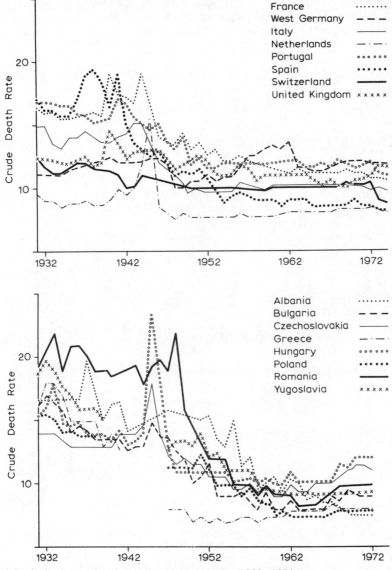

1.4 Crude death rates in selected European countries, 1932–1974.

1,000), Albania (7·9 per 1,000) and Poland (8·1 per 1,000). By contrast, rates in excess of 11 per 1,000 are found in six West European countries, together with the more industrialized East European states (Czechoslovakia, Hungary, and East Germany). Infant mortality has also declined substantially in response to better medical care and hygiene. The highest rates are still found in eastern and southern Europe, for example, Romania (49·5 per 1,000), Yugoslavia (56·3 per 1,000), Portugal (58 per 1,000) and Albania (86·8 per 1,000) compared with

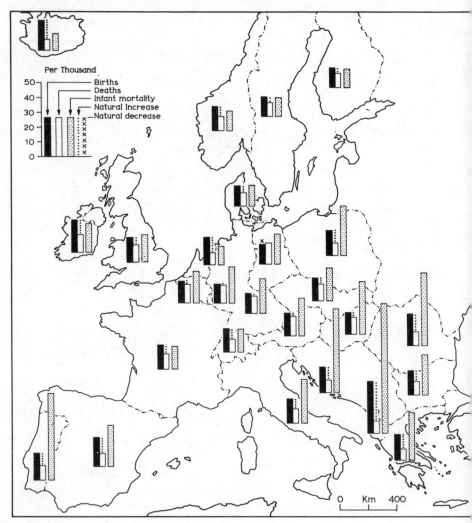

1.5 Europe: aspects of natural change, 1970.

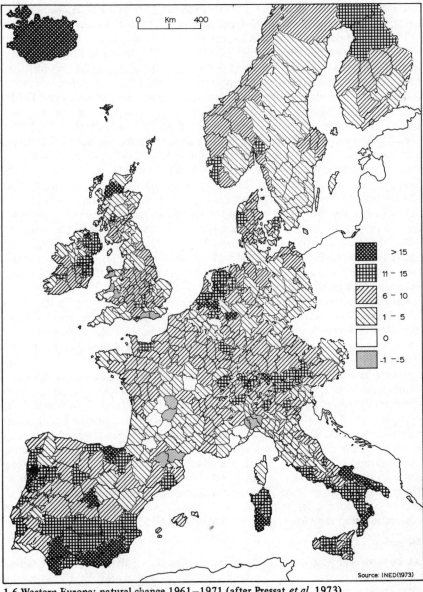

1.6 Western Europe: natural change 1961–1971 (after Pressat *et al.* 1973).
Calculated as $\dfrac{\%\ \text{natural change}}{\text{population 1961}}$

Source: INED(1973)

Legend:
> 15
11 – 15
6 – 10
1 – 5
0
-1 – -.5

low rates in Sweden (11·1 per 1,000), Finland (11·3 per 1,000), Netherlands (11·5 per 1,000) and Norway (12·8 per 1,000).

The over-all pattern of natural change for 1970 is shown in Figure 1.5. Both extremes were encountered in Eastern Europe, with Albania having the highest rate of natural increase (27·6 per 1,000), but with deaths exceeding births in East Germany. In the West, very low rates of natural increase were recorded in Austria and Luxembourg, and West Germany suffered a decrease (Festy, 1974). However, there was no clear distinction in rates of natural increase between Eastern and Western Europe. Comparatively high rates (10–15 per 1,000) were found in Iceland, the Netherlands, the Republic of Ireland, Romania, and Spain, and low rates (2–5 per 1,000) in Belgium, Czechoslovakia, Finland, Hungary, Sweden, and the United Kingdom (Fig. 1.5). In the more industrialized parts of Europe, with legacies of good health services, ageing of the population has accelerated the mortality rate, which now runs roughly parallel with family limitation. In less developed parts of the continent, the age structure is younger, but the demographic effects of this are partly offset by higher infantile mortality rates. In the countries of Eastern Europe changing population policies (sometimes favouring birth control and abortion, sometimes being pro-natalist) have produced quite striking changes over short periods as these societies have become increasingly urbanized.

The distribution of rates of natural increase in Western Europe for the 1960s (Fig. 1.6) demonstrates the continuance of higher rates in two types of areas. The first includes some parts of the rural periphery of the continent—as in southern Italy, Iberia, Ireland, Sweden, and Finland. The second comprises some major industrial employment areas which contain large numbers of young and middle-aged couples and which have attracted young people of employable and marriageable age from provincial areas. Increasingly, however, the central areas of conurbations have experienced sharp falls in natural increase, and even natural decrease, as the fertile age groups have migrated to suburban and outer metropolitan areas. Deaths exceed births in severely depopulated rural areas such as those in the Pyrenees, the Massif Central, and upland Wales. Here, selective outmigration of the young and ambitious in search of work has led to a distortion of the age—sex pyramid and removed the capacity for regeneration. Other areas, such as parts of Sussex and the Alpes-Maritimes also display an excess of deaths over births because they have functioned as retirement destinations and their age structures have become distorted.

Migration

As we have seen, the analysis of natural change of population in Europe during the twentieth century, and especially since the end of World War II, indicates a clear convergence of trends in birth and death rates between countries. Although within individual countries there are still substantial regional variations in rates of natural increase these are more often than not the result of selective migration flows. In fact, both directly and indirectly, migration has become the key element in the explanation of regional variations in population change in Europe. As successive countries have emerged from the demographic transition the problems of population growth resulting from high birth rates have become less important. Instead redistribution of population through migration has come to the fore as the main demographic feature.

Migration occurs at a range of scales and for a variety of reasons. Differences in opportunities between countries have led to and maintained a high level of international movement. In the nineteenth and early twentieth centuries this movement tended to be away from Europe altogether. In recent decades it has predominantly been from the Mediterranean lands, including the North African coast, to industrial north-west Europe. At the same time population has become more mobile within countries and strong inter-regional migration currents have developed. Much inter-regional migration has been from rural to urban areas, but in addition many older industrial areas have lost population to those with greater locational advantages. However, in post-industrial societies it seems that increasingly there are complex flows of migrants between areas with similar economic characteristics. The flows mentioned so far have been long-distance ones, involving change in the social and economic milieu of migrants, but much migration remains short-distance and of an intra-urban variety. Especially important is the movement to the suburbs that characterizes most large cities. As indicated in the Introduction, these short-distance movements will be referred to only in passing in this book.

The reasons for the longer-distance migrations are complex, but two main sets of motives stand out: political and economic.[2] Much of Europe's international migration during the twentieth century has been politically inspired. The occurrence and aftermath of two major wars saw to that, although Europe's political migrations have by no means all been connected with wars. Economic reasons, especially the search for work, have guided many migrants, ranging from rural workers seeking urban jobs, to the great mass of international labour migrants of the 1960s. A myriad of other personal reasons needs to be considered. For many migrants, geographical migration and social mobility have been seen as interconnected, and passage up the social ladder may only be achieved through a move to another area.

International migration

Emigration has been a persistent theme in the history of European population change. It has been linked to a wide range of overseas colonization ventures, to the impact of political and economic crises at home, and to perceived variations in opportunities abroad. Annual variations in net loss from Europe (including Russia) through emigration have been charted by Kosiński (1970) for the periods 1891–1920, 1921–39, and 1946–63. Losses were particularly pronounced in the first period, with Italy, the British Isles, the Austro-Hungarian Empire, Iberia, and the states of Eastern Europe being the main supply areas. The upheavals of World War I contributed to this outflow and will be mentioned in a little more detail below. The depressed years of the 1920s and 1930s, together with the impact of the U.S. Quota Law of 1921, reduced average outflows for those decades, with the British Isles continuing to form the largest source of emigrants. In the early years after World War II, the picture was severely affected by migrations consequent upon the war, but again it is clear that the British Isles was a principal source of migrants, with, for example, assisted passages to the 'Old Commonwealth' and the 'brain drain' to North America playing important roles. The Mediterranean lands continued as important areas of emigration, for example to Australia, although labour movements to industrial Europe came to play a more dominant role in their demographies than trans-oceanic emigrations. Political changes in Eastern Europe brought overseas emigration virtually to a halt from Communist countries.

Migration flows between the countries of Europe have long occurred. Industrializing nations in the nineteenth century drew workers from neighbouring countries, with Irish moving to Britain, Italians to France, and Central Europeans to the German empire. But such embryonic economic flows were of small significance when compared with political migrations associated with the two World Wars in the present century and the labour migrations of the post-war years.

Kosiński (1970) has estimated that 7,700,000 people were involved in intra-European population movement associated with World War I. When German-occupied territories, such as Alsace-Lorraine and parts of Poland, were reconquered, residents there were given the choice of taking the nationality of the conquering powers or migrating to Germany. Disintegration of both the Austro-Hungarian and Ottoman Empires was followed by the creation of new states and was accompanied by considerable adjustments of population which were neither regulated by international treaties nor recorded in detail. In south-eastern Europe a succession of regional wars, in addition to World War I, produced flows of perhaps 200,000 Turks who were repatriated from the European continent. The Treaty of Lausanne in 1923 stimulated the movement of 1,000,000 Greeks from Asia Minor to Greece with about 300,000 Turks moving in the opposite direction. At the same time some 250,000 Greeks were returning from other parts of the Balkans. Such movements continued in the 1920s and 1930s. Hardening political policies in central Europe provoked outflows of Jews, especially from Poland, Spain, and Germany. Between 1927 and 1938 almost 200,000 Jews left Poland (with only 19,000 going to other European states, 74,000 to Palestine and 106,000 to non-European countries). Nazi legislation in 1933, and especially in 1935, produced the outflow of 400,000 refugees from the 'German lands' by May 1939. Only about 10 per cent of these were not Jewish. Some 283,000 fled from Germany, 95,000 from Austria, and 23,000 from the Sudetenland. A very large number of Czechs (perhaps 400,000) shifted from the Sudetenland into Bohemia following the Munich Pact in 1938. Elsewhere in Europe, political changes in Italy led to the emigration of 60,000 people after the establishment of the Fascist regime in 1924; and perhaps 300,000 Spaniards moved into France during and after the Spanish Civil War. At the same time the *Volksdeutsche* (ethnic Germans) were gathered back into Germany from the Baltic states in 1939–40 and from western parts of the U.S.S.R., Romania, Bulgaria, Hungary, and Yugoslavia. Israeli data register the flow of 365,000 immigrants to Palestine in the inter-war years, of whom 235,000 arrived between 1933 and 1939 with the great majority coming from Europe. The main migration flows during the 1920s and in 1930 have been summarized by Kirk (1946).

World War II was accompanied by massive shifts of population involving more than 25,000,000 people, mainly in east-central Europe. Many of these were temporary movements with complicated readjustments following. For example, 7,000,000 foreign workers were transported to work in war-time Germany, and these comprised 5,000,000 civilian workers and 2,000,000 P.O.W.s at the end of the war, when one fifth of workers in the German lands were made up of these groups.

In the years following the cessation of hostilities Europe's population, especially in the centre and east of the continent, was in a state of turmoil. Much of the migration that ensued was politically inspired, although it is not always possible to separate political from economic motives. For example, many refugees who moved from East to West Germany were motivated by the latter's prosperity as well as purely political reasons.

A major problem in assessing the direction and extent of the migrations consequent upon the conclusion of World War II is that the data are of limited accuracy. As had happened in the years after World War I, agreements for population exchange were made without a clear idea of how many were involved, and the volume of some movements went unrecorded. What is certain is that numbers were large. Between 1945 and 1949, for example, 3,000,000 Germans were transferred from the redrawn boundaries of Poland following the Potsdam Agreement and 4,800,000 Poles, plus 1,000,000 Germans claiming Polish nationality, were resettled in the northern and western territories of the new Poland. Some 1,500,000 people moved back into areas in western Czechoslovakia vacated by the Germans, from other parts of the country and from abroad. Between 1944 and 1946 about 500,000 Lithuanians, White Russians, and Ukranians were transferred from Poland to the U.S.S.R., and between 1946 and 1948 about 1,500,000 Poles and Jews were repatriated from former eastern Polish territories annexed by the Soviet Union. Many others are known to have been forcibly repatriated to the U.S.S.R. in 1945–6 and subsequently disappeared. Other exchanges were between Czechoslovakia and Hungary, Czechoslovakia and the U.S.S.R., and Hungary and Yugoslavia. Later, the Greek Civil War caused the displacement of about 700,000 people. Between 1950 and 1951 150,000 of Turkish descent were expelled from Bulgaria and a further 600,000 Turks were estimated still to be there when Bulgaria closed its borders to further emigration in 1951.

The main migrations in central and eastern Europe during 1944—51 are depicted in Fig. 1.7, based on Broek and Webb (1968). The biggest movements

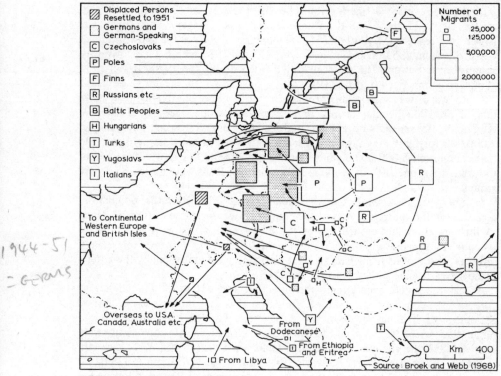

1.7 Europe: migrations,   1944—1951

involved Germans, and among the countries of asylum after 1945, West Germany occupies an exceptional place. The absorption of refugees became its basic economic and social problem. At the end of the war the Allies organized the removal of ethnic Germans from Poland, Czechoslovakia, and Hungary, while at the same time hundreds of thousands more from other east and south-east European territories were forced to evacuate. By 1950 West Germany recorded 7,800,000 refugees and East Germany had about 3,500,000 more. But the movement was still not complete and between 1950 and 1955, the number of refugees in West Germany increased by 1,000,000, making them 17·4 per cent of the total population. Most of West Germany's refugees after 1950 came from East Germany; between 1950 and the building of the Berlin Wall in 1961 an estimated 3,000,000 East Germans crossed to the West, mainly via Berlin. Only a very small number moved in the opposite direction (Rose, 1969). In 1956 West

Germany and other West European states received about 200,000 Hungarians, fleeing after the abortive uprising.

Although the political migrations so far discussed involved exchanges of population within Europe, there were others involving European population outside the continent. In the period since 1945 colonial powers, especially France, the United Kingdom, the Netherlands, and Belgium, have received back many of their former nationals who had either gone as administrators and settlers, or had been born and bred in colonial areas. As the political change of decolonization dictated, so the volume of this movement has varied; perhaps the most dramatic movement was that of almost 1,000,000 *pieds noirs* from Algeria to France after the conclusion of the Treaty of Evian in 1962 (McDonald, 1965). The Netherlands repatriated about 38,000 Dutch from Indonesia in 1958 and another 20,000 in 1962 from West New Guinea (Rose, 1969). Power (1972), however, has estimated that in the post-war years no fewer than 300,000 Indonesian refugees were absorbed in the Netherlands. The United Kingdom has also provided a home for many thousands of Asians from East Africa, consequent upon 'Africanisation' there, perhaps the notable movement being that of about 20,000 Ugandan Asians in 1972.

The international migrations so far described have been tied to particular political events. They by no means account for all international migration in Europe and, since the years immediately after World War II, have been relatively unimportant in the face of more 'normal' economically inspired movements. The economic migrations that had preceded World War I continued afterwards. France, for example, with its cruelly distorted and truncated population pyramid, found itself short of both workers and eligible bachelors—and encouraged immigration. It contained 2,800,000 foreign-born folk in 1931, with Italians (900,000) and Poles (500,000) making up half that amount. Belgium's declining workforce was supplemented by Dutch, Poles, and Italians, particularly in the mining areas. England continued to receive Irish immigrants.

Kirk (1946) summarized these inter-war labour flows as being 'typically a movement from countries of lower levels of living and agrarian over-population to those of slower population growth and greater economic opportunities' (p. 242). Where natural increase was slow or even non-existent, as in France for certain years of the 1930s, migration inflows were decisive in maintaining or increasing population. Emigration was already a contributory but not definitive solution to problems of population pressure in eastern and southern Europe's areas of high natural increase, although it was not great enough to prevent further accumulation in already overcrowded lands. By the end of World War II it was becoming obvious that further outmigration from areas with high birth rates and low levels of industrialization would be necessary and, even if birth rates fell, changes in employment structure would become necessary to lessen dependence on agriculture and provide labour for industrial growth. This view was propounded by Kirk (1946) who argued that an increase in migration in Europe generally would ensue. He believed that the reappearance of pressure to migrate from eastern and southern Europe to western Europe was highly probable although he supposed that the new role of the Soviet Union in Europe would strengthen political deterrents to emigration from this region. He correctly prophesied continuation of Soviet policy to forbid free emigration altogether, maintaining that closer economic and political ties with the U.S.S.R. seemed likely to encourage similar policies and attitudes towards migration among its smaller neighbours. The result of these policies in Eastern Europe has been a diversion of emigration flows from these countries away from the west and towards the east.

A consequence of this political schism of the European continent in recent decades has been the development of separate international migration fields on either side of the Iron Curtain. That to the east is on a much smaller scale, reflecting generally lower levels of economic development. Within Eastern Europe migrations between countries are treated primarily as a form of co-operation in the field of manpower utilization (ILO, 1973). As a general principle, the socialist governments reckon by judicious planning to arrive at manpower balances within their own frontiers without need for immigration or emigration. Movements tend to be regarded as short-term rather than permanent and take the form either of 'export' of specialized technical services or of transfers of groups of workers primarily motivated by the objective of acquiring advanced training. Polish engineers working in East Germany and Bulgarian construction workers in the U.S.S.R. are examples (see Chapter 6). East Germany has developed during the 1960s as the main recipient of nationals of other East European countries, especially from Hungary. However, Bulgaria and Czechoslovakia have recently started organized immigration of manpower from Egypt. Projections of the future labour market situation in Eastern Europe suggest that pressures exist which might lead to increases in migration (Danieli, 1972). East Germany, Czechoslovakia, Hungary, and Bulgaria are most likely to be the countries of immigration, while Poland and Romania seem likely to continue having surpluses of workers, and therefore to offer scope for emigration.

In the rest of Europe, and beyond its southern fringes, the period since World War II has seen major growth in international migration for economic reasons. Although many migrants have ended up by settling permanently in a new country, the majority have been more transient. Voluntary migration for work purposes between countries in Western Europe started almost as soon as World War II ended. In the years since, certain countries, namely Sweden, Switzerland, France, West Germany, and Belgium, have become characterized as countries of immigration; others, especially Finland, Ireland, Portugal, and Italy, became sending countries. A third group, including the United Kingdom and the Netherlands, at various times since 1945 have functioned as both receiving and sending countries.

As the amount of cross-national migration has increased, especially since the late 1950s, so it has been governed by 'a complex of multilateral and bilateral treaties, national statutes, administrative regulations and informal administrative and police practices' (Rose, 1969, p. 44). Some countries, notably the United Kingdom and Switzerland, have developed more stringent controls against immigration than others, largely for political reasons. Alarmed at the build-up of a foreign minority of 700,000 in a country of only 6,000,000, Switzerland began to take steps to reduce its immigrant population in 1963. A succession of restrictive measures followed, with referenda on the issue. The United Kingdom faced a different situation. There the problem was not a large volume of temporary immigrants but a steady increase in the numbers of Commonwealth citizens, often with different racial backgrounds, wishing to settle permanently. In 1962 and again in 1968 Commonwealth Immigration Acts drastically curtailed immigration, a process followed up by the 1971 Immigration Act which, incidentally, resulted in United Kingdom legislation recognizing no fewer than six types of aliens!

Rose (1969) attempted to summarize the openness of policy towards immigrants in the main host countries. As far as new immigration was concerned, France seemed to be most open, whilst Switzerland and the United Kingdom were the most closed. The situation was a little different when policies to aid in the acceptance and integration of immigrants were considered. France emerged as the country apparently making the greatest efforts, followed by Sweden and the United Kingdom. Switzerland did least to aid the integration of its foreign workers, then the Netherlands. West Germany came in an intermediate position, with conditions being complicated by the Federal structure of government which leaves much in the hands of individual employers as far as the social and economic well-being of immigrants is concerned.

International migration since World War II has been a major influence in population redistribution in Europe as a whole. Although important at the time and often having involved demographic influences subsequently, the coercive political migrations of World War II and its aftermath have diminished in significance in the face of voluntary movements primarily for work reasons. Not only have these movements changed the balance of population growth and livelihood between individual countries, but by the selective nature of origin and destination areas they have had important regional impacts within individual countries.

Internal migration

These international movements must be seen in the light of more profound migratory trends that have characterized population change within individual European countries in recent decades. In fact, important though international movements have been, in sheer volume they have paled before the vast amount of inter-regional movement that has taken place. It is these internal movements that have been most responsible for regional variations in population change. Figure 1.8 summarizes regional net migration change in Western Europe between 1961 and 1971, although a note of caution needs to be sounded on the matter

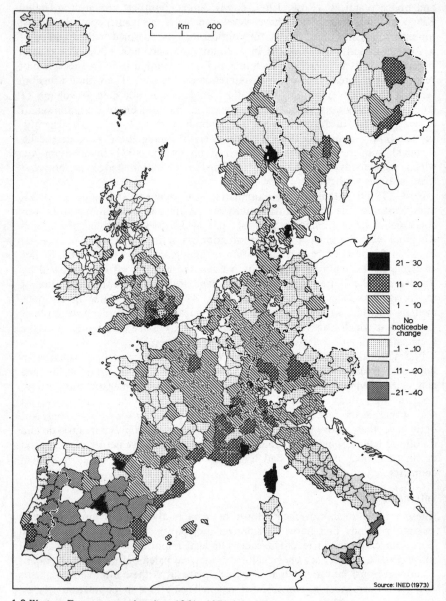

1.8 Western Europe: net migration, 1961–1971 (after Pressat *et al.* 1973).

Calculated as $\dfrac{\text{pop. 71–pop. 61 natural change}}{\text{population 1961}}$

of its interpretation. The scale of administrative units used varies between countries: for example, in countries such as Norway and Denmark, individual cities may be distinguished whilst elsewhere the units bear little relationship even to city regions. Also by illustrating net migration as a percentage, the absolute numbers involved and the volume of gross flows are missed. Certain generalizations may, however, be made. The over-all pattern displayed is one of migration gain in the central industrial areas of Western Europe and along the Mediterranean coast of northern Spain, France, and northern Italy. These are surrounded by a predominantly rural periphery of migration loss. The areas with the highest net gains include favoured areas for retirement such as the Mediterranean coast and the Channel coast of England, and some capital city regions such as those around Madrid and Oslo. Other areas of high migration gain are newer industrial areas, such as much of central and southern England, southern Germany, the Barcelona and Valencia areas of Spain, France's 'Grand Delta' area and the Paris basin, and Switzerland's more urbanized zones. In contrast, the areas of biggest net emigration are mainly peripheral agricultural or silvicultural areas, such as those of interior Spain and Portugal, most of Norden, southern Italy, Scotland, and Ireland. More modest losses are found in older industrial areas, such as north-west England, Lorraine, the Belgian Limburg, and the French Nord, and also in less remote rural areas such as parts of western France, Alsace, northern parts of the Netherlands, north-western parts of West Germany, and Alpine areas. In general terms, the pattern of net migration reflects the pattern of total population change (Fig. 1.1), emphasizing the significant role of migration in contemporary changes in population distribution.

To a considerable extent inter-regional migrations within countries reflect spatial differences in levels of earnings and job opportunities, although such differences by no means represent the principle motivation of all individuals and households who move. In an industrial economy a large volume of migration occurs because technological and ensuing industrial change necessitate redistribution of labour, both occupationally and geographically, in accordance with changes in demand. During the last half-century many of Europe's old industrial areas and its agricultural areas have suffered decline in demand for labour; in contrast, other areas have come to specialize in new light industry and in service provision and have had a growing need for more workers. Thus there have been regional shifts in the demand for labour. These have not been matched by parallel trends in natural change of population and as a result, migration has ensued. Hence, although natural increase is an important element in aggregate population change it is migration which largely brings about local divergences from national trends.

Because of the existence of spatial imbalances in job opportunities, most European governments have adopted some kind of migration policy. Klaasen and Drewe (1973) have said that such policies have a dual objective: to raise the mobility of labour in general and to provide incentives for people intending to move in so far as this move accords with government regional development targets. Migration policies are thus linked closely with regional policies. In effect, the migration policies adopted by governments have been of a restricted nature. For the most part they have been geared to aiding unemployed people, or those in insecure jobs, who wish to move out of areas designated as ones of high unemployment. Occasionally the policies have been linked to counter-congestion measures; in the Netherlands for example, assistance is not given for unemployed people wishing to migrate to the 'over-urbanized' Randstad area (Klaasen and Drewe, 1973; OECD, 1967). In France, assistance is given to companies decentralizing from the Paris area who take their labour forces with them. In most countries, however, migration policies are little developed. Emphasis is put instead on capital mobility, thus moving work to the workers. Only Sweden has a comprehensive migration policy closely linked with national and regional full employment policies and involving large numbers of people. Most inter-regional migration in Western Europe therefore takes place without official sponsorship and with little attempt by governments to channel movements along lines regarded as 'desirable' for policy objectives. The result is that rates of population change tend closely to reflect regional and local changes in economic circumstances, and these can conflict with such social objectives as the provision of housing in areas of inmigration and the maintenance of service levels in areas of outmigration.

Conclusion

This brief overview of twentieth-century demographic trends in Europe has provided a context for studying some of the more important recent migration trends. By way of summary, several important points may be made. The first is that, taken as a whole, Europe's population growth rate has been slowing down. As the demographic transition has worked its way across the continent there has been a convergence of national experience in terms of both fertility and mortality rates; none the less, there are still some very significant differences in rates of population change between countries, with some having rapid increases, and a few undergoing population loss. Secondly, there has been a tendency for population to redistribute itself spatially in accordance with the needs of industrial development and its associated economic and social changes. At both national and regional levels lack of coincidence between rates of economic change and of population change have led to substantial movements of people in response. Sometimes such migrations have been transient; more usually, especially at the intra-national level, they have been permanent. Thirdly, underlying population changes since 1945 have been the traumatic effects of wars and the conflict of political ideologies. The latter has, for all practical purposes, divided the continent into two power blocs, espousing different methods of social and economic organization and allowing little contact between the population of the two sides. It is against this background of demographic changes and events that the study of various migration themes in post-war Europe can now be set.

Notes

[1] Geographical names are presented according to the following rules. The names of official regions and provinces are always indicated in the appropriate national language; however names of islands, rivers, towns, etc. are given in the conventional English form (e.g. 'Copenhagen') where such an English form exists.

[2] In this respect we are reminded of the early migration of our illustrious predecessor Captain Alexander Maconochie, first Professor of Geography at University College London, who was captured by the Dutch in 1812, was then handed over to the French and, together with fellow officers and men, was forced to march in the depth of a bitter winter from Holland to Verdun, where he was held prisoner of war for over two years. Later in his life he became a more permanent labour migrant and occupied the post of Superintendent of Norfolk Island.

References

Biraben, J. N., Peron, Y., and Nizard, A. (1964) 'La Situation démographique de l'Europe occidentale', *Population*, 19, 439−84.

Bodrova, V. (1972) 'La Politique démographique dans les républiques populaires d'Europe', *Population*, 27, 1001−18.

Broek, J. O., and Webb, J. W. (1968) *A Geography of Mankind*, McGraw-Hill, New York.

Danieli, L. (1972) 'Labour scarcities and labour redundancies in Europe by 1980: an experimental study', in Livi Bacci, M. (Ed.), *The Demographic and Social Pattern of Emigration from the Southern European Countries*, Department of Statistics and Mathematics, University of Florence.

Festy, P. (1974) 'La Situation démographique des deux Allemagnes', *Population*, 29, 795−824.

International Labour Office (1973) *Some Growing Employment Problems in Europe*, ILO, Geneva.

Kirk, D. (1946) *Europe's Population in the Interwar Years*, Gordon & Breach, New York.

Klaasen, L. H., and Drewe, P. (1973) *Migration Policy in Europe: a comparative study*, Saxon House, Farnborough.

Kosiński, L. (1970) *The Population of Europe*, Longman, London.

McDonald, J. R. (1965) 'The repatriation of French Algerians', *International Migration*, 3, 146−57.

Organization for Economic Co-operation and Development (1967) *Manpower and Social Policy in the Netherlands*, OECD, Paris.

Power, J. (1972) *The New Proletarians*, British Council of Churches, Community and Race Relations Unit, London.

Pressat, R. (1967) 'La Suppression de l'avortement légal en Roumanie; premiers effets', *Population*, 22, 1116−18.

Pressat, R., Biraben, J. N., and Duhourcau, F. (1973) 'La Conjoncture démographique: l'Europe', *Population*, 28, 1155−69.

Rose, A. M. (1969) *Migrants in Europe: problems of acceptance and adjustment*, University of Minnesota Press, Minneapolis.

2. RURAL-URBAN MIGRATION IN WESTERN EUROPE

HUGH CLOUT

Introduction

Western Europe, as one of the most urbanized sections of the Earth's surface, has experienced important flows of migrants from the countryside to its towns and cities for many centuries. E. G. Ravenstein (1885) formulated his seven 'laws of migration' almost a century ago on the basis of evidence from nineteenth-century Britain, and rural—urban migration in the past has been studied in various ways and at several levels ranging from the local to the regional and national scales (Lawton, 1967; Merlin, 1971; Saville, 1957). But such flows of population are not only historical phenomena. The popular image of rural Europe being relatively stable and slow-changing becomes less appropriate with every year that passes (Pitié, 1971). Millions of European countryfolk have moved from their farms, villages, and home regions since World War II in search of social and economic advancement which town life can bring. In Sweden, for example, 30 per cent of the national population now lives in the three largest cities (Stockholm, Gothenburg, and Malmö) and partly as a result of continuing rural—urban migration, they may contain 50 per cent of the total by the year 2000 (Törnquist, 1970). Flows from rural to urban areas predominate not only in less developed parts of Western Europe, such as Portugal, Spain and the Italian Mezzogiorno, which are characterized by high birth rates, low wages, limited job opportunities, and poor living standards, but also from many other rural areas where birth rates are low and wage levels are moderate when judged by Europe-wide standards.

By contrast, a range of new factors has come into operation in highly urbanized and industrialized areas, such as parts of the United Kingdom, West Germany, France, and the Netherlands. These factors interact to distort and even to reverse the traditional balance of migration from the countryside to the town. In theory the process of rural—urban migration is simple in the extreme but in practice it is exceedingly difficult—if not indeed impossible—to define with any degree of precision. Six important groups of factors are responsible for this dilemma.

Rural—urban migration: an elusive phenomenon

First, there is no internationally recognized definition of 'rural' and 'urban' areas. At various times in the past, each country independently devised its own criteria for making this distinction. Sometimes it was derived from numerical thresholds, as was the case in France where the long accepted but recently changed definition of an urban unit was a *commune* with at least 2,000 people living in its main settlement. But in many other countries, such numerical logic is lacking. In most cases the legal status of being a 'town' or 'city' was conferred centuries ago and has since become seriously inadequate to describe the spatial extent of modern urban systems. For this reason, official statistics may indicate stability or decline in numbers of urban residents at the national or regional level or even at the scale of an individual city. Such figures are, of course, illusory since they merely reflect changes in the spatial structure of modern cities, as residential functions decline in inner city areas but disperse outwards into what is still recognized officially as 'rural' suburbia (Johnson, 1974). This problem affects the majority of Western Europe's towns and cities but is particularly well illustrated by the tiny German *Länder* of Bremen and Hamburg which exclude the partially urbanized districts around them that are at present profiting from a decongestion of population and employment from central areas.

The second complicating factor is that rural—urban migration is frequently confused with rural depopulation or with the decline of the agricultural workforce. These processes are intimately associated with rural-urban migration but are not synonymous with it (Vincienne, 1972). Rural depopulation may be produced by any one of the following conditions: outmigration exceeding inmigration; more deaths than births; migratory loss exceeding natural increase; or net outmigration combining with natural decrease. Contraction of the agricultural population, in turn, involves only one professional component in the much wider phenomenon of rural depopulation. It may result from the death or retirement of farmers and farmworkers but does not necessarily provoke rural—urban migration. Alternative employment may be found in nearby towns within commuting distance or may even be available in the heart of the countryside, although the latter situation is rare. None the less, the decline of agricultural employment is a crucial element in the general retreat of population from rural areas and offers the specific advantage of being readily determined from statistical sources. For these reasons it will be retained for discussion in later paragraphs.

Third, not all national censuses in Western Europe record internal migration and for those that do, there is little standardization of inquiry or presentation (Fielding, 1972, 1975). The system of population registration operated in West Germany, Belgium, the Netherlands, and especially in Scandinavia, requires each move to be recorded. Detailed flows to and from administrative units may be retrieved as well as the movements of individuals for the duration of their lifetime (Hägerstrand, 1957). The excellence of such registration systems has undoubtedly contributed much to the high quality of migration studies emanating from Northern Europe. Inquiries in France and recent censuses in the United Kingdom (1966, 1971) included questions on place of residence at the time of the previous census and thus allow migration flows to be determined. But such material does not capture each stage in migratory movements and may have been gathered, or at least analysed, on a sample basis. It is therefore inappropriate for use in studying changes in small areas. The popular 'residual method' for calculating net migration involves computing intercensal changes in population for appropriate areas and then subtracting natural increase or decrease in order to determine the migratory balance (Pitié, 1971). Figure 1.8 was compiled on this basis. It has the quality of indicating regional patterns of gain and loss through migration during the 1960s but is nevertheless deceptive since it deals with net results rather than with actual volumes of inward and

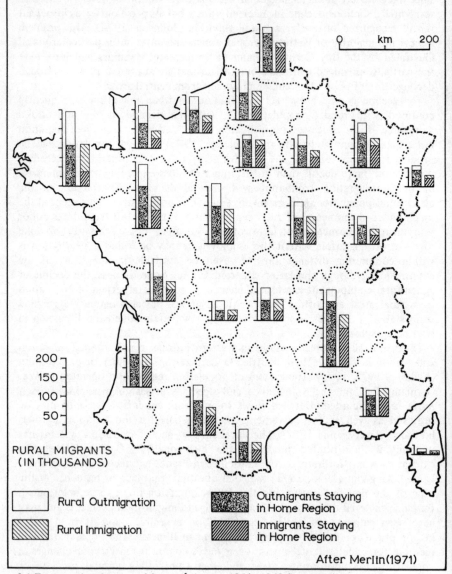

0   km   200

200 ┐
150 ┤
100 ┤
50 ┤

RURAL MIGRANTS
(IN THOUSANDS)

☐ Rural Outmigration   ▒ Outmigrants Staying
                                in Home Region

▨ Rural Inmigration   ▨ Inmigrants Staying
                                in Home Region

After Merlin (1971)

2.1 France: migration to and from rural areas, 1954–1962 (by region).

outward flow. Various other sources may be exploited to compensate for deficiencies in census material. Electoral registers provide a good example, having been used in one case study to examine the migration behaviour of 110,000 Auvergnats from 450 *communes* in the mountains of the Massif Central (Estienne, 1958).

The fourth complication stems from the fact that important urban—rural flows of population have operated in recent years, which make statistics on migratory balance quite inadequate indicators of rural—urban flow for all except the most remote areas of countryside in which significant counter-flows were absent (*Atlas of Social and Economic Regions of Europe*, 1964). To take a single national example, 2,360,000 migrants left officially defined 'rural' areas in France between 1954 and 1962 but these flows were partially compensated for by a further 1,354,000 people settling in the countryside to give a net rural loss of only 1,006,000 (Merlin, 1971). Every region, except Provence-Côte-d'Azur experienced less rural inmigration than outmigration from their country areas (Fig. 2.1). In the following six years, 2,010,000 migrants left the French countryside and a further 1,205,000 moved out from towns and cities to give a net loss of 705,000 (Tugault, 1974).

Such compensating, or at least partially compensating, flows are in response to three processes. The first, and probably the most important, involves the spread beyond urban limits of new areas of suburbia and more widely dispersed zones of commuter settlement made possible by rising rates of car ownership as well as the existence of adequate systems of public transport. The second type of process includes the migration of families of workers who move to employment facilities in remote rural areas. Numbers involved in this kind of counter-current are undoubtedly small. In addition, increasing numbers of elderly people move to the countryside on retirement, often to the regions from which they originated or to attractive areas that they visited whilst on holiday (Bernard and Auriac, 1970; Cribier, 1970; Lepape, 1970). There is, indeed, an important age difference between migrants from the countryside and those returning to it. As Friedlander and Roshier (1966) have reported, rural outmigration on the whole consists of young, unmarried migrants but population dispersal from the main urban centres is mainly of married people.

The true volume of rural—urban migration is disguised in many areas by important local flows which redistribute population in the countryside as has been the case for centuries. For example, 1,541,000 people moved between rural *communes* in France between 1962 and 1968. Little is known in any detail of these movements but other, more dramatic, rural—rural migrations have been investigated. Large numbers of refugees from the East were resettled on farm holdings in many western parts of West Germany after World War II and in Finland new farms were cleared by farmers who had been displaced as a result of international boundary changes. Under less urgent circumstances, farmers moved from densely populated areas of Armorica and from harsh conditions in the Massif Central to occupy vacant farmland in Aquitaine. Important contrasts in

settlement policy developed in Northern Europe, with new farms being cleared
in parts of Norway and Finland, while rural policy in Sweden was geared to
reducing agricultural output, abandoning marginal land, and rationalizing
settlement patterns.

The fifth complicating factor is that rural–urban flows may be impossible to
disaggregate from available migration statistics (see Chapter 3). Inter-regional
flows incorporate rural–urban movements to a varying degree depending on the
nature of the regions involved (Tugault, 1973). In highly urbanized countries,
such as the Netherlands and the United Kingdom, by far the greater proportion
of inter-regional movement comprises inter-urban flows. By contrast, in
countries with less pronounced urban development such as Italy, Portugal, and
Spain, most inter-regional movement represents flows from rural to urban areas.
Outmigration from the countryside of these less developed parts of Western
Europe frequently involves migrants moving to urban destinations in other
countries where there are large demands for labour. Such moves therefore
qualify as examples of international labour migration and are discussed in more
detail in chapters 4 and 5. For example, many rural migrants leave the
Mezzogiorno to find work in the cities of northern Italy, but others move to
urban destinations in Switzerland or West Germany. In similar fashion, large
numbers of migrants from rural Iberia move to cities in France, rural migrants
from Ireland find work in the cities of the United Kingdom, and rural Finns,
especially those from the Swedish-speaking, south-western parts of the country,
migrate to Stockholm and other Swedish cities.

The final complication involves the fact that many forms of rural employment
have declined and contribute to rural–urban migration. Agriculture undoubtedly
accounts for the greater proportion of this decline but jobs have also been lost in
traditional industries in response to competition from urban factories, and in
rural services because local demand has fallen below critical thresholds. The
process of 'ruralization' has become established in many parts of Western Europe
and broad-based rural communities have given way to employment patterns
based more exclusively on agricultural production (Pinchemel, 1957). In spite of
the fact that they relate to only one section of the rural population, figures on
primary employment indicate the order of magnitude of one of the most
important processes contributing to the decline of population in the countryside. Rates of loss in primary work depend on several factors, including among
others, the health of the international economy and the appropriate national
economy, and the availability of alternative employment. Outflow from
agricultural employment decelerated markedly during the critical decade of the
1930s and smaller economic fluctuations since World War II have had a similar
effect.

In 1950, 30,000,000 people were involved in farming, forestry, and fishing in
the six original member nations of the European Economic Community. Within
ten years, this figure had fallen by one half and had almost halved again by
1972, when it stood at 8,400,000. From representing 28·9 per cent of the

workforce, this primary employment declined by almost two-thirds to 11·2 per cent (Table 2.1). When the three new members are included, the workforce of the Nine engaged in farming, forestry, and fishing, involved 17,047,000 people (17·1 per cent) in 1960 and declined to 9,655,000 (9·4 per cent) twelve years later. Agriculture was still highly important as an employer in the peripheral parts of the Community, which comprised the Republic of Ireland, western France, and southern Italy (Fig. 2.2), and it is these areas from which rural–urban migration in the Nine is operating with great intensity (Commission of the European Communities, 1973). When Western European nations beyond

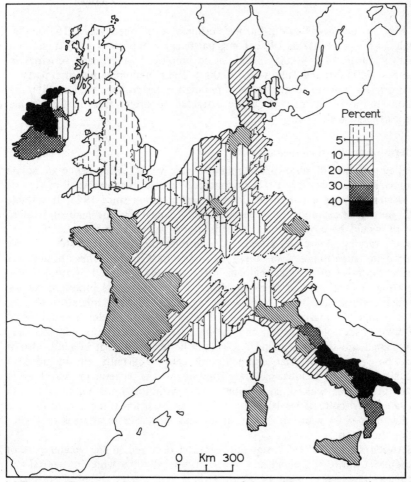

2.2 European Economic Community: proportion of the workforce in farming, forestry, and fishing, 1972.

TABLE 2.1 *Employment in farming, forestry, and fishing as percentage of labour forces*

	1950	1960	1972		1960	1972		1960	1972
Belgium	12·6	8·7	4·1	Austria	23·0	17·9	Portugal	41·0	31·1
France	27·6	22·4	12·6	Denmark	18·1	9·7	Spain	40·0	29·1
West Germany	22·1	14·0	7·5	Finland	25·0	22·3	Sweden	16·0	8·0
Luxembourg	25·9	16·3	9·3	Greece	54·0	45·8	Switzerland	11·0	6·7
Italy	43·9	32·8	17·5	Republic of Ireland	37·3	24·1	Turkey	79·0	71·5
Netherlands	14·3	10·0	6·9	Norway	16·0	13·8	United Kingdom	4·2	2·7

the EEC are included, Western Europe's primary workforce involved 16,000,000 people (12·5 per cent) in 1972, being particularly important in Portugal and Spain. A further 11,490,000 people were employed in primary activities in Greece (1,740,000) and Turkey (9,750,000). These predominantly rural parts of Mediterranean Europe form a series of population reservoirs, containing literally millions of potential migrants to be attracted to urban areas in their home countries or abroad.

Patterns of rural—urban migration

Detailed patterns of rural—urban migration are virtually impossible to isolate from available statistics, but it is undoubtedly correct that almost all rural parts of Western Europe experienced flows of outmigration since 1945. If suitable data were to exist and could be subjected to analysis, the map of Western Europe would be covered by thousands of migration fields focused on urban centres, varying in size and attraction, with migration fields generated by large cities being superimposed on those of smaller settlements. These hinterlands exist irrespective of broader regional losses or gains produced by rural—urban migration. Figure 2.3 has been simplified from the results produced by the 'residual method' and serves to pick out regional patterns of migratory change, but it completely masks the existence of actual migration fields. In addition to the countryside, old industrial and mining areas also lost more migrants than they gained and Figures 1.8 and 2.3, should be read with that in mind. Also, it must be remembered that compensating counter-currents are included in calculations for the residual method. They distort the patterns produced, as do rural—rural flows, which may originate from within national boundaries, as in the case of agricultural resettlement in Italy, or from across them, as in the case of the *pieds noirs* who left North Africa and settled in rural areas of France during the 1960s.

Between 1960 and 1971, net outmigration occurred in the greater part of Scandinavia, most of Ireland and Scotland, virtually the whole of central and southern Italy, great areas of Iberia (where the greatest rates of loss were recorded), Austria, much of western France and the Massif Central, and

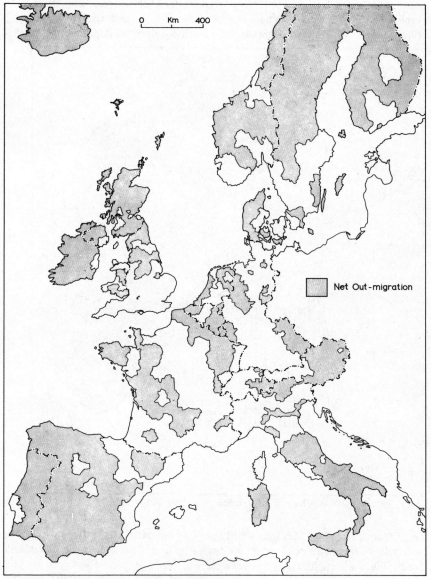

2.3 Western Europe: regions of net outmigration, 1961–1971

relatively small areas in West Germany, the Netherlands, and the United Kingdom. These zones vary greatly with respect to their physical resource base, socio-economic characteristics, and spatial extent. They are all distinguished by a predominance of agriculture and a relative lack of services and alternative employment, but the farming systems they support and the environmental conditions in which they operate are extremely diverse. Population densities

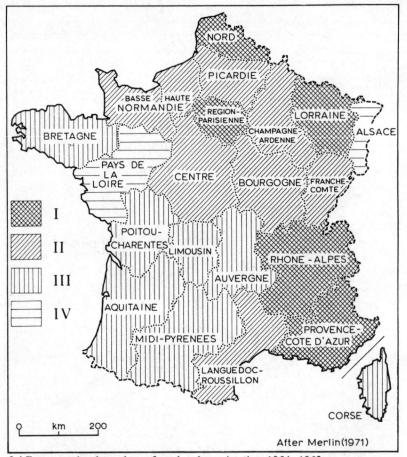

2.4 France: regional typology of rural—urban migration, 1954–1962

range from more than 100 inhabitants per km^2 in parts of the Italian south, to well below 20 persons per km^2 in the empty lands of Scandinavia, Scotland, and Spain (Fig. 1.2). High rates of natural increase build up population pressure and serve to accentuate outmigration from parts of Iberia, southern Italy, and the Republic of Ireland, but conversely, deaths exceed births in some other areas of serious outmigration (Fig. 1.8). Mean incomes are relatively low in all the departure zones, but what a Swede may perceive as 'poverty' would be viewed very differently by a farmworker from the Spanish interior. Finally, each of the departure areas is located in relative isolation from major poles of urban industrial growth and from the axes of transportation that link them together.

Examining the case of France in more detail, Merlin (1971) devised a fourfold regional typology, according to characteristics of rural–urban migration between 1954 and 1962 (Fig. 2.4). Five highly urbanized regions experienced strong flows of rural outmigration and managed to retain a high proportion of their migrants in regional employment centres (Type I). A second group of regions also underwent important rural–urban migration but lacked suitable urban centres to provide employment for more than a small proportion of migrants (Type II). Flows to the capital predominated from six of these regions, located in the Paris Basin. Languedoc–Roussillon dispatched large numbers of migrants beyond its borders to Marseilles, and many migrants from Franche–Comté moved either to Paris or to Lyons. The under-industrialized agricultural West, together with Corse, experienced less intense rural outmigration but its component regions managed to retain only a limited proportion of migrants (Type III). Very important long-distance flows linked Bretagne, Limousin, and the Auvergne with Paris. Other parts of the West dispatched migrants to cities in neighbouring regions, as in the case of the link between parts of Poitou–Charentes and the city of Bordeaux. The remaining two regions (Alsace and the Pays de la Loire) underwent relatively slight rural outmigration and retained a high proportion of their migrants (Type IV).

Whilst such aggregate patterns may be depicted at a regional level, relatively little is known of the actual flows of rural–urban migrants and the precise distances travelled. Not surprisingly, sample studies demonstrate an increasing importance of long-distance rural–urban migration as transport conditions have improved with the passage of time. Large urban areas and especially capital cities offer higher incomes than regional centres and medium-sized towns and draw migrants from very wide areas (Châtelain, 1960). In addition, such large centres are particularly attractive to rural migrants by virtue of the wide range of public service jobs that they offer in public transport, the civil service, post office, and domestic service (Bertrand, 1970). Pourcher's (1970) analysis of migrants resident in Paris confirmed this idea, with flows directed from all parts of the country but especially from Brittany, central France, and the Loire valley. The pull of Paris was felt above all in rural areas and small towns, with 55 per cent of the provincial migrants living in Paris having been born in rural *communes*.

Nevertheless, there is still abundant reason to stress the significance of short-distance rural–urban movements, which sometimes serve as preliminaries to subsequent moves over greater distances. The first point may be illustrated by the 'colonies' of Bretons that have become established in the towns of the Mayenne and in other neighbouring *départements*, where many rural–urban migrants have taken jobs as petty officials and in other service activities, preferring life in a country town to the anonymity of Paris, even though wages in the capital would be higher. Many other case studies demonstrate short-distance moves, for example from country areas in western France to nearby market towns and from relatively harsh upland environments, such as the Auvergne or the Durance plateaux, to lowland towns in the Limagnes or the plains of the Rhône and Basse-Provence (Estienne, 1958; Merlin, 1965). By way of illustration to the second point, Pourcher (1970), found that only 41 per cent of migrants to Paris, from both rural and urban sources, had made the transfer directly. The rest stayed temporarily at one or two, rarely more, places on the way. These stopping places were markedly more urban than the birthplaces of most migrants. Although 55 per cent of migrants had been born in rural areas, only a quarter arrived in Paris directly from the country. Many other migration studies emphasize the existence and importance of stepwise moves, which were, for example, in evidence at all levels of migration in Finland during the 1960s. Migrants from rural districts moved first to local centres, next to large centres, and finally many moved to Helsinki (Hautamäki and Viitala, 1970).

Causes of migration and characteristics of migrants

The diversity of reasons behind the decision to leave the countryside for the town have been elucidated by researchers from many branches of the social sciences. In the words of S.A. Stouffer (1962), '. . . nobody who contemplates the multiplicity of economic, political, social and psychological factors that must enter into the personal contemplation of any prospective migrant would expect any simple model using only two or three variables to account for everything' (pp. 109–10). Numerous classifications of these variables have been devised, but in the following paragraphs, factors are arranged in descending order of scale from highly generalized economic arguments, through community and social factors, to personal and psychological ones.

TABLE 2.2 *Reasons for Scottish farmworkers leaving farms (%)*

Pay	35	Living too far from the farm	4
Hours	11	Farm too remote	11
Inadequate housing	6	Bad relations with employer	20
Promotion	13		

Source: McIntosh, F. (1969), 'A survey of farmworkers leaving Scottish farms, *Scottish Agricultural Economics*, 19.

Reasons that may be broadly classified as economic, being linked to the nature of rural employment and remuneration, emerge at the head of virtually every list. Rural wages are almost universally low, job opportunities are limited, and farmwork is arduous. These points dominated a survey of reasons for Scottish farmworkers leaving farms on which they had been employed during the middle 1960s (McIntosh, 1969) (Table 2.2). Alternative employment in urban areas offers the prospect of a higher standard of living for the intending migrant and his family (Fielding, 1966). In addition, a range of subsidiary economic reasons might be quoted which include the diminishing demands for labour in mechanized farming and in old-established rural industries and services.

Beneath this broad range of economic factors, there occur important variations in what may be termed community conditions. These, in turn, may be subdivided into two groups. The first relates to material disadvantages of living in rural areas and includes poor housing, absence of piped water supply, electricity and mains drainage, and lack of adequate public transport and local shopping and education facilities. Important though these deficiencies may be in contributing to the decision for a rural dweller to migrate, there is no simple correlation between paucity of facilities and intensity of outmigration (Bracey, 1958). The second group includes parameters such as community spirit and quality of leadership which are difficult to define and measure from readily available statistics but are none the less vital in influencing rural residents to move or stay (Mitchell, 1950; Thorns, 1968).

Social variables include the sex, age, education, and residence of potential migrants. As E. G. Ravenstein (1885) noted in his seventh 'law', almost a century ago, rural–urban migration is a sex-selective process, with women being more migratory than men. The prospect of inheriting land and eventually managing a farm may offer a considerable attraction for a young man to remain on the land. By contrast, farm girls do not share in this reaction, being more influenced by the relatively poor living conditions that their mothers may have had to endure. Most country areas fail to offer adequate employment opportunities in manufacturing and tertiary activities, and many young women therefore see their future in the town rather than on the farm. They tend to move at an earlier age than their male counterparts who, if they choose to leave the countryside, may at least postpone migration until military service has been completed. Women also tend to migrate longer distances than men, as they seek employment from the range of tertiary jobs that are available only in capitals and other large cities. However, there are cases in which sex-selection does not operate in this way. Weight of tradition or family constraints may keep young women at home, and in cases where rural–urban migration extends into international labour migration, young men are primarily involved (Mabogunje, 1970).

No matter how sex-selective outmigration operates, imbalances are produced in rural communities. Normally, more men than women of marriageable age remain, but the prospect of being unable to find local marriage partners may provide a powerful stimulus for young men to leave for urban areas (Saville, 1957). The net result is to remove a significant proportion of the young adult population and to reduce the capability of the departure community for natural increase, so that the number of deaths may eventually exceed the number of births. It is of course less complicated for young, single people to migrate than for parents with children. A young person's range of commitment to and degree of involvement in his home community is almost certainly less. The decision to leave is often associated with critical stages relatively early on in the life cycle, such as leaving school and looking for a first job, settling down after military service, or finding suitable work and accommodation for a wife and young family. Provincial migrants to Paris were particularly numerous in the 20—25 year age group (Pourcher, 1970). Some 45 per cent had migrated alone to the city, 28 per cent were accompanied by husband or wife and children, and 27 per cent had arrived as children with their parents. Other studies broaden the age group for rural—urban migration to 15 to 30 years (Wendel, 1953). In many cases, counter-flows to the countryside involve a surplus of elderly people who simply cannot compensate for the young people who have departed.

Variations in education are also of critical importance in encouraging movement. The higher the level of education, the greater the probability that young people will migrate to urban areas in order to find the kind of work that will allow them to make use of their schooling (Hannan, 1969). Indeed, parents in some rural areas encourage their children to continue their studies so that they may train as nurses, teachers, or other types of white-collar workers and thus have marketable skills that will be in demand in urban areas (Jones, 1965). Long-distance migration to regional or national capitals may result. Sometimes parents encourage their daughters to pursue their studies and equip themselves for urban jobs, whereas boys are not encouraged to stay on beyond the minimum leaving age, since they are expected to stay on the land. Certainly, traditions regarding land inheritance and duty to one's parents on the one hand and parental attitudes regarding the future viability of agriculture and rural life on the other are crucial in affecting young people's views of rural—urban migration. But in many cases, as Beijer (1963) remarked, '. . . as soon as contacts with the outside world are established, migration . . . depletes the area as regards both quantity and quality, for it is mainly the most active elements who will seek to escape the poor conditions' (p. 322).

Size and degree of isolation of the home community may be of importance in affecting the decision to migrate. At a regional scale, net outmigration is most pronounced from the agricultural periphery of Western Europe, but when examined in detail there is evidence that young people living within easy access of urban areas leave the countryside more readily than their counterparts in remote areas where facilities may be poorer and the future be viewed more exclusively in terms of agriculture and the rural life. However, there is also clear evidence that the smaller the settlement, the greater the possibility of its decreasing in size, for large villages present a much better social and economic base for life and are able to retain population more easily than smaller settlements. In Spain, for example, few settlements with fewer than 2,000 inhabitants increased their population during the 1960s (Ruiz, 1972).

Ultimately, there are intensely personal and psychological variables which differ for each potential migrant. Variations in satisfaction with rural life and ambitions for the future are partially in response to an individual's character and intelligence but are also linked to the range and volume of information about urban life that are at his disposal for sampling. Research in the Netherlands showed that while migrants out of rural areas were significantly more intelligent than those who remained, migrants to other rural areas or moving only short distances were not (Lijfering, 1968). Formal education, the mass media, contacts with family and friends, and holiday travel provide images of an alternative urban way of life that offers both advantages and disadvantages when compared with the countryside. Personal contacts are particularly significant in this respect, since many rural–urban migrants (and international labour migrants) find initial accommodation and employment with the help of friends or family members who are already established in the city. In Pourcher's words (1970) provincials who decide to migrate to Paris are '... not going into the great unknown; 77 per cent of them have spent holidays or paid visits to relatives in the capital and 58 per cent already know someone who can assist them. A favourable environment on arrival helps the settling process; 41 per cent of the migrants find their first job through contacts or relatives. Furthermore, one-third of the provincials are put up, to begin with, by their friends or family. Despite this, the problem of accommodation is often mentioned as one of the main difficulties encountered by migrants. But the inconvenience of bad housing conditions is eventually accepted, counterbalanced as it is by the prospect of financial improvement' (p. 194). Long-distance rural–urban migration may often be explained by personal information flows and contacts which, in turn, may have stemmed from earlier forms of seasonal migration to urban work. Moves from northern Italy to France, West Germany, and Switzerland, or from the Massif Central to Paris exemplify this situation perfectly.

The impact of rural–urban migration

Migration from the countryside has important implications for the migrants themselves and for both departure and reception areas. The general assumptions are that migrants obtain better-paid employment, have access to improved social facilities, and enjoy better living conditions in the city. To an extent, each of these ideas is ultimately correct, but migrants often undergo a difficult and painful process of adjustment to city life and may initially have to occupy inadequate accommodation (Duocastella, 1957). Certainly, large rural flows of migrants to the cities of northern Italy and other parts of Western Europe place severe strains on local authorities to provide additional housing, educational, and welfare facilities that growing concentrations of population require. Naturally, the costs of building and maintaining facilities are higher in major urban areas

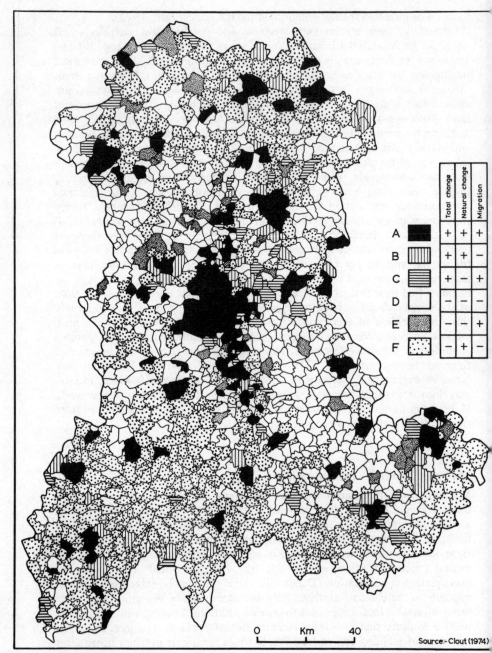

	Total change	Natural change	Migration
A	+	+	+
B	+	+	−
C	+	−	+
D	−	−	−
E	−	−	+
F	−	+	−

0   Km   40

Source:- Clout (1974)

2.5 The Auvergne: regional typology of migration and natural change, 1954–1968 when compared with their installation in smaller urban centres. As Kötter (1962) has argued, '... migration of surplus rural manpower to areas of concentration is no remedy, but merely aggravates the already difficult problems of the cities' (p. 3). A particularly severe example is provided by the *gecekondus*, or squatter colonies, that have proliferated around many Turkish cities as a result of intense rural–urban migration. They lack transport facilities, supplies of water and electricity, and function as transition points between traditional rural ways of life and more progressive urban housing which may be obtained later in the assimilation process. Similarly, there is evidence from northern Italy of southerners newly arrived from the countryside being exploited and paid wages below the normal rates.

However, the implications of rural–urban migration are equally profound for departure areas, which are affected with respect to size and structure of their resident population; pressure on land resources for agriculture and other uses; and provision of services for remaining rural residents. Since rural–urban migration is both age and sex selective, it has the effect over time of reducing rates of natural increase. Rural communities, such as 'Forestville' in northern Sweden, become increasingly old-aged (Rundblad, 1957). Strong outward flows of migrants have contributed to the recent reduction of birth rates in southern Italy and similar results have been recorded in many other regions. In parts of

TABLE 2.3 *Matrix of types of population change in the Auvergne, 1954–1962, 1962–1968*

		1962–8							% non-changers
		A	B	C	D	E	F		
	A	88	15	9	19	0	30	161	54·7
	B	18	13	4	14	1	29	79	16·5
1954–62	C	5	1	18	26	6	5	61	29·5
	D	8	3	40	290	50	57	448	64·7
	E	1	0	9	19	10	2	41	24·4
	F	38	22	15	205	14	242	536	45·1
		158	54	95	573	81	365	661	

Source: Clout, H. D. (1974), 'Population changes in the Auvergne region of central France 1954–68', *Erdkunde*, 28.

the Massif Central and central Wales the process has gone even further with deaths exceeding the number of births each year.

Below the regional level, there are important local variations in demographic 'health' which may be illustrated by reference to a sixfold typology of migration and natural change in 1,326 *communes* in the Auvergne region of the Massif Central between 1954 and 1968 (Fig. 2.5). The Cantal upland in the south-west represents a rapidly declining population reservoir that has been tapped by other parts of France for many centuries. Net outmigration involves most Cantalien *communes* and is greater than natural increase (Type F). Outmigration is less intense than natural increase in another group of *communes* (Type B) but in the eastern uplands of Forez and Livradois the cumulative legacy of decades of rural—urban migration has produced an elderly residual population and natural decrease now combines with net outmigration to form a veritable demographic disaster zone (Type D). It is clear when population changes between the periods 1954—62 and 1962—8 are examined in detail that many *communes* were changing from natural increase to natural decrease so that the demographic disaster zone expanded at the expense of the declining reservoir (Table 2.3) (Clout, 1974). Relatively few areas of the Auvergnat countryside experienced both natural increase and net inmigration (Type A). These were mainly commuter *communes* located in the lowland Limagnes close to Clermont-Ferrand or around other employment centres. This range of experience might be reproduced in many other parts of Western Europe (Duboscq, 1972; Nadasdi, 1974).

By releasing population pressure on land resources, rural—urban migration opens the way for farms to be amalgamated and enlarged and other types of structural change to take place that are desirable for the future viability of farming in Western Europe. But informal rationalization of this kind can be very slow to operate and in some countries has been accelerated by policies which offer annuities to elderly farmers, provided that they lease or sell their land for farm-enlargement schemes, and which supply practical retraining and financial help for younger farmers and farmworkers who agree to find employment outside agriculture. Very often, such men and their families need to move to urban areas in order to do so. In some areas pressure on land resources has declined so drastically that the demand for making agricultural use of it has contracted. Under such conditions, small patches of land, and eventually broad areas, will be abandoned. Alternative schemes for rational afforestation or the designation of recreation space need to be devised if the land is not to remain idle. Nevertheless, much abandoned land is still in the possession of individual or collective owners and maintenance of their rights poses complications for land-use planning.

In addition, contraction of the resident rural population may reduce but does not erase the demand for commercial, social, medical, and transport services in small settlements. But as thresholds of economic viability are passed, rural service functions may be withdrawn or not replaced. This adds to the inconvenience and isolation of the increasingly aged residual population (Lecoh, 1970). Contraction of services operates in a vicious downward spiral which may encourage even more rural–urban migration for those among the rural population who are able to move.

Implications for rural policy-making

It is clear that rural–urban migration is a powerful force for change in the countryside and that policies for rural management should take full cognizance of its implications. Various kinds of scheme have been implemented in individual countries for promoting change in farm structures, but in most cases inadequate attention has been paid both to local needs for alternative employment for those of a suitable age to continue working and to regional and national implications of rural–urban migration if sufficient manufacturing and tertiary employment is not installed in the countryside. Neither has the spatial impact of the declining but still surviving demand for rural services been appraised adequately and incorporated in rural management schemes.

In order to rectify these deficiencies, greater attention needs to be paid to establishing alternative employment at small towns or holding points which would also offer a range, albeit a restricted one, of shopping, health, educational, and other facilities. As Alberoni (1970) remarked with respect to Italy, '. . . the rural world must be urbanized if it is to become hospitable once more' (p. 306). Establishment of small holding points will prove a major challenge for industrial relocation schemes which have displayed considerable success in building up major growth poles in various parts of Western Europe but are less well geared to tackling the problems of smaller foci. In addition to economic policies with spatial implications for the surrounding countryside, new social policies need to be implemented effectively to help rural dwellers adjust from work on the land to alternative employment in workshops, on building sites, in transport, and in service activities. Certainly, these are the main conclusions from a UNESCO study of depopulation of mountain areas in Switzerland. Agricultural problems . . . cannot be resolved in the context of agriculture alone . . . Only long-term rural development and improved infrastructure can stop depopulation' (Biucchi, 1968, p. 235).

Schemes of this kind combining social, spatial, and economic approaches to rural problems have been attempted in several countries and perhaps with greatest success in Sweden. Now the revised Common Agricultural Policy for the enlarged Common Market is moving away from its past obsession with supporting commodity prices, towards implementing farm enlargement, defining priority agricultural areas for special assistance, and allocating finance for retraining rural workers and encouraging rural industries to be developed. This kind of policy is needed throughout the countryside of Western Europe but perhaps nowhere more urgently than in the Mediterranean lands. In the words of agronomist René Dumont (1961), '. . . the Mediterranean countryside appears to be dangerously overpopulated and definitely incapable of usefully employing all of its present population, even when current land improvement schemes are completed. Three forms of action need to be taken: industrial development (especially in Spain), planned outmigration, and birth control (especially in Italy). Without these, living standards cannot hope to be raised and will in fact decline rapidly' (p. 600).

Looking into the future it is possible that three elements of change may modify recent trends in rural—urban migration. First, rates of natural increase may well decline in some departure areas in response to local distortions of population structure. Some of these areas will register more deaths than births and will no longer function as reservoirs of potential migrants. However, unless attitudes toward family planning are radically changed, problems of rural overpopulation may well continue in Mediterranean Europe. Second, flows of migrants away from country areas may well be reduced in volume and distance, provided that rural holding points can be equipped with services and employment facilities, and adequate systems of private and public transport can be operated to allow daily commuting from rural hinterlands. As Hannan (1970) has remarked, with reference to rural Ireland, '. . . if enough factory jobs with a sufficient range of skills and paying satisfactory wages had been available in the home community, it is very likely that the great majority of boys and girls who had received only a primary education or a vocational education would not have migrated' (p. 252). Schemes for rural industrialization have been effective in Brittany and in other regions in absorbing young, relatively untrained labour, and together with the declining birth rate and increasing return flows of retired people, have contributed to the decline in net migratory loss recorded in the peninsula during the 1960s. Finally, urban—rural counter-currents may increase in intensity, with greater numbers of elderly people retiring to the countryside and 'dispersed cities' of commuter homes spreading even further from major employment centres. In any case, systems of interaction will become more intense and widespread by the end of the century so that our traditional notions of 'rural' and 'urban' environments will have to be radically revised.

References

Alberoni, F. (1970) 'Aspects of internal migration related to other types of Italian migration', in Jansen, C. J. (ed.), op. cit., 285—316.

Atlas of Social and Economic Regions of Europe (1964) Nomos Verlagsgesell-schaft, Baden-Baden.

Beijer, G. (1963) *Rural Migrants in an Urban Setting*, Martinus Nijhoff, The Hague.

Bernard, M-C., and Auriac, F. (1970) 'Les Retraités en milieu rural: exemple en montagne lozérienne et gardoise', *Bulletin de la Société Languedocienne de Géographie*, 4, 115–34.

Bertrand, P. (1970) 'Le Deséquilibre des migrations Paris–Provence s'attenue', *Économie et statistique*, 10, 3–26.

Biucchi, B. M. (1968) 'Exode rural et dépeuplement', in Commission Nationale Suisse de l'UNESCO, *Exode rurale et dépeuplement de la montagne en Suisse*, Fribourg, 211–37.

Bracey, H. E. (1958) 'A note on rural depopulation and social provision', *Sociological Review*, 6, 67–74.

Châtelain, A. (1960) 'La Géographie des salaires en France et son incidence sur les migrations de population', *Revue de géographie de Lyon*, 35, 381–93.

Clout, H. D. (1974) 'Population changes in the Auvergne region of central France 1954–68', *Erdkunde*, 28, 246–59.

Commission of the European Communities (1973) *Report on the Regional Problems of the Enlarged Community*, Brussels.

Cribier, F. (1970) 'Les Migrations de retraite des fonctionnaires parisiens', *Bulletin de l'Association de Géographes Français*, 381, 135–43.

Duboscq P. (1972) 'La Mobilité rurale en Aquitaine', *L'Espace géographique*, 1, 23–42.

Dumont, R. (1961) 'Les Excédents démographiques de l'agriculture méditer-ranéenne', *Population*, 6, 587–600.

Duocastella, (1957) 'Problèmes d'adaptation dans le cas de migrations inter-ieures: un exemple en Espagne', *Population*, 12, 115–28.

Estienne, P. (1958) 'L'Émigration contemporaine dans la montagne auvergnate et vellave', *Revue de géographie alpine*, 46, 463–94.

Fielding, A. J. (1966) 'Internal migration and regional economic growth: a case study of France', *Urban Studies* 3, 200–14.

Fielding, A. J. (1972) 'Internal Migration in Western Europe', paper to International Geographical Union, Commission on Population Geography, University of Edmonton.

Fielding, A. J. (1975) 'Internal migration in Western Europe', in Kosiński, L. and Prothero, R. M. (eds.), *People on the Move*, Methuen, London, 237–54.

Friedlander, D., and Roshier, R. J. (1966) 'A study of internal migration in England and Wales' part I, *Population Studies*, 19, 239–80.

Hägerstrand, T. (1957) 'Migration and area', in Hannerberg, D., *et al.* (eds.), *Migration in Sweden: a Symposium*, Lund Studies in Geography: Series B, 13, 27–158.

Hannan, D. F. (1969) 'Migration motives and migration differentials among Irish rural youth', *Sociologia Ruralis*, 9, 195–220.

Hannan, D. F. (1970) *Rural Exodus: a Study of the Forces Influencing the Large Scale Migration of Irish Rural Youth*, Chapman, London.

Hautamäki, L., and Viitala, P. (1970) 'Mechanism of migration in Finland in the 1960s', *Fennia*, 99(7), 1–41.

Jansen, C. J. (ed.) (1970) *Readings in the Sociology of Migration*, Pergamon, Oxford.

Johnson, J. H. (ed.) (1974) *Suburban Growth: Geographical Processes at the Edge of the Western City*, Wiley, London.

Jones, H. (1965) 'A study of rural migration in Central Wales', *Transactions of the Institute of British Geographers*, 37, 31–45.

Kötter, (1962) 'Economic and social implications of rural industrialization', *International Labour Review*, 86, 1–14.

Lawton, R. (1967) 'Rural depopulation in nineteenth century England', in Steel, R., and Lawton, R. (eds.), *Liverpool Essays in Geography*, Longmans, London, 227–55.

Lecoh, T. (1970) 'La Population des ménages agricoles: émigration et vieillissement', *Population*, 25, 497–516.

Lepape, L. (1970) 'Étude de la population des retraités et des personnes âgées inactives dans les villes touristiques littorales', *Bulletin de l'Association de Géographes Français*, 381, 123–33.

Lijfering, J. (1968) 'Selective migratie. Een empirische studie van de samenhang tussen plattelands migratie en selectie naat intelligentie in Nederland', *Meded. Landb.-Hogesch. Wageningen*, 68, 1–148.

Mabogunje, A. (1970) 'Systems approach to a theory of rural/urban migration', *Geographical Analysis*, 2, 1–15.

McIntosh, F. (1969) 'A survey of farmworkers leaving Scottish farms', *Scottish Agricultural Economics*, 19, 191–97.

Merlin, P. (1965) 'La Dépopulation des plateaux de la moyenne Durance', *Annales de géographie*, 74, 431–46.

Merlin, P. (1971) 'L'exode rural', *Cahiers de l'Institut National d'Études Démographiques*, 59, 1-228.

Mitchell, G. D. (1950) 'Depopulation and rural social structure, *Sociological Review*, 42, 69–85.

Nadasdi, M. (1974) 'La Situation démo-géographique en Belgique et au Grand-Duché de Luxembourg 1968–71', *Hommes et terres du Nord*, 1, 91–112.

Pinchemel, P. (1957) *Structures sociales et dépopulation rurale de la plaine picarde de 1836 à 1936*, Armand Colin, Paris.

Pitié, J. (1971) *Exode rural et migrations intérieures en France: l'exemple de la Vienne et du Poitou-Charentes*, Éditions Norois, Poitiers.

Pourcher, G. (1970) 'The growing population of Paris', in Jansen, C. J. (ed.), op. cit., 179–202.

Ravenstein, E. G. (1885) 'The laws of migration', *Journal of the Royal Statistical Society*, 48, 167–235.

Ruiz, M. P. (1972) 'Notas sobre el exodo rural y la evolución de la población en una comarca de tierra de campos', *Revista de Estudios Agro-Sociales*, 81, 23–60.

Rundblad, B. G. (1957) 'Problems of a depopulated rural community', in Hannerberg, D., *et al.* (eds.), *Migration in Sweden: a Symposium* Lund Studies in Geographye, Series B, 13.

Saville, J. (1957) *Rural Depopulation in England and Wales, 1851–1951*, Routledge and Kegan Paul, London.

Stouffer, S. A. (1962) *Social Research to Test Ideas*, Free Press, Glencoe.

Thorns, D. C. (1968) 'The influence of social change upon the farmer', *Farm Economist*, 11, 337–44.

Törnquist, G. (1970) *Contact Systems and Regional Development*, Lund Studies in Geography, Series B, 35.

Tugault, Y. (1973) 'La Mesure de la mobilité: cinq études sur les migrations internes', *Cahiers de l'Institut National d'Études Démographiques*, 67.

Tugault, Y. (1974) 'Croissance urbaine et peuplement', *Population*, 29 (numéro spécial La Population de la France), 207–38.
Vincienne, M. (1972) 'La Mobilité des agriculteurs', *Études rurales*, 45, 48–61.
Wendel, B. (1953) *A Migration Schema: Theories and Observations*, Lund Studies in Geography, Series B, 9.

3. INTER-REGIONAL MIGRATION IN WESTERN EUROPE: A REAPPRAISAL

PETER WOOD

Internal migration is a relatively neglected component of population studies in Western Europe, being a victim of deficiencies of data and of confusions between a variety of causes and types of movement. At present, 'internal migration' must be defined to exclude population movements between countries, although a time may eventually arrive when such a distinction becomes obsolete in Western Europe. A distinction should also be drawn between short- and long-distance moves. Short-distance residential migration, the greater part of which in Western Europe takes place in and around large cities or conurbations, has a very different social and economic significance from long-distance migration. The present chapter will focus on the latter type of movement, which is often yet misleadingly regarded as being synonymous with 'inter-regional' migration. Here it will be regarded as being the same as 'labour migration', whereby migrants change their places of employment and residence simultaneously. Such an approach possesses the virtue of defining relatively long-distance movement in terms of its economic and social significance, as well as its characteristic geographical scale. As a consequence, such migration can be viewed as a process of social change in itself, capable of being related to other changes in society, rather than as a mere symptom of regional disparities. Rather less weight than normal will therefore be placed upon the classic 'migration problem' regions, which suffer large net losses of population through migration. Instead, the characteristics of highly industrialized urban regions in north-west Europe will be given particular attention. Although in these regions migration imbalances are relatively insignificant, labour migration involves large numbers and is an increasingly important social trend. Clearly, regions of heavy population loss through migration need special attention, but their experience may be better comprehended in the context of an understanding of the causes of migration on a continental scale. Perhaps this theme can be best illustrated by reference to the conventional interpretations of inter-regional migration which have become widely accepted.

There is little doubt that the absence of suitable data has severely hampered the study of internal migration in Europe. Nevertheless, the situation improved considerably during the 1960s, with regard both to studying particular countries and gaining a panoramic view of the continental situation. In particular, the *Regional Statistics* (European Communities), which were first published in 1971, provide data on gross inter-regional flows and 'come as close as possible at the present time to achieving comparability of regional population statistics for a number of European countries' (Fielding, 1972, p. 1). Even so, the study of internal migration *per se*, examining individual and group movements and their relationships with other social trends, still has to be carried out in the framework of individual countries, each with its own population records and traditions of social survey.

Taking Western Europe as a whole, two apparent explanations of migration seems to be accepted widely, being derived from patterns of net inter-regional movement. Such patterns are illustrated in Figure 3.1 for the EEC and in

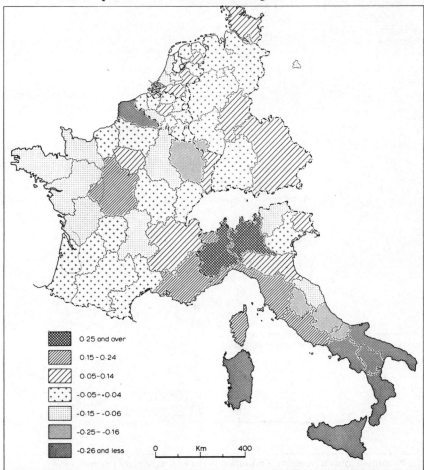

0.25 and over

0.15 - 0.24

0.05-0.14

-0.05-+0.04

-0.15 - -0.06

-0.25 - -0.16

-0.26 and less

O   Km   400

3.1 Regions of net loss and gain from internal migration in the EEC in the late 1960s

Figure 3.3 for Great Britain, using data for various periods in the late 1960s. (See Figure 3.2 for the dates relating to the continental countries.) The index shown in these maps divides the net balance of migration (in−outmigration, positive or negative) by the total number of migrants in each region (in+out

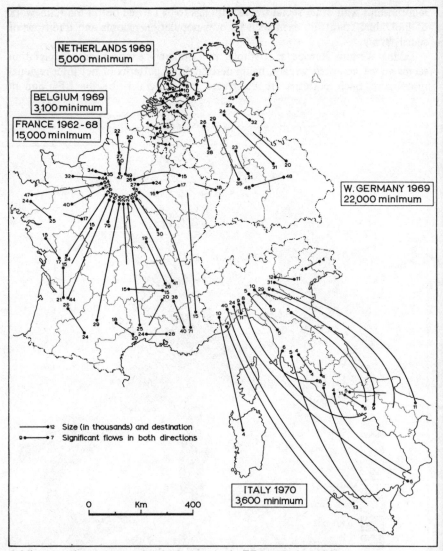

3.2 Patterns of gross inter-regional migration in the EEC in the late 1960s

migration). The first popular explanation of these patterns is based on the observation that migration takes place from declining rural regions to zones of industrial or commercial growth. Such a pattern dominates flows in Italy (from the south to the northern industrial areas), as well as in Spain (to the Mediterranean coast, Barcelona, Madrid, and the industrial area of Bilbao),

Portugal (to Lisbon and Oporto), and the Republic of Ireland (to Dublin and Cork). These countries also contribute appreciable numbers of migrants to the international flows of workers which have become so marked in the last two decades (see Chapters 4 and 5).

The second type of net inter-regional migration flow seems to take place from urbanized regions, characterized by old industries or mining, to economically or environmentally more attractive regions, with rapidly growing industrial or commercial activities. Moves from Scotland, northern England, and Wales to the

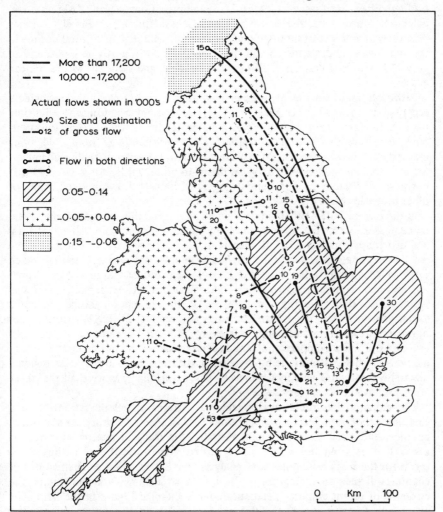

3.3 Net balance and gross flows of internal migration in Great Britain, 1965–1966

Midlands and southern England have long been explained in this way, as has the more recent relative shift of population from London to East Anglia and the South-West. Similar explanations for the predominant patterns of inter-regional movement have been employed in the Netherlands, Belgium, and West Germany (where the southern *Länder* have gained. at the expense of the Saarland, Nordrhein—Westfalen, and Rheinland—Pfalz.

In Scandinavia and the Alpine countries, internal migration combines net losses from rural regions with marked net movements to growth zones around leading cities, such as Stockholm, Gothenburg, Copenhagen, Oslo, Vienna, Salzburg, Innsbruck, Zurich/Basle, and Geneva/Lausanne. Finally, France illustrates most types of inter-regional movement, with regions of rural decline in the north-west and centre, of industrial decline in the north and east, and of growth in the Paris Basin, around Lyons—Grenoble, and along the Mediterranean coast.

Although these images of internal migration in Western Europe are widely accepted at a broad level of generalization, closer examination suggests that they may be fundamentally misleading as a guide to the nature of migration itself. Such is certainly the case if regional characteristics (e.g. 'rural', 'declining industrial', 'growing metropolitan') are associated directly with the characteristics of the migrants moving between them—in other words, if it is assumed that migrants in Western Europe consist largely of industrial unemployed, rural, or other low-paid workers.

In the case of 'rural—urban' inter-regional migration, this association may seem to be reasonable at first glance, since the social and economic milieux of rural and urban areas may still be sufficiently distinct in some parts of Europe for the 'area' to represent adequately the 'life' of its people. But even here there is much evidence that rural—urban migration is a complex process, and in any case 'rural' regions are becoming increasingly heterogeneous in economic and social structure so that migration to or from them can no longer be explained exclusively in terms of rural social change (see chapter 2). Explanations of net migration flows from declining to growing industrial regions must take into account still more complex and varied social processes. Simple economic theory has led to such patterns being associated with absolute and relative regional unemployment rates and income levels. Not surprisingly, as we shall see, these attempts have not been very successful.

The common interpretations of regional patterns of net migration loss and gain have, therefore, led to oversimplifications of the social processes at work in advanced industrial societies. Fundamentally, the study of internal migration as a social process requires a generally accepted framework of explanation which can form the basis for comparative analysis on a European scale. The rest of this chapter will seek to sketch the outlines of such a framework, drawing on the evidence of recent empirical, statistical, and sociological work in the field. The views put forward by A. H. Richmond (1969), on the nature of internal migration in industrial and post-industrial societies, will then be evaluated in the light of this disparate evidence. Finally, recent evidence from England and Wales will be used to illustrate the scale of inquiry at which progress in the study of internal migration trends in Western Europe can be expected.

Empirical evidence for inter-regional flows

Figure 3.2 uses EEC data on gross inter-regional migration to indicate the most important flows of population that were taking place during the late 1960s. It shows the pattern of actual flows, upon which the net balances of Figure 3.1 were based. Figure 3.3 depicts a comparable picture for Great Britain, derived from the 1966 Census of Population (Central Statistical Office, 1970). For each country, 'significant' flows are shown as those with more than a defined minimum level of inter-regional movement, allowing for the different numbers of regions in each country and the total gross movement between them.[1] In Great Britain, where cartographic clarity permits, a lower threshold is also used to indicate significant subsidiary patterns.

The varied scale of regional subdivision in each country makes direct international comparison impossible, especially between the extreme cases of West Germany and the Benelux countries, but a common and very significant feature of patterns in West Germany, Belgium, the Netherlands, and Great Britain is the high level of interchange between regions. In West Germany the *Länder* provide unsatisfactorily large units, compared even with the regional definitions employed in other countries. But the map shows how the net pattern of movement to the south during 1969 was only a marginal effect, compensated by considerable reverse gross movements. For example, Nordrhein–Westfalen lost 35,000 to Baden–Württemburg and 31,000 to Bayern, but received 29,000 and 24,000 respectively from these *Länder*. In Belgium and the Netherlands, the main flow consisted of exchanges between adjacent regions, but the small scale and high urbanization of these countries makes the concept of long-distance inter-regional migration difficult to separate from residential movement around major metropolitan areas. In Great Britain, a high level of gross exchange between Standard Regions was evident in 1965–6, with the major net balances favouring the South-West, East Anglia and the East Midlands.

As might be expected, the differential net effect of migration between the regions of Italy is much greater than in the countries of north-west Europe. Losses from Sicilia, Calabria, Campania, Puglia, Basilicata, and Sardegna are very large. In 1970, for example, Calabria lost 41,000 people through migration to other parts of the country but gained only 15,000 in return. In Sicilia the corresponding figures were 66,000 and 29,000, in Campania they were 65,000 and 30,000, while Puglia lost 52,000 and gained 26,000. Not only were the losses enormous but the turnover represented by these figures was also very great. The nature of migration even in these regions must therefore account for the considerable numbers of arrivals as well as for the losses. The patterns of exchange within the northern half of Italy are comparable to those in the industrial regions of north-west Europe, with marked net gains over-all in

Lombardia and Piemonte (which are merged together in Europe Figure 3.2, for convenience of mapping).

The pattern of migration in France for 1962–8 was dominated by the attraction of the Paris Region, although every other region apart from Alsace, Franche-Comté, and Corse received more than 15,000 people from the capital, as well as dispatching more than this number there. The largest net losses were recorded in Basse-Normandie, Nord, Bretagne, Pays-de-la-Loire, Poitou-Charentes, Lorraine, and Auvergne, while Centre and Provence-Côte-d'Azur gained markedly. Other significant moves in France were mainly between adjacent regions, although Provence-Côte-d'Azur, and Rhône-Alpes benefited considerably from exchanges with industrial regions in northern and eastern France and with Aquitaine and Midi-Pyrénées.

In general, there is an appreciable level of population exchange between the variously defined regions of Europe, although striking imbalances of flow are associated only with the peripheral non-industrial regions. Within the main body of Western European industrial society, exchanges of people between regions represent a more important feature of migration than any net losses or gains of population by regions—a fact of great significance in understanding the nature of migration. Statistical analysis of migration flows in recent years has tended to confirm the importance of this conclusion.

Statistical evidence on the nature of inter-regional flows

As empirical evidence for the directions and volume of inter-regional movement improved during the 1960s, so efforts were made to apply techniques of statistical modelling to available data. The purpose of much of this work was to discover which dominant characteristics of origin and destination regions (sometimes referred to as the 'push' and 'pull' causes of migration) 'explain'—in statistical terms—the major patterns of flow between them. In this manner it was hoped to find some basis for predicting inter-regional migration, which is one of the least understood and least predictable elements in demographic and economic planning. Rather than provide a brief review of all the work carried out in this field, the present section will concentrate on experience in Great Britain, where important developments have taken place in recent years. Comparisons will be drawn from the evidence of similar analysis in other countries at a later stage. The emphasis will remain on the contribution that these techniques have made to understanding migration patterns themselves rather than on the more general discussion of the place of migration in regional or economic policy.

Weeden (1973) has outlined and compared three approaches to inter-regional migration modelling. (a) *Ad hoc* models which use the regression upon net or gross migration flows of other variables, selected *a priori* because they represent factors which should influence migration. Such variables include relative unemployment rates, changes in employment or in total population over a prior period of time, wage rates, incomes, social structure, or even the physical characteristics of regions, as well as various measures of distance or contiguity. (b) Gravity models, based on the analogy with physical interaction, employing logarithmic derivatives of distance and other indices of the relative attractiveness of origin and destination regions (especially population size). These models of gross flows between regions are again calibrated by regression or analysis of covariance methods. They usually contain similar variables of relative attractiveness to those listed under (a). (c) Markov chain models, based on the assumption that the pattern of exchange between regions in the past may reveal structural constants which can be used or modified in a controlled manner to predict future probabilities of migration. Although Weeden does not consider them, (b) might also include the various 'intervening opportunity' models, stemming from the work of S. A. Stouffer (1960), which are log-linear in form but do not explicitly include distance as a variable (Galle and Taeuber, 1966). In practice, linear regression models have most frequently been applied to the British situation, although Hart (1970) used a gravity model as the basis for his study of gross inter-regional migration in 1960—1.

British work in the 1960s applied these methods to the variously defined Standard Regions, following the readier availability of migration data after the 1961 Census and the 1966 Sample Census. Much of it was concerned with net migration patterns between regions, but, as will be discussed shortly, Hart (1970) has demonstrated convincingly the value of investigating gross flows in the context of modern patterns of migration exchange.[2] Considerable effort was first expended on examining the effects upon migration in the United Kingdom of relative regional unemployment levels. The work of Oliver (1964), like the later work by the Scottish Council (1966), was heavily influenced by regional policy considerations, and revealed the conceptual and technical problems which this bias raises (Jack, 1968). Oliver's paper demonstrated some association between differences in unemployment rates and net inter-regional migration, but also how difficult it was to separate unemployment as a 'cause' of migration from other factors with which it is highly correlated, such as the industrial composition of regions, their social infrastructure, or even their weather (Hart, 1972, p. 156). More recently, Jack (1970) and Hart (1970, 1972) attempted to incorporate measures of relative 'employment opportunity' to explain migration patterns. Jack, however, used a measure of the change in average regional unemployment rates during the 1962—4 period, so that interpretation of the significance of unemployment indices remained a problem. Either relative unemployment levels merely reflect more general characteristics of the regions with which unemployment itself is highly correlated (since migrants, as Hart (1970) points out, are not usually themselves unemployed in large numbers) or unemployment levels are likely to be influenced by net migration and therefore cannot be regarded as independent variables. Doubt has therefore been thrown fairly comprehensively upon the unemployment 'explanation' of inter-regional migration, so beloved of labour economists.

Following this rather negative point, perhaps the most positive progress in this field has been made by Hart, using various statistical approaches for analysing inter-regional migration flows after the 1966 Sample Census (although his 1970 paper was based mainly on 1961 Census data). First, he attempted to avoid the problems associated with unemployment measures by using independent measures of changing 'employment opportunities' between regions. His first paper used a distance-based gravity model formulation combined with other variables chosen in effect on the basis of the pattern of residuals from the migration/gravity model relationship (Hart, 1970). Thus, the simple gravity formula provided a 43 per cent 'explanation' of the gross volume of migration between the regions of England and Wales in 1960/1. This level was raised to 56 per cent by adding a measure of the rate of industrial building since 1945 per manufacturing worker in origin and destination areas. Once the size and proximity of regions had been taken into account, the highest propensity to move was between regions with similarly high long-term rates of industrial building, while low migration took place between regions of slow growth. Further refinement, including *differences* in the rates of industrial building between the origin and destination regions (to allow for the element of movement from slower- to faster-growing regions) and the proportion of service industries in each region, added to the over-all level of explanation. Unemployment and indices of relative earnings, however, provided no significant extra explanation of gross migration patterns.

In summary, Hart (1970) states: 'it is clear that the migration pattern in England and Wales is different from the one which is popularly emphasized. While there is certainly a fair degree of movement from underemployed to prosperous regions, by far the most significant degree of movement is taking place between prosperous and prosperous regions' (p. 292).[3]

The statistical analysis of gross migration flows therefore suggests that the social and occupational structure of modern movement favours high levels of mutual exchange between prosperous regions, rather than the pattern of 'push'–'pull' from depressed to prosperous regions which forms the popular image. Although the limited value of unemployment indices now appears to have been generally accepted, the sociological evidence for the detailed nature of inter-regional migration has still to impinge itself fully on economic thinking. However, two further papers by Hart indicate that some progress has been made.

In the second paper Hart (1972) attempted to analyse migration at a more detailed geographical scale than that of Standard Regions, by using county data for Great Britain taken from the 1966 Sample Census. Unfortunately, net migration patterns for the year 1965–6 had to be used because of problems of obtaining sufficiently accurate gross inter-county migration data. The main conclusion that is relevant here was that changing employment opportunities in a previous period (measured according to the increase in county employment between 1961 and 1966) provide the main measurable impetus to labour movement. Unemployment (or the conditions which this measure represents) has some influence, but differential wage rates, given theoretical prominence by

Hicks (1963), again showed no influence whatever.[4] The degree to which, at this scale, short-term employment growth and migration (or labour demand and supply) are independent, and also how far inter-county movement is in fact simple residential migration rather than labour migration are both open to serious question in evaluating this analysis. In his conclusions, Hart points to the need for a more careful consideration of lagged effects on migration, representing perhaps the accumulated build-up of labour demand in excess of supply after a period of growth or even a response to the changing 'image' of regions. In addition, he emphasizes the value of further investigations into the experience and behaviour of different socio-economic groups. In this he was echoing Raimon's (1962) conclusions from ten years earlier, and he went on to produce, in another paper, evidence for the different migration behaviour of professional, intermediate, and manual workers (Hart, 1973). The analysis was of net migration by Standard Regions for Great Britain in 1966, and his conclusion confirmed that some priority should be given to the development of a more dynamic view of the influences on migration derived from sound time-series data (for example, Bennett, 1974).

The statistical modelling of British migration data has been reviewed in detail because there has been some coherence of effort since the mid-1960s in applying these methods to specific data sources in the context of regional development problems in Great Britain. The limitations of the approach have, however, also become progressively evident, but clear lines of useful development certainly remain for the future. Elsewhere in Western Europe complementary if somewhat more diverse and scattered attempts have been made to produce valid generalizations about aggregate inter-regional patterns of migration (Fielding, 1972). The failure of unemployment and related indices to explain migration patterns has been noted by Sommermeyer (1970) in the Netherlands and by Termote (1968) in Belgium. Again, more elaborate indices of changing employment opportunities or of urbanization seem to provide better statistical models, as also do religious and language differentials in appropriate circumstances (Jansen and King, 1968).

The availability of suitable data has allowed some workers to examine the migration patterns of different groups in far more detail than is possible in Britain. The studies by Jakobsson (1970) in Sweden and Courgeau (1970) in France of migration fields of population in differing circumstances have revealed how long-distance migration is likely to take place from isolated locations by young unmarried adults and by relatively more educated white-collar workers. The increasing mobility of the population over time has also been clearly demonstrated where suitable historical data have been analysed (for example, by Courgeau).

Models that place increasing emphasis upon the disaggregation of socio-economic groups, as well as upon gross migration between smaller areas than Standard Regions, may in the future be based more profitably on principles of 'intervening opportunity' rather than on elaborate modifications of distance-decay functions. Intervening opportunity models have been widely applied in the United States and have also been successfully experimented with in Belgium by Jansen and King and in France by Courgeau (Jansen, 1969). Like other methods which attempt statistical 'explanations' they suffer from the same problems of 'circularity of argument' as gravity and regression models. It is difficult to employ statistically defined variables for origin and destination regions that are convincingly independent of each other in their supposed influence on migration. Nevertheless, intervening opportunity approaches may provide models that are more sensitive in the use of disaggregated data in different regional situations, as well as allowing such work to be related more directly to the results of micro-scale social survey work on the causes of migration by different groups.

Willis (1968, p. 58) has pointed out that American developments of highly disaggregated gravity and interaction models (such as by Lowry, 1966, and by Rogers, 1965) lead strongly to the implication that gross outmigration depends more on the size and structure of the residential population of the origin area than on absolute or relative levels of economic opportunity, and that gross inmigration is to be explained by the size and condition of the labour market of the destination area. The conclusion from Hart's (1970) paper seems to point in a similar direction, even though his analysis has a very different basis. Apart from work on migration differentials in Sweden and France the effect of the structure of the residential population in the origin area upon its propensity to migrate is a question that has so far been confined largely to sociological studies.

Sociological evidence for the nature of inter-regional flows

Detailed questionnaire surveys of samples of migrants have been carried out in increasing numbers on both sides of the Atlantic since the early 1950s (Johnson, Salt, and Wood, 1974).[5] Although the desire to forecast group behaviour has undoubtedly influenced this trend, the tradition of social inquiry has tended to place the weight of conclusions from such surveys on the description of migrants' experiences without extending the implications towards aggregate models of migration. Nevertheless, some well authenticated generalizations have resulted from this work, regarding the propensities of different groups to migrate at various times in their lives, and their experiences when moving. In general, these accord with the results of analyses of aggregate data when they are able to probe into the patterns of movement displayed by various socio-economic groups in different regional situations. The prospects for integrating the macro- and micro-approaches to inter-regional migration study are therefore generally encouraging. Once more, this section will draw heavily upon British survey experience, and will later refer to other European evidence.

Two general comments about the evidence need to be made at this point. First, both the socio-economic factors that encourage or constrain migration and the individual and group motivations that are influenced by them are compound in character. 'Explanation', therefore, in terms of measurable indices such as employment opportunities, vacancies, unemployment, and so forth, which have a statistical meaning at an aggregate level, cannot be transferred simply to individual experience. At best these indices only provide surrogates for the variety of influences that affect individuals and groups. (This is, of course, equally true where models based upon multiple indices are concerned.)

A second consideration that needs to be kept in mind when macro- and micro-scales of evidence are being compared, and perhaps reconciled, is that geographical variations in the characteristics of migrants and in labour market conditions may cause the predominant influences on the pattern of movement in some areas to differ considerably from those in other areas. This is particularly likely when comparing evidence on a European scale, but many subtleties are likely to emerge even in a country such as Great Britain. If the social and economic characters of origin and destination areas do determine the structure of migration flows this is only to be expected. One study of migration between labour market areas in Britain, which will be referred to in more detail at the end of this chapter, found it necessary to employ a fivefold classification of areas, based on their employment, housing, and migration characteristics in the mid-1960s, and this only partially reflected the full variety of conditions found throughout the country (Johnson, Salt and Wood, 1974, chapter 3).

The compound nature of reasons for migration emerges consistently from empirical studies. Perhaps the most universally accepted explanations involve life-cycle stages and career patterns. The first of these reflects changing circumstances that follow marriage, an expanding family, middle age, and retirement. In general, mobility is highest in the early years of single and married life. Age is thus also reflected in contrasted patterns of mobility, and of course there are also differences between single and married groups. Life-cycle changes are common to all socio-economic groups but do not, of themselves, necessarily create long-distance labour migration; residential mobility is all that is required. Career patterns, on the other hand, are widely contrasted between different occupation and income categories and seem to differentiate between those who are or are not likely to undertake major relocations around the country. Educational background and training are obviously related to career pattern, as is income and the past experience of moving that migrants possess. Each of these characteristics might equally well be chosen to 'explain' inter-regional migration. Evidence indicates overwhelmingly that long-distance migration tends to take place most frequently among higher-income, managerial, and professional workers, especially in the younger age groups (below 35—40). The mechanism of 'spiralism' is classically invoked to explain this feature, since the motivations of such groups tend to be towards work improvement (Watson, 1964; Porter, 1968). On the other hand, manual workers are much more sedentary and orientated towards stable social relationships in their home area, except when young and single and perhaps aspiring to a different life-style.

These archetypes combine the results of several influences, as well as career pattern, on the propensity of the two groups to migrate. At one extreme, managerial and professional workers possess career incentives and financial resources to move; and, generally speaking, the location of suitable jobs, concentrated in major urban centres, may necessitate frequent migration from one city to another. Conversely, poorly developed career structures, relatively low incomes, and the ubiquitous availability of semi-skilled and unskilled manual work (at least in times of high employment) provide little incentive to move. This contrast is reinforced by the higher value usually placed upon social ties in an area by manual groups and by their relatively restricted access to information about opportunities elsewhere. Both of these conditions, of course, are probably by-products of a tradition of low mobility. Institutional factors, especially those associated with the housing market, may also add further disincentives to move. In general, the mechanisms that allow families to change house over long distances in Great Britain are heavily biased in favour of relatively well-off groups that can obtain mortgages for owner-occupied property.

The two categories described here oversimplify the situation, especially in the way they exaggerate the apparent importance of extreme groups in terms of income and occupational status. The 'intermediate' occupations from this point of view, consisting of skilled manual and technical workers and the lower-paid white collar groups, form a heterogeneous category which probably has an even greater contemporary significance in changing patterns of labour migration than its large numbers would suggest. In 1966 48 per cent of the working population in England and Wales were in socio-economic groups 5–9 (intermediate non-manual, junior non-manual, service and skilled manual workers, foremen and supervisors). Most of the factors which combine to explain inter-urban migration, and which work together to 'polarize' the experience of professional and managerial from manual workers, seem to act in conflicting ways for the intermediate groups. Perhaps the main factor which differentiates 'intermediate' households in their attitudes towards long-distance migration is degree of education and training, through its effects upon aspirations towards upward social mobility. In the long term, families in these occupational groups are more likely to make a radical change as a result of widening educational opportunities than are the families of semi-skilled and unskilled manual workers. On the other hand, social ties and traditions may still discourage many households from making significant long-distance moves, especially when suitable employment opportunities are available fairly widely in most parts of the country. There is, however, some evidence that the effects of housing constraints are most frustrating for some categories of intermediate workers in Britain (Harris and Clausen, 1967, p. 26). While often possessing the aspirations to migrate for career and social reasons, these households may not possess adequate resources to move as freely in the housing market as professional and managerial groups. Sociological evidence has therefore tended to confirm the pattern of behaviour of both relatively affluent and poor groups, without throwing a great deal of light on the complexities that differentiate between various categories of intermediate worker. One reason is the technical difficulty of applying the questionnaire survey method to those who have not migrated, even though they might have done so in other circumstances. Yet the most significant changes in attitudes and in the ability to migrate are likely to be taking place amongst these categories of workers and their families.

The situation of the intermediate groups also highlights the importance of the varying attitudes of workers to migration in different regions. Unlike socio-economic groups with extensive or very localized patterns of migration behaviour, they depend particularly on the opportunities that may be available within some defined regional compass. Such a range of opportunities varies widely between regions. In the south-east of England, for example, a technical or white-collar worker is more likely to be able to achieve his aspirations without moving out of the region than is a similar worker in the North. This situation also, of course, affects the attitudes of the other occupational groups to some extent, and also the prospects that are available for young workers entering the labour market.

This summary of sociological evidence about inter-regional migration rests on the results of work in Great Britain and in the United States. Perhaps the main needs now are for an accurate picture of the contribution of different groups to the total picture of change, and for a better understanding of the effects upon migration patterns of changes in the economic and social forces which underlie them. In continental Western Europe there is no evidence to suggest that these forces are working in markedly different ways, although the balance between the contributions of different groups to migration patterns may differ from country to country. For example, the high standard of living and close proximity of many nodes of growing industrial and commercial activity in north-west Europe points towards a high level of 'spiralism' and of mutual exchange of middle-class workers between regions. This may also include appreciable international movement. In addition, the large number of immigrant workers, often single and relatively young, seems likely to produce high levels of mobility by manual workers between regions, especially in West Germany and the Benelux countries. The influences of religious and language differences must also create their own localized patterns. On the other hand, the populations of some regions remain loyal to the values of rural and small-medium town ways of life, so that their attitudes to long-distance migration cannot be associated simply with the norms of industrial-urban society which may predominate in the major urban regions.

In many ways, the experience of West Germany would be most interesting in making comparisons with the Anglo-American pattern of migration, but unfortunately adequate sociological evidence is not available. Elsewhere, such evidence emphasizes the preoccupations of demographers and planners: in Italy, the drain of population from south to north; in France, the dominance of Paris. In Sweden, Gerger (1968) has provided a useful summary of the work that has been carried out on the motivations for labour migration (both within and between regions) arising largely from surveys carried out by the Research Department of the Labour Market Board. An interview survey of migrants between 1964 and 1967 showed that 52 per cent of moves took place for work or wage reasons, 20 per cent for housing reasons, and 15 per cent for family reasons. Forty-five per cent of the moves were over distances of less than 50 km, and among these housing motivations were more dominant especially where movement was to large cities and was by married families with children. More generally, migration was high (in terms of the sample proportion that had moved) for women (presumably associated with marriage), the young, the unmarried, couples without children, and among more highly educated and trained groups. It was also higher in towns than in rural areas. Another study of the migration experience of skilled manpower confirmed that training 'directs' skilled manual and technical workers to particular areas of demand for their services, as commonly do earlier personal contacts with the destination region.

The well-known survey of French migration motivations and experience by Girard, Bastide, and Pourcher (1964) has the rare advantage of examining moves that did not end in Paris, as well as those that did. Nevertheless, it concentrated heavily on small towns (70 per cent of the sample was taken from areas with less than 20,000 population) so that the extent of movement between the main industrial-urban areas is still largely uncharted. The results of the survey cannot be reported fully here, but, like the Swedish evidence, they illustrate general similarities with British surveys and also highlight particular differences of emphasis. Only one-third of those questioned were manual workers and these, along with farmers, artisans, and shopkeepers, were the least likely to migrate. Among mobile groups, young adults predominated and the motives of half of them for moving were based on work reasons. Finding work or career improvement were particularly important to those moving to Paris and other large cities. Personal reasons, including marriage, explained one-quarter of the moves, and these were more concentrated into small town and rural destinations. Other personal attitudes to movement are revealed by the relative willingness to move of those who had already done so at some time in the past, and the importance, for half of the cases, of pre-existing acquaintances in the destination areas, especially when these were Paris or other large cities. This factor may be particularly significant in France, contributing to the 'psychological' importance of Paris.

The comparison of different social survey results even within one country is difficult enough, and the problems are compounded in international comparisons. This seems to be inherent in the method of detailed social survey itself. The two easily accessible examples described here provide no more than an impression of the types of similarity and difference that might emerge from European-wide analysis of long-distance migration patterns within individual countries. Even though the aims of the Swedish and French surveys may have differed, the social character of migration shows marked similarities with the British and North American experience. Needless to say, the truth is far from the popular image of inter-regional migration being undertaken mainly by the unemployed or otherwise underprivileged. To a large extent, inter-regional migration is an integral part of the prosperous life-style of Western Europe. The evidence of large-scale analyses of aggregate data and of surveys of individual migrant groups therefore raises the issue of what 'generally accepted framework of explanation' can provide the basis for further progress in the study of internal migration in industrial and post-industrial societies.

Towards a framework of analysis

This review of inter-regional migration studies in Western Europe has juxtaposed evidence from various sources over the past two decades on gross movements. In some respects the disparate contributions, improved sources of data, progressive testing of statistical models at the macro-level of analysis, and social survey evidence, point encouragingly towards a consensus of opinion about the processes of social and economic change that underlie long-distance internal migration. They also highlight the significance of exchanges of population within urban-industrial Western Europe, as distinct from the more obviously important centre—periphery pattern that results in the net shift of population from backward regions. The fact that the contributions are disparate, however, also indicates a major reason for the confusions and oversimplifications which have been outlined. The evidence, at whatever scale of analysis, does not provide an interpretation in itself of the significance of internal migration in Western Europe. Something more imaginative is required.

In fact, an imaginative context for the analysis of internal movement has been presented by Richmond (1969) in discussing the sociological nature of migration (international as well as internal) in industrial and post-industrial societies: 'Internal migration . . . is multi-way, inter-urban and occupationally selective' (p. 239). He suggests that in post-industrial society only a residual of rural—urban movement remains as a last reminder of the predominant pattern of flows during the 'industrial' period of the nineteenth and early twentieth centuries (Richmond, 1969, p. 245). Contemporary movement is dominated by inter-urban flows between cities and metropolitan areas, resulting in comparatively small net gains and losses. The traditional search for 'push' and 'pull' factors to explain internal migration flows is no longer realistic, since migration, like other forms of occupational and social mobility, has become a functional imperative in advanced, post-industrial societies. Its role is to facilitate the allocation of human resources in a way which is not only economically more productive but also provides opportunities and choice for individuals. In Richmond's view, migration flows are only partly governed by geographical distance and are increasingly affected by the range of opportunities that is available in alternative places, in competition with other migrants (See Table 3.1 for a summary of the characteristics of relevance to migration).

Less convincing, perhaps, is his suggestion that, since the demographic and occupational characteristics of inter—urban migrants are very similar, the structural characteristics of the urban population are not affected by the large gross exchanges involved (Richmond, 1969, p. 245). He also emphasizes

TABLE 3.1 *Societal determinants of migration patterns*

	Type of Society		
	Traditional	*Industrial*	*Post-industrial*
Form of organisation	Gemeinschaft	Gesellschaft	Verbindungsnetzschaft
Typical locus of interaction	Communities	Associations	Social networks
Principal mode of production	Agricultural	Mechanical	Automated
System of stratification	Quasi-feudal	Class	Meritocracy
Main means of communication	Oral	Written	Electronic
Main means of transportation	Horse and sail	Steam-propelled	Jet and rocket
Population movement	Rural–rural	Rural–urban	*Inter-urban*
Type of migration	Forced (push)	Voluntary (pull)	*Transilient (two-way)*
Mode of coaptation of migrants	Assimilation/isolation	Pluralistic integration	*Active mobilization*

Source, A. H. Richmond, 'Sociology of migration in industrial and post-industrial societies', in J. A. Jackson, *Migration*, (1969), 238–81. Richmond explains that most societies today have sectors participating in all three 'stages of development'. Thus, most countries will exhibit patterns of migration that are characteristic of all three types of society and stages of development.

however, the selective nature of the movement; in current circumstances when, as Richmond himself admits (pp. 278–9), the transition to a 'post-industrial' state is not complete, the selective nature of inter-urban migration probably does have important implications for inter-regional changes in economic and social structure, quite apart from the continuing existence of net shifts of population arising from imbalances in gross flows between urban labour market areas.

In his conclusions on the prospects for post-industrial societies, Richmond adopts a 'McLuhanesque' interpretation of migration trends in which migration becomes the norm of behaviour and is multi-directional, *at least for selected age and occupational groups* (p. 280) (my italics). Individual migrants will not be tied to any one locality, but neither will they be 'rootless', alienated or 'marginal men' in the sense in which these terms were understood in the context of traditional or industrial phases of development. Instead they are involved in the world-wide communications network (*Verbindungsnetzschaft*-like social system) that is the characteristic form of social organization in post-modern society (Table 3.1). One likely consequence of the revolution in communications and organization, of which increased inter-urban migration by an elite or 'meritocracy' is but one symptom, is that educational systems will require extensive adaptation to meet the needs of new occupational structures. Training and retraining periods will extend, while the length of labour force participation is likely to contract. It is likely that the number and proportion of the population involved in inter-urban migration will grow substantially.

One does not have to accept Richmond's more grandiloquent interpretations of the effects of these trends in order to agree that inter-urban migration is symptomatic of a style of social and economic organization that is peculiar to the latter half of the twentieth century.[6] Nor is it necessary to find Richmond's view of the future attractive before one appreciates that increased mobility carries with it perceived benefits to which a growing proportion of the population may aspire. In these circumstances, workers who are tied to particular areas for most of their lives are increasingly likely to be viewed as under-privileged. On the other hand, Richmond's view is an oversimplification, understating the variety of social and economic patterns that may provide satisfactory life-styles for many people in different regions, and tending to accelerate the apparent process of transition towards the complete form of post-industrial life. In fact, at this stage, such a way of life must be regarded as little more than an 'ideal type' which spells out the logical consequences of certain current trends. The value of this scenario, however, lies in the questions that it raises about the extent and character of internal migration, and in the prominence that it gives to this neglected aspect of migration study.

Inter-urban migration: the case of England and Wales

From the view put forward by Richmond, the study of inter-regional migration should focus much more explicitly on inter-urban gross labour migration; that is, on moves between labour market areas, which usually involve changes in the place of employment, as well as of residence. Hence much of the work discussed in this chapter approaches this phenomenon at best obliquely, sometimes in association with short-distance inter-metropolitan shifts, which are predominantly residential moves without job changes, or with rural–urban migration, with its peculiar economic and social basis. Alternatively, the study of inter-regional moves that are not defined in terms of functional labour market criteria produces results that depend heavily on the regional system adopted.

The aggregate study of inter-urban migration should therefore begin with some functionally based definition of urban regions as labour market areas. This issue poses a number of well-known conceptual and technical problems. These have become more acute in recent decades, as journey-to-work patterns have become more complex. It is true, as several workers have pointed out, that the concept of the self-contained 'closed' labour market area is increasingly irrelevant as a model of the real labour market conditions found in advanced industrial and 'post-industrial' societies (Cullingworth, 1969; Kerr, 1954; Goodman, 1970; Hunter and Reid, 1968). Nevertheless, the commuting tolerances of individuals, of particular occupational groups, or of the working population as a whole do indicate the most appropriate *scale* at which to study labour market behaviour. Clearly, the more comprehensive the occupational composition of the commuting group being discussed, the less precise can statements be about its behaviour, but this is a problem that is not peculiar to labour market definition. In modern circumstances, private transport and the dispersion of employment locations have undoubtedly reduced the degree of self-containment of labour supply areas around particular nodes of demand, especially large metropolitan areas such as London (Lawton, 1967). Also, when the occupational structure of labour demand is very heterogeneous, any particular definition of labour market areas is likely to reflect the search area of some occupational groups for employment more accurately than others. White-collar workers, for example, generally have a greater tolerance of commuting than manual workers (at least in terms of distance and cost).

While emphasizing these reservations, however, the value of a functionally relevant geographical framework for studying migration patterns should also be stressed, as opposed to arbitrary definitions which may create even more problems of interpretation. In the United States, various definitions of 'metropolitan areas' have been accepted as representing functional urban units, defined on the basis of the size of employment centres and the patterns of journey to work into them. Until recently, this approach has been surprisingly neglected in Europe in spite of much discussion of 'city regions' as a possible basis for administration (Royal Commission on Local Government in England, 1966–69). Little attempt has been made to collect statistics and base analysis on such units. In Britain, this omission has appeared even more glaring since suitable data for metropolitan area definition have been available since 1921. Not surprisingly therefore, a recent comprehensive survey of urban developments and functions in England and Wales found it necessary to define urban labour market

areas, based generally on significant urban cores of more than 20,000 population
in 1961 and the associated surrounding areas that sent more than 15 per cent of
their residential working population to the core area (Hall *et al.*, 1973). One
hundred such Standard Metropolitan Labour Areas (SMLAs) were thus defined.
As Figure 3.4 shows, these did not cover the whole of the country, although
they contained 70 per cent of the population of England and Wales.

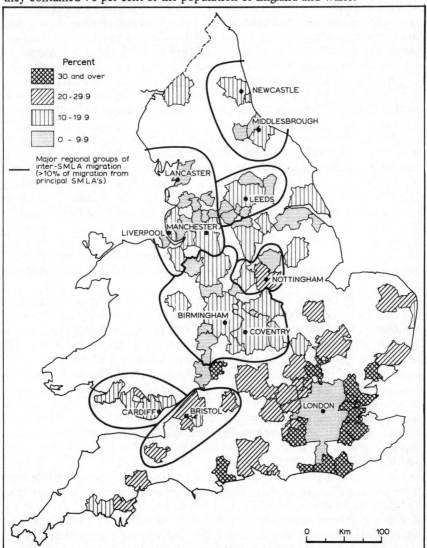

3.4 Patterns of migration between Standard Metropolitan Labour Areas, 1965–1966.
Percentage of outmigrants moving to London; and major regional groups.

These units represent the best available definition of functioning urban areas in England and Wales so that, for example, migration between them might be regarded as reflecting major patterns of nationally significant labour migration, eliminating a large proportion (although certainly not all) of the purely residential migration around towns and cities. Migration between the labour market areas so defined provides an important economic mechanism through which the supply of labour as a factor of production may be matched to the geography of demand. Its importance for individuals and families, on the other hand, lies in the magnitude of the decision, associated with long-term changes in family life-cycle and in career patterns. There are of course, other reasons for inter-urban migration, especially retirement, but there is ample evidence that employment reasons, in association with stages in family life-cycles, dominate the motivations for long-distance movement, unlike residential moves within metropolitan areas which are more frequently related simply to family life-cycle changes.

Following the definition of these SMLAs, direct evidence for the volume of inter-urban migration in Europe is largely confined to recent work in England and Wales. Because it is so highly urbanized, much migration within Britain is inevitably inter-urban in character, with rural—urban flows now being relatively insignificant. The largest volumes of movement, however, remain those within individual regions, involving mainly residential moves around and away from the large cities and conurbations.

The pattern of migration between the hundred SMLAs in 1965/6 is shown in Figures 3.4 and 3.5. The details have been examined closely elsewhere, but a number of salient points may be summarized here (Johnson, Salt, and Wood, 1974).

(i) The size of the SMLAs ranged from over 9,000,000 in the case of London, and between 1,000,000 and 2,500,000 for Newcastle, Leeds, Liverpool, Manchester, and Birmingham, to around 70,000 for the smallest SMLAs, such as Stafford, Kidderminster, Taunton, Shrewsbury, and Barrow-in-Furness. The character of the SMLAs, therefore, varied very widely in both the number and likely range of jobs they had to offer. The larger cities (most obviously in London) contained a number of sub-market areas for particular occupational groups, reflecting the location of employment centres and residential areas and the local conditions which govern commuting travel.

(ii) High levels of population growth in the SMLAs were concentrated in areas adjacent to London in the early 1960s, excluding London itself, and in the Midlands and southern England.

(iii) Only 51 per cent of the gross migration into the SMLAs during 1965/6 came from other SMLAs in England and Wales. Twenty-four per cent came from elsewhere in the British Isles (mainly Scotland and Ireland, of which some was also effectively inter-urban) or from abroad; and another 25 per cent came from the non-SMLA areas of England and Wales. The share of inter-urban migration, as we have defined it, was therefore high but not overwhelming—a significant

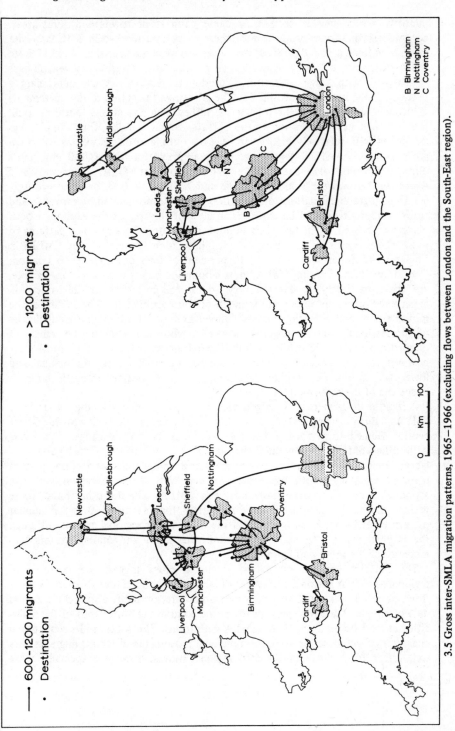

3.5 Gross inter-SMLA migration patterns, 1965–1966 (excluding flows between London and the South-East region).

minority of inmigrants to SMLAs came from small towns and rural areas, although an unknown proportion of these must have worked in SMLAs before moving. In total, over 600,000 people moved between SMLAs in the year 1965/6. (iv) As Richmond (1969) suggests, the pattern of inter-urban movement was 'multi-way' with large gross flows producing relatively small net balances between individual pairs of SMLAs. The adjustment function of the movements is strongly suggested by these patterns, rather than any strong 'push' or 'pull' factors. High net inmigration to the SMLAs around London, for example, was associated with relatively high levels of gross outmigration, as well as with high gross inmigration. High Wycombe, for example, attracted 10,000 inmigrants during 1965/6 but also sent 6,500 outmigrants to other SMLAs. The comparable figures for Luton were 8,000 and 6,800; and 7,200 and 6,000 for Guildford.

(v) The geographical pattern of migration flows was dominated by moves to and from London. This is to be expected in view of the size of the capital's labour market area, and exchanges with London dominated the migration patterns of most places south of the Wash–Severn line. More generally, few SMLAs in England and Wales sent less than 10 per cent of their outmigrants to London. Conditions in the London SMLA, in its labour and housing markets for example, are therefore likely to exert a very widespread influence on the migration experience of people moving over much of southern Britain. A good deal of the movement to and from this broadly defined London labour market area must be of professional and managerial workers, who can exploit the range of opportunities available in the capital. The definition of the London SMLA may, however, be too general to identify significant market areas for manual and lower-paid white-collar workers—these may be more confined to particular areas or sectors of the metropolis.

(vi) Significant patterns of migration flow also surrounded the other large SMLAs, Birmingham, Manchester, Liverpool, Leeds, and Newcastle. These centres seemed to perform a dual role, acting as foci for exchanges of workers with other SMLAs nearby and also as nodes in the inter-regional pattern of labour migration. Thus, for example, the Birmingham-centred flow pattern involved exchanges with other parts of the West Midlands region, but also attracted a net flow from more northerly SMLAs. On the other hand, more people moved to London from Birmingham than returned there. A similar pattern of exchange occurred around the other major regional centres, although the importance of the net flow towards the south and Midlands tended to increase for the more peripheral cities.

The patterns centred on major provincial cities suggest the existence of regional as well as national exchanges of labour migrants, although short-distance flows between adjacent SMLAs, as measured here, probably also include a good deal of simple residential movement, as the commuting hinterlands of the major cities extend beyond the 1961 SMLA definitions. The social and occupational character of the more localized intra-regional movements of labour migrants may well differ from those of the inter-regional moves, however, especially those based upon London. Regional systems of exchange were evident in the North West, the West Midlands, the North Midlands (including Burton-upon-Trent, Derby, and Nottingham), the West Riding of Yorkshire, the North East, South Wales, and the Bristol region (Fig. 3.4). Obviously, more evidence is needed to investigate the structure of these two scales of movement. The net effect of the national influence of London (i.e. outside the South East region) was to produce a marked flow to it from the North, the Midlands, and Wales, while net outmigration took place to such southern SMLAs as Bristol, Bournemouth, Portsmouth, and Southampton. Taken together with the other elements of the net southward flow from the large provincial cities, the result is a complex but persistent pattern of southward movement arising from a large number of balancing and crossing gross flows.

Conclusion

In attempting to examine various types of evidence from different disciplines and at different scales for the nature of internal migration in Western Europe, this chapter has inevitably become involved with methodological issues. In broad terms the factual situation is relatively clear, now that better data have become available during the 1960s, but the significance of such movements and what constitutes a reasonable basis for their prediction are still unresolved issues. This is partly because of disciplinary divisions within the study of migration, but also because migration is too often regarded as a symptom of something more important, rather than a force for social and economic change in itself. Migration is a social process which can be understood only in the context of a wider view of social developments as a whole.

Nevertheless, the evidence seems to point in similar directions; towards the study of migration patterns in industrial Western Europe as exchanges between areas, that is, gross flows rather than their net effects. It also points towards the study of the socio-demographic structures of the origin areas of movement and the relative economic opportunities which are available there and in the destination areas. A disaggregated mode of analysis of large-scale trends is required, at least according to socio-economic and age groups, with the lagged effects of changes in social and economic circumstances also being taken into account. These suggestions highlight the inadequacy even of data that have become available in recent years. If local labour market conditions are so critical in generating exchanges between regions then more attention needs also to be paid to geographical variations in these conditions at the appropriate scale of regional analysis, based upon labour market areas. A wide spectrum of such conditions can be postulated for Western Europe, from the periphery—centre exchanges that result in the marked net imbalances which occur between Scotland and southern England, or between southern and northern Italy, to the equal exchange of 'spiralist' middle-class families in the urban-industrial heartland of the continent, as envisaged by Richmond's post-industrial ideal. Between these extremes, every variety of economic and social structure may be combined. A comparison of Figures 3.3 and 3.5 for England and Wales suggests, very generally to be sure, the greater clarity that may be gained from regarding internal migration in these ways, even within the limited range of conditions found in that country.

It should be obvious from the suggestions made here that the scenario for post-industrial society (and for the transition to that state) suggested by Richmond is an oversimplification. But it seems to provide a more dynamic and imaginative stimulus to further work on internal migration than have regional migration studies in the past. The migration process is, of course, much more varied in its causes and consequences than he suggests, even in the highly urbanized British Isles. Elsewhere in Europe, more diverse social structures and trends provide still greater variation. Migration is a reflection of the variety of society, according to occupations, demographic structure, and human geography. Its explanation must therefore be sought in terms of these variations. Whether Western Europe is becoming more uniform socially or not, enough evidence has been reviewed in this chapter to confirm that diversity rather than uniformity of explanation is still more likely to produce valid generalizations about migration.

Notes

[1] The 'expected' level of migration exchange was defined as: Gross Number of inter-regional migrants ÷ possible maximum number of inter-regional flows in each country (proportional to the number of defined regions).

[2] One of Weeden's main conclusions is that models of net migration should be derived from gross migration models, rather than independently.

[3] American analyses of inter-state migration tend to confirm a 'push'–'pull' hypothesis, whether based on differential unemployment (e.g. Blanco, 1963) or income inequalities (e.g. Raimon, 1962, Okun, 1968). The explanation of this apparent contrast with British findings is probably revealed by Raimon's study, where relative wage levels seemed to affect long-distance movement (in a U.S. context) of white-collar workers, but were less effective in predicting short-distance movements. The latter scale provides a better point of comparison with the U.K. evidence.

[4] But compare with Raimon, 1962, where the effect of wage differences on long-distance migration was confirmed in the U.S.

[5] This section attempts to summarize the major conclusions from a variety of sociological studies. For a more detailed review, see Johnson, Salt, and Wood (1974), chapters 5 and 7. The expanding literature on the general state of migration studies, with some reference to internal migration, includes Mangalám and Schwarzweller (1969, 1970), Jansen (1969, 1970), Lee (1969), and Mangalam (1968). A useful bibliographic guide, up to the mid-1960s, is Welch (1970).

The main detailed sociological study of internal migration in America is Rossi (1955), which has exerted an important influence on empirical work in the sociology of migration. In Britain, two detailed studies are Jansen (1967) and Taylor (1969). At a higher level of aggregation: Friedlander and Roshier (1966). Influential studies in America, again from a decade earlier, include Leslie and Richardson (1961) and Rose (1958).

A good deal of investigation in the 1960s has been into the migration of workers: Harris and Clausen (1966), Ladinsky (1967), Lansing and Mueller (1967), Hunter and Reid (1968), Cullingworth (1969), Klaasen and Drewe (1973). A well-known review of social trends in industrial society, which points out their significance for migration, is Watson, (1964).

[6] Richmond (1969, p. 280): 'The migrants perform a catalytic function, instigating processes of change at the technological, economic and social levels that have profound repercussions throughout society ... [they are] agents of the post-industrial revolution itself.'

References

Bennett, R. J. (1974) 'Process identification for time-series modelling in urban and regional planning', *Regional Studies*, 8, 157–74.

Blanco, C. (1963) 'The determinants of inter-state population movements', *Journal of Regional Science*, 5, 77–84.

Central Statistical Office (1970) *Abstract of Regional Statistics*, London.

Courgeau, D. (1970) 'Les Champs migratoires en France', *Cahiers de l'Institut National d'Études Démographiques*, 58.

Cullingworth, J. B. (1969) *Housing and Labour Mobility*, OECD, Paris.

European Communities (1971) *Regional Statistics*, Brussels.

Fielding, A. J. (1972) 'Internal migration in Western Europe', Paper to International Geographical Union, Commission on Population Geography, University of Edmonton.

Fielding, A. J. (1975) 'Internal migration in Western Europe', in Kosiński, L., and Prothero, R. M. (eds.), *People on the Move*, Methuen, London, 237–54.

Friedlander, D., and Roshier, R. J. (1966) 'A study of internal migration in England and Wales', Part II, *Population Studies*, 20, 45–59.

Galle, O. R. and Taeuber, E. (1966) 'Metropolitan migration and intervening opportunities', *American Sociological Review*, 31, 5–13.

Gerger, T. (1968) 'Investigations into the migration of manpower', *Geografiska Annaler*, 50(B), 27–31.

Girard, A., Bastide, H., and Pourcher, G. (1964) 'Mobilité géographique et concentration urbaine en France—une enquête en province', *Population*, 19, 227–66. Also translated into English in Jansen, C. J. (ed.) (1970), *Readings in the Sociology of Migration*, Oxford, 203–53.

Goodman, J. F. G. (1970) 'The definition and analysis of local labour markets: some empirical problems', *British Journal of Industrial Relations*, 8, 179–95.

Hall, P. *et al.* (1973) *The Containment of Urban England*, I, Allen and Unwin, London.

Harris, A. I. and Clausen, R. (1967) *Labour Mobility in Great Britain, 1953–63*, Government Social Survey, London.

Hart, R. A. (1970) 'A model of inter-regional migration in England and Wales', *Regional Studies*, 4, 279–96.

Hart, R. A. (1972) 'The economic influences on internal labour force migration', *Scottish Journal of Political Economy*, 19, 151–73.

Hart, R. A. (1973) 'Economic expectations and the decision to migrate: an analysis by socio-economic groups', *Regional Studies*, 7, 271–85.

Hicks, J. R. (1963) *The Theory of Wages*, Macmillan, London.

Hunter, L. C., and Reid, G. L. (1968) *Urban Worker Mobility*, OECD, Paris.

Jack, A. B. (1968) 'The Scottish Council study of migration within the United Kingdom: some comments', *Regional Studies*, 2, 21–6.

Jack, A. B. (1970) 'A short run model of inter-regional migration', *The Manchester School*, 38, 15–28.

Jack, A. B. (1971) 'Inter-regional migration in Great Britain: some cross-sectional evidence', *Scottish Journal of Political Economy*, 19, 147–60.

Jackson, J. A. (ed.) (1969) *Migration*, Cambridge University Press.

Jakobsson, A. (1970) *Omflyttningen i Sverige, 1950–1960*, Statistika Central-bryn, Stockholm.

Jansen, C. J. (1967) *Social Aspects of Internal Migration*, University of Bath.

Jansen, C. J. (1969) 'Some sociological aspects of migration', in Jackson, J. A. (ed.); *Migration*, Cambridge, 61–2.

Jansen, C. J. (1970) 'Migration: a sociological problem', in Jansen, C. J. (ed.), *Readings in the Sociology of Migration*, Pergamon, Oxford, 3–35.

Jansen, C. J., and King, R. C. (1968) 'Migration et occasions intervenantes en Belgique', *Recherche économique de Louvain*, 4.

Johnson, J. H., Salt, J., and Wood, P. A. (1974) *Housing and the Migration of Labour in England and Wales*, Saxon House, Farnborough.

Kerr, C. (1954) 'The Balkanisation of labor markets', in Bakke, E. W. (ed.), *Labor Mobility and Economic Opportunities*, M.I.T. Press, Cambridge, Mass.

Klaasen, L. H., and Drewe, P. (1973) *Migration Policy in Europe: a Comparative Study*, Saxon House, Farnborough.

Ladinsky, J. (1967) 'Occupational determinants of geographic mobility among professional workers', *American Sociological Review*, 32, 253–64.

Lansing, J. B., and Mueller, E. (1967) *The Geographic Mobility of Labor*, Univ. of Michigan Press, Ann Arbor.

Lawton, R. (1967) 'The journey-to-work in Britain, some trends and problems', *Regional Studies*, 2, 27–40.

Lee, E. S. (1969) 'A theory of migration', in Jackson, J. A. (ed.) (1969), *Migration*, Cambridge, 282–97.

Leslie, G. R., and Richardson, A. H. (1961) 'Life-cycle, career pattern and the decision to move', *American Sociological Review*, 26, 894–902.

Lowry, I. S. (1966) *Migration and Metropolitan Growth: two analytical models*, Institute of Government and Public Affairs, University of California.

Mangalam, J. J. (1968) *Human Migration*, Univ. of Ohio Press, Lexington.

Mangalam, J. J., and Schwarzweller, H. K. (1969) 'General theory in the study of migration. Current needs and difficulties', *International Migration Review*, 3, 3–18.

Mangalam, J. J., and Schwarzweller, H. K. (1970) 'Some theoretical guidelines towards a sociology of migration', *International Migration Review*, 4, 5–20.

Oliver, F. R. (1964) 'Inter-regional migration and unemployment, 1951–1961', *Journal of the Royal Statistical Society*, Series A, 127, 42–75.

Okun, B. (1968) 'Inter-state population migration and state income inequality', *Economic Development and Cultural Change*, 16, 297–313.

Porter, J. (1968) 'The future of upward social mobility', *American Sociological Review*, 33, 5–19.

Raimon, R. L. (1962) 'Inter-state migration and wage theory', *Review of Economics and Statistics*, 44, 428–38.

Richmond, A. H. (1969) 'Sociology of migration in industrial and post-industrial societies', in Jackson, J. A. (ed.), *Migration*, Cambridge, 238–81.

Rogers, A. (1965) *An Analysis of Inter-regional Migration in California*, Center for Planning and Regional Development, University of California.

Rose, A. M. (1958) 'Distance of migration and socio-economic status of migrants', *American Sociological Review*, 23, 420–23.

Rossi, P. H. (1955) *Why Families Move: A Study in the Social Psychology of Urban Residential Mobility*, Free Press, Glencoe.

Royal Commission on Local Government in England (1966—9) *Report*, I; and II *Memorandum of Dissent* (D. Senior), HMSO, London.

Scottish Council (1966) *Emigration and Immigration: the Scottish Situation*, Edinburgh.

Sommermeyer, W. H. (1970) 'Multi-polar human flow models', unpublished paper, Regional Science Association meeting, Rotterdam, March 1970.

Stouffer, S. A. (1960) 'Intervening opportunities and competing migrants', *Journal of Regional Science*, 2, 1—21.

Taylor, R. C. (1969) 'Migration and Motivation' in Jackson, J. A. (ed.), *Migration* (1969), Cambridge.

Termote, M. (1968) *Un Modèle de migration pour la Belgique*, Université Catholique de Louvain.

Watson, W. (1964) 'Social mobility and social class in industrial communities', in Gluckman, M. (ed.), *Closed Systems and Open Minds*, Oliver and Boyd, New York, 129—57.

Weeden, R. (1973) 'Inter-regional migration models and their application to Great Britain', *NIESR, Regional Papers*, 2, 51—67.

Welch, R. (1970) *Migration Research and Migration in Britain: A Bibliography*, University of Birmingham, Centre for Urban and Regional Research, Occasional Paper, 14.

Willis, J. (1968) *Population Growth and Movement*, Centre for Environmental Studies, Working Paper, 12.

4. INTERNATIONAL LABOUR MIGRATION: THE GEOGRAPHICAL PATTERN OF DEMAND

JOHN SALT

Introduction

In the long history of human migration in Europe, many themes have been enacted. Refuge from war, flight from religious persecution, dispossession from the soil, attraction of the town, search for the sun, or simply escape from hard environment have all motivated waves of migrants from time to time. For several centuries an underlying theme has been the allure of lands of opportunity. Some of these have been at a great distance, for example North America in the nineteenth century and Oceania in the twentieth; others have been much closer at hand. The spirit of liberalism that prevailed in all nations into the twentieth century allowed relatively free movement of people between states to live and work. Consequently the literature on European migration is replete with examples of European nationals—northern, western, eastern, and southern—who have moved from their mother countries to gain livelihoods elsewhere in the Continent, where better economic and social opportunities were thought to prevail.

Since 1945, the industrial countries of continental Europe, in their search for economic growth, have taken advantage of the long-established tendency for some migrants to better themselves by seeking job opportunities in other lands. First one country in north-west Europe, then another, sought to orchestrate the diverse patterns of movement, to guide, to channel, to attract. The inducements have been high pay and steady jobs offered to willing hands around the Mediterranean Basin and even across the Sahara Desert. The rewards to the industrial countries have been high—often prodigious—rates of economic growth, and relief for their own people from dirty, boring, and otherwise undesirable jobs. Only recently have the costs begun to hit home, especially the difficulties of assimilating large numbers of often transient foreign workers, who have seemed increasingly to incur economic liabilities for the host country as well as plucking the strings of social conscience.

The theme of labour migration is not a new one in Europe but during the last two decades the voluntary search for permanent work in other countries has achieved massive proportions. In western and northern Europe, gross annual movement of foreign workers has recently been averaging between 2,000,000 and 3,000,000 per annum. The whole of north-west and Mediterranean Europe, North Africa, and even Francophone West Africa, have been incorporated into one vast labour market. Manpower decisions taken in one country can have a direct bearing on levels of employment and unemployment in any one of a dozen others. Migration flows can be quickened, slowed, or reversed by a twist of the tap.

The situation has not gone unnoticed and an increasing volume of literature has been devoted to a wide range of aspects of this contemporary international movement (for example, Bouscaren, 1969; Rose, 1969; Böhning, 1972; Castles and Kosack, 1973; Böhning and Maillat, 1974; a useful bibliography is Hogarth and Salt, 1973). The economic reasons for, and especially the social problems arising from, migration have been debated at length. However, there have been few attempts at a geographical synthesis of modern European labour migration and this chapter and the next add to the literature by stressing the spatial structure of migration streams, and the conditions with which they are associated in both destination and origin areas.

In this chapter attention is devoted initially to a broad view of the evolution of labour migration since 1945, including the main reasons for the movement, the development of its geographical pattern, and some of its principal social consequences. The second part of the chapter will focus on the situation in West Germany, where the immigration of foreign workers (*Gastarbeiter*) has assumed very great importance. Particular attention will be paid to a hitherto neglected branch of the study of foreign worker migration, namely the patterns of areal differentiation that have developed within the immigration country. Throughout, emphasis will be on migrants seeking permanent work and not on daily cross-frontier movements or on migration for purely seasonal work.

In very general terms, contemporary labour migration in Western Europe is of a fairly well-defined type. Most migrants are unmarried, unskilled workers, usually from the Mediterranean area, who have been drawn into the industrial powerhouse of north-west Europe. Most of the migration is not seasonal, but neither can it strictly be termed permanent since, initially at any rate, few of those moving intend to settle permanently in the host country. Thus, an annual turnover of about 50 per cent is average. Migration to the United Kingdom is an exception; a majority of its immigrants during the last two decades seem to have moved with the intention of settling permanently in the mother country of the Commonwealth. To this end family settlement has been the rule in the United Kingdom, and this probably explains the greater stability of the geographical flow pattern of migrants to this country, compared with others in north-west Europe (see below, especially Figs. 4.8 and 4.9).

Number of foreign workers

As yet only approximate estimates can be made of either the numbers of workers migrating in any one year, or of the total numbers of migrants currently working in the countries of north-west Europe, because of lack of data. For 1971, official statistics suggested about 6,500,000 foreign workers in West Germany, France, Switzerland, Benelux, and the United Kingdom. Allowing, however, for the large amount of clandestine migration, which either enters official statistics belatedly or not at all, this figure is almost certainly an underestimate. It has been suggested, for example, that the Austrian and French figures are 20 per cent below reality (ILO, 1973). Hume (1973) estimated the total numbers of foreign workers in north-west Europe in 1973 was about 8,000,000 (plus 1,000,000 dependants). The International Labour Office (1973) estimated that for the EEC plus Austria, Norway, Sweden, and Switzerland the figure was 7,500,000. An article in *Time* (1973) estimated that about 7 per cent of the labour force of the countries of the EEC consisted of foreigners and that, in total, the migrant workers constitute the EEC's sixth largest 'country', between the Netherlands and Belgium in size of population. The United Nations is reported to have forecast that by 1980 the total immigrant labour force in Western Europe could reach 22,000,000, although in the light of recent events this now seems unlikely. What is clear is that in certain countries and industries migrant workers are a large and potentially powerful group. Table 4.1

TABLE 4.1 *Foreign workers employed at the end of 1973*

	Number (000s)	% of labour force
West Germany	2,500	12
France	2,300	10
Switzerland	600	30
Sweden	220	6
Belgium	200	7
Netherlands	80	2
Luxembourg	33	30
Italy	33	0·3

summarizes the number of foreign workers employed at the end of 1973 in the main labour-importing countries. France and West Germany are clearly the major immigration countries, followed by Switzerland, Sweden, and Belgium. The dependence on foreign labour is better illustrated if the proportion of the total labour force accounted for by aliens is considered (column 2). They make up about one-third of the labour force in Switzerland and Luxembourg, while West Germany, France, Belgium, and Sweden exhibit a heavy dependence on them. Even Italy, traditionally a labour-exporting country, has markedly increased its immigration of foreign workers in recent years. During 1973–4, however, there were signs of a slowing down in rates of recruitment. To some extent, this can be attributed to fears of industrial recession, but it also reflects increasing concern in the destination countries with the problems of assimilating a large, if temporary, foreign minority. (See Postscript p. 220).

Reasons for labour migration

At the heart of the explanation for the migration of labour is the demographic fact that in recent decades the growth of population in the industrial countries of Europe has been slight and shows few signs of increasing. A natural consequence has been a slow-growing indigenous labour force: between 1960 and 1970 the European labour force as a whole grew at only 0·6 per cent per annum. Some countries (Austria and East Germany) actually experienced decline; increases in West Germany and the United Kingdom were only 0·3 per cent and 0·4 per cent per annum respectively. Only Turkey, with 1·9 per cent per annum, had a high growth rate in its indigenous labour force. Projections by the International Labour Office suggest a continuation of this trend to 1980, with Europe's labour force growing only one-third as fast as that of the rest of the world (ILO, 1973).

With indigenous labour force growth failing to keep pace with burgeoning economic growth, it was natural for industrial north-west Europe to look elsewhere for labour supplies. Initially, the resettling of wartime displaced persons and the transfer of labour from agriculture satisfied increasingly labour-hungry urban areas, but the inadequacy of these sources was soon manifest. To the south, around the Mediterranean and in Africa, were countries with different population/employment relationships. Not only were population growth rates higher than to the north, but widespread unemployment and slow economic growth meant a reserve of labour only too willing to explore the *El Dorados* of Paris, Stuttgart, Geneva, and elsewhere. What could be more natural than for the countries of labour shortage to co-operate with those of labour surplus in bringing about greater equilibrium in the European labour market?

It would be wrong to assume that immigration of foreign labour means there are no indigenous labour surpluses in the host countries. In fact, concurrent surpluses and shortages of labour have usually been the case. To some extent these imbalances have been regional and countries have encouraged the immigration of foreign labour into some regions while their own workers were experiencing unemployment elsewhere. In other cases, imbalances have been occupational, with the indigeneous population refusing to accept some of the low-paid, dirty jobs on offer. Hence in 1964 Belgium had 61,000 unsatisfied job applications, but still issued 40,700 working permits to foreign workers (Bouscaren, 1969); in 1970, France had 262,000 registered unemployed but received between 600,000 and 700,000 foreign workers; in West Germany in 1970, the figures were 144,000 and 700,000. Many of the indigenous unemployed would be either unemployable or just changing jobs, but undoubtedly many more were in economically depressed areas and were geographically immobile. In the United Kingdom, for example, many immigrants came to work in the labour-short service sector in London during the 1960s, at the same time as unemployment rates of 5 per cent were common in the development areas. Thus, labour migration from abroad has helped smooth out spatial and occupational imbalances between labour demand and the indigenous supply.

By the 1970s, recruitment of foreign workers had become a central plank for continued growth and prosperity in much of north-west Europe. It started, however, as a short-term economic expedient to ease what seemed a partial labour shortage for certain unpopular jobs, especially in areas of strong labour demand such as southern Germany and the Paris basin. Rather than encourage permanent settlement, which might have caused long-term social problems of assimilation, countries preferred to admit foreign workers under contract, usually lasting a year but renewable for further periods. The policy had another advantage in that foreign workers could provide a buffer against the vagaries of the economic cycle for the indigenous labour force. In times of unemployment it was assumed that the nationals of the host country could be protected by the release from employment of aliens—the so-called *konjunkturpuffer* approach. Thus began what Böhning (1972) has called 'the self-feeding process of economic migration'. From being concentrated in only a few sectors of the economy foreigners have increasingly penetrated into all sectors because rising standards of living have induced a flight from the dirty and otherwise undesirable jobs that occur universally. Not only have these been the purely labouring jobs, but also the boring production line jobs where mass-production techniques are often composed of a series of simple tasks for which unskilled foreigners are easily trained. Thus there has occurred an exodus of indigenous workers from 'blue-collar' occupations, their places being taken by migrants who have been able to exert little pressure for an upward revision of wage rates. Many of the economies of north-west Europe have thus ensured themselves of a plentiful supply of cheap, low-skilled labour. What started as a partial shortage of labour has become a general shortage, ironically increased by the additional demands created by the build-up of ethnic communities of migrants.

The process can be observed in the occupations and economic sectors entered by migrants. Most of them have entered the low-status, poorly-paid, unattractive jobs shunned by the indigenous population. Throughout the 1950s migrants worked mostly in labouring jobs in agriculture, mining, construction, and services, where the most unpleasant and worst-paid jobs were to be found. Until 1954, agriculture was the main employer of migrant workers in France, while even in 1956, 95 per cent of foreigners recruited for employment in West Germany were seasonal agricultural workers. In Switzerland, domestic service, agriculture, and the catering trades were the chief employers of migrants in the early years. In Belgium, the attraction of the coalmining industry was paramount until the Marcinelle colliery disaster of 1956 deterred many migrants.

What has happened over the years is an increasing penetration of foreign workers into all branches of the economy. Agriculture, mining and services have recruited proportionately fewer migrants, while manufacturing has recruited more, although there are signs in the mid-1970s that this balance may be changing as more migrants are recruited into the mining and service sectors. In Switzerland, the proportion of aliens working in factories rose between 1952 and 1963 from 10 per cent to 35 per cent (Mayer, 1965). When the Swiss government, alarmed at the impact of a large foreign labour force in a country of only 6,000,000 people, finally called a halt in 1965 to the increase in numbers of migrant workers, they accounted for more than half the labour force in several industries. In France, during the 1960s, employment of migrants in metal industries has increased and these now form the second largest employer of aliens after construction. In Sweden, 60 per cent of foreign workers are in manufacturing industries. For West Germany, the more comprehensive data allow a clearer picture to be presented of the penetration of foreign workers in the economy. It is clear from Table 4.2 that by 1973 foreign workers were to be found in all major sectors of the economy, though there was a marked

TABLE 4.2 *Employment of foreign workers in West Germany by industrial sector*

Sector	1973 Numbers	%	1966 %	1960 %
Metal industries	836,539	35·7	33·2	25·6
Other manufacturing	565,865	24·1	26·2	19·7
Construction	389,854	16·6	18·8	25·7
Commerce	147,266	6·3	4·6	5·4
Social services	137,867	5·9	4·1	2·9
Private services	126,811	5·4	4·6	7·5
Mining	70,991	3·0	4·9	7·9
Transport	52,577	2·2	2·4	2·2
Agriculture	19,030	0·8	1·2	3·1
TOTAL	2,346,800	100·0	100·0	100·0

Source: Bundesanstalt für Arbeit, *Ausländische Arbeitnehmer.*

concentration of them in manufacturing, especially in metal industries. Construction was also a significant employer of immigrants. Comparison of the situation in 1973 with those in 1960 and 1966 illustrates how the present situation has come about. Manufacturing as a whole increased its proportion of all foreign workers from 45·3 per cent in 1960 to 59·8 per cent in 1973, mainly through increased employment in the metal industries. Most of this increase occurred between 1960 and 1966. Between 1966 and 1973, the proportion of foreign workers in manufacturing as a whole remained stable, although the percentage in metal industries increased slightly and that in other manufacturing decreased. While the manufacturing sector was increasing its share of the foreign workforce, other sectors, notably construction, mining, private services, and agriculture, fell behind. Commerce and social services increased their representation, while transport remained fairly static. If the period since 1960 is looked at as a whole, it is clear that the major changes in the balance of foreign recruitment between sectors of the economy occurred before the 1966/7 recession; by then the present sectoral distribution pattern of foreign workers had become established.

At the beginning of 1973 foreign workers represented 10·8 per cent of the total labour force in West Germany, but their importance in some industries, especially those with inferior conditions of work or pay, was much greater than in others. Most of the manufacturing sector had a larger proportion of foreign workers than the economy as a whole. In metal industries the percentage doubled to 15·2 per cent between 1968 and 1973 and there was concentration in the heavier (and dirtier) branches, especially iron and steel production. Amongst other industries, 20·6 per cent of the workforce of the synthetic fibre, rubber and asbestos industries was foreign; glass and ceramics had 18·5 per cent; textiles and clothing had 17·4 per cent. Although the foreign worker proportion of the labour force in service industries as a whole was low (4·9 per cent), certain branches had heavier concentrations. Hotels and catering, for example, had 20·5 per cent, medical services 9·8 per cent, and sanitation 9·4 per cent. Most service industries, although having comparatively low proportions of foreign workers, had experienced rapid increases since 1968; for example, the Federal railways up from 2·1 per cent to 5·3 per cent.

Concentrations of immigrants among certain employers and in certain factories have been even higher than the figures above would suggest. For example, by 1966 the Ford Motor Company at Cologne already employed 5,000 Turks, and in 1973 the figure had risen to 11,500 out of a foreign workforce of 15,000 and a total workforce of 33,000. In 1974 the BMW factory at Munich had 11,000 immigrants on its payroll of 17,000.

In the foregoing, emphasis has been placed on the tendency of migrants to enter as unskilled workers and to take the low-status jobs on offer. In fact, there is less homogeneity about the skill levels of migrants than much of the writing on the subject would suggest. To some extent this reflects the varying characteristics of migrants from different source regions, but it is also owing to the differential skill demands of the industries they enter. The bulk of evidence about migrants' skills relates to their situation upon entering the host country (a useful summary is in Castles and Kosack, 1973). Less appreciated, however, are the skill levels reached by migrants during their sojourn in north-west Europe, although it has long been known that most of them are manual workers. Recently, some information on the skill levels of migrants at work in West Germany and on the variations between industries and national groups has become available. The first information was, in fact, obtained in 1968, but it was not until publication of the results of a Survey carried out in 1972 that reasonably comprehensive statistics on skill levels of the foreign labour force became available (Bundesanstalt für Arbeit, 1973). The 1972 Survey, carried out by the Bundesanstalt für Arbeit, found that 88 per cent of male foreign workers were in the manual category and only 11 per cent were classed as white collar (1 per cent were apprentices). Eighteen per cent of the manual workers were skilled, most of them having entered West Germany as skilled workers already; only 6 per cent became skilled after migration. At the other end of the spectrum, 35 per cent were classed as unskilled, a surprisingly small percentage in the light of the popular view that migrants are predominantly recruited for the lowest-grade jobs. A large number of the manual workers were thus regarded as semi-skilled, the high proportion (47 per cent) probably resulting in large measure from their recruitment into many light industries, especially engineering, where at least some training or experience is necessary in using production line techniques. Such training can be easily obtained on the job and no less than 37 per cent out of the 47 per cent had increased their status from 'unskilled' to 'semi-skilled' since entering West Germany. In all, 45 per cent of the manual workers bettered their skill status after migrating; to that extent there is training of the migrant workforce in the host country.

The different levels of skill were not balanced evenly between industries. Skilled workers, for example, were concentrated in construction, and in the production of machinery; in these two 37 per cent and 29 per cent respectively of foreign workers were skilled, compared with an average of 18 per cent. The semi-skilled tended to be in all manufacturing industries, especially textiles and electrical engineering, which had 61 per cent and 60 per cent respectively, compared with an average of 47 per cent. Unskilled workers were to be found particularly in private services—65 per cent—and in agriculture—61 per cent—compared with an average of 35 per cent.

There were also differences in levels of skill between national groups. Skilled workers were more likely to be from West Germany's immediate neighbours (excluding Italy)—44 per cent—or from Yugoslavia—32 per cent—compared with the average of 18 per cent. Other national groups contained about the same level of skilled workers, though there were slightly fewer skilled Greeks and more skilled Turks. The pattern for unskilled workers was in partial contrast to that for skilled. A low proportion of unskilled workers came from neighbouring states and from Yugoslavia, but again there was not much difference between the other national groups. The distribution of semi-skilled workers by nationality was similar to that for the unskilled, although the Greek contingent contained a slightly higher proportion than the rest.

Geographical pattern of flows during the post-war period
The growing use of foreign labour described above has led to a changing geographical pattern of migration. In 1945 the economy of Europe was either in ruins or needing large-scale reconstruction. There was also a strong demand for goods and services. Those countries in Europe with economies undamaged by direct enemy action (Sweden and Switzerland) were happy to allow labour immigration in order to meet this demand. Sweden took about 10,000 workers per annum between 1946 and 1950, mainly from Finland; during the 1950s and 1960s, the pace of immigration quickened and by 1973 Sweden had 250,000 foreign workers. As early as October 1945, Switzerland entered into agreements with neighbouring countries for the immigration of workers to fuel the Swiss economy. In 1946, Switzerland received 50,000 foreign workers and within a year the number trebled. Thereafter Switzerland continued to rely on aliens as a source of labour: numbers of foreign workers reached 363,000 in 1958 and 721,000 in the peak year of 1964. Meanwhile, the victorious Allies were also experiencing labour shortages. France, for example, accepted 214,000 foreign workers between 1946 and 1949, especially from Spain and Turkey. Between 1951 and 1957 the United Kingdom, France, and Belgium played host to an annual average inflow of 37,000, 45,000 and 42,000 permanent workers respectively (Hunter and Reid, 1970).

During this time, Italy was the main source of migrant labour. Poverty, especially in the South, and rampant unemployment provided a willing pool of potential migrants anxious to seek out the jobs and pay that were to be found to the north. As a result, Italian workers migrated freely, especially to Switzerland and France. Between 1946 and 1956 an annual average of 150,000 Italians migrated elsewhere in Europe.

In West Germany in the 1950s, the economic miracle had hardly begun. With the German economy devastated by the war, a major problem between 1945 and 1950 was the need to resettle 8,500,000 refugees from the East. The unemployment rate was high—9 per cent in 1951—and West Germany had little need to import foreign workers in the decade after the war ended. Nonetheless, there was some inflow of labour to West Germany; by 1954 there were 70,000 aliens employed there and in 1955 a labour immigration agreement was concluded with Italy. In 1957 more workers entered than left and from then on their numbers increased rapidly, in tune with the economic miracle; unemployment, at 3·4 per cent in 1957, was down to 1·2 per cent in 1960.

Labour migration during the 1950s was, therefore, of fairly limited geographical extent. Italy furnished over half the supply, Switzerland and France were the main host countries, with France also receiving migrants from its North African territories. Belgium imported some labour, especially from Italy, for work in coalmining areas. The Netherlands, with a serious unemployment problem, was a net exporter of labour during the 1950s. But in the late 1950s a change began to occur in the over-all pattern. As all the European economies began to grow faster, their labour shortages became more acute and their need for migrant workers increased. The German economic miracle proved to have a remarkable appetite for 'guest workers' (*Gastarbeiter*) as the migrants were called. In 1958, 55,000 foreign workers entered West Germany; just two years later this figure had shot up to 250,000. Figure 4.1 shows the principal sources of migrant labour to France and West Germany, the main importers in 1960. Already the flow of Italians to West Germany exceeded that to France and movements from further afield (for example, Spain and Greece) were beginning. For France, Spain, and Italy were the main European sources, although, of course, North Africa continued to furnish workers.

The rapid growth of the West German economy had one immediate and profound effect. By drawing in such large numbers of migrant workers, it changed the main flow pattern. France and the other main importers of the 1950s found their traditional source—Italy—beginning to dry up from about 1958 onwards, in the face of the West German recruiting effort. Not only were the Germans more efficient in this respect, but the pay and conditions they offered were superior to those offered by the French. Switzerland suffered similarly, though to a lesser extent because the Swiss already paid better wages than the French. Furthermore, in the early 1960s the Italian economy was beginning to boom and it was not unknown for trainloads of southern Italians going to work in Germany or France to be 'hijacked' by Piedmontese

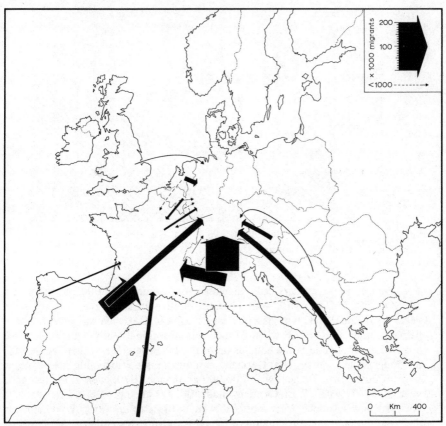

4.1 Labour migration to France and West Germany, 1960

industrialists anxious to recruit men for their own factories in northern Italy. Between 1958 and 1964, Italian wage rates increased by 80 per cent, a faster rate than in the other EEC countries (for example, France 60 per cent, West Germany 67 per cent) (Bouscaren, 1969). It was not surprising then that the early 1960s saw a marked downturn in Italian emigration, and because of this and the West German competition, other importing countries turned to alternative sources. Between 1960 and 1964, the annual entry of Spaniards into France increased from 90,000 to 170,000 and into Switzerland from 6,000 to 80,000, while Portuguese entry into France rose from 5,000 to 48,000. In 1965 there was some increase again in Italian migration to France and West Germany, the result of recession in Italy and restrictions on immigration into Switzerland, a traditional destination for Italians.

The changing patterns of labour migration during the 1960s are summarized in Figures 4.2 and 4.3 illustrating the annual flows into the largest host countries.

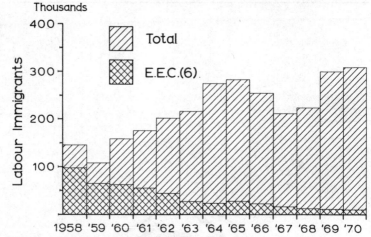

4.2 Annual flows of labour migrants to France, 1958–1970

For France, there was a steady increase from around 150,000 per annum in 1958 to 300,000 in 1970, a trend interrupted only slightly by the recession years 1967 and 1968. It is also interesting to note that such was French labour demand, that in 1962/3, when France was absorbing nearly 1,000,000 *pieds noirs* who left Algeria at the conclusion of the Evian agreement, there was no fall in foreign worker entry. West Germany exhibits a more remarkable rise in annual migrant entry than France, with 700,000 coming in 1970. Even in the recession year of 1967, when West Germany had 500,000 unemployed, there were still 150,000 new entrants. Very noticeable in both cases, however, is the steadily declining number and proportion of migrants moving from other EEC countries, despite the freedom of movement between member states.

The decline in numbers of newly entering foreign workers to West Germany in 1971 and 1972 affected citizens of the EEC less than those from elsewhere; it remains to be seen whether this indicates a further basic change in the pattern of migration. It may be that free movement between member states of the EEC means that migration within the Community is less sensitive to economic fluctuations than migration from elsewhere.

Quite clearly, by the end of the 1960s, movement between states in the EEC was of small consequence compared with movements from elsewhere. These new sources were the predominantly rural countries of the Mediterranean. To many of the inhabitants of these countries, poverty and unemployment could only be relieved by migration to the northern industrial economies. Figure 4.4 shows the large amount of labour coming into France in 1970 from Spain and Portugal, and the innovation since 1960 of substantial flows from Yugoslavia and Turkey. France's special relationship with Algeria is also well illustrated, although since

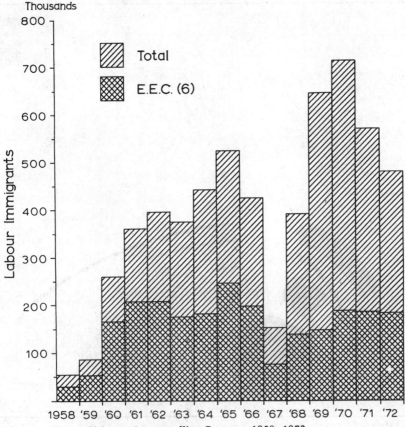

4.3 Annual flows of labour migrants to West Germany, 1958–1972

1973 that movement has been halted. The map for West Germany in 1970 is even more dramatic (Fig. 4.5). Yugoslavia had taken over from Italy as the main source, while Turkey, Greece, Spain, and Portugal became of major importance. Clearly then, the dominant pattern of European labour migration in 1970 was from the peripheral south to the industrial heartland on a scale not seen before. This was shared by all of the original Six members of the EEC; the Netherlands, for example, drew substantially from the Mediterranean countries compared with the situation a decade earlier (Figs. 4.6 and 4.7). In contrast, the pattern for the United Kingdom changed very little between 1960 and 1970 (Figs. 4.8 and 4.9).

The last two decades have thus seen a spatial evolution in labour migration streams. The rise of West Germany as a major destination and the eclipse of Italy

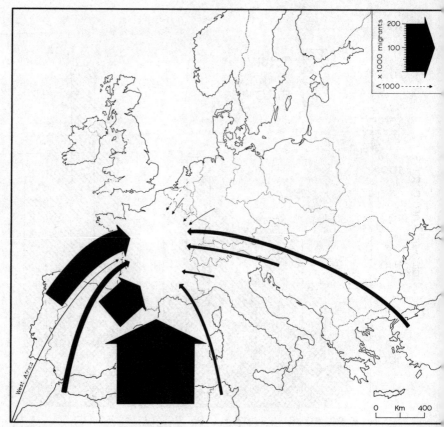

4.4 Labour migration to France, 1970

as the principal source of supply, together with increasing labour hunger in north-west Europe, have created a new pattern of movement whose hallmark is large-scale migration over long distances. By the early 1970s a broad range of supply countries regularly dispatched workers to satisfy a wide spectrum of demand.

Institutions of labour migration

Parallel with the broad evolution in volume and direction of migration has been the establishment of a set of institutions designed to regulate and facilitate movement between states. Two forces lie behind this development. The first is primarily economic; it is important to have some organization in what is effectively a multi-national labour market, in order to ease flows of workers in the directions required. Secondly, there is a social need to provide the right

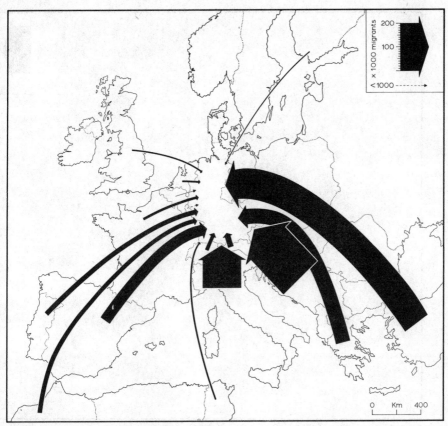

4.5 Labour migration to West Germany, 1970

assistance and adequate safeguards for the individual worker in the unfamiliar surroundings of a foreign land. The agreement for free labour movement between the countries of the EEC is the best known and most comprehensive, but several others exist. In practice, these agreements have been largely overtaken by events and have proved less effective as agents for promoting and facilitating migration than was originally supposed.

Two main sets of institutions may be recognized. The first consists of the common labour markets established between groups of states with the prime intention of allowing unrestricted movements of member nationals. Four of these agreements have been set up. Two of them, between the Benelux countries and within the European Coal and Steel Community, have been of little importance, being superseded by the EEC scheme. The Nordic Common Labour Market, established in 1954 by Norway, Sweden, Denmark, and Finland, was the

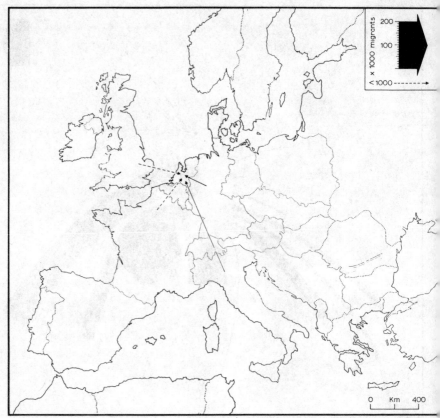

4.6 Labour migration to the Netherlands, 1960

first common labour market. Its aim was to allow workers from any of the signatory countries to travel freely to seek and accept employment within the common labour market. In practice, Sweden has been the main host country and Finland the main supplier.

Unlike the Nordic Common Labour Market, the development of free labour movement within the EEC must be seen as part of a larger integration movement, both economically and politically. Indeed, it may be argued that the provision for free movement of population between the member states of an economic union is the best way to create the 'European spirit' necessary for ultimate political union (Feldstein, 1967). The details of the free movement provision have been recounted elsewhere (for example, Böhning and Stephen, 1971) and only the salient points need to be mentioned here. The basis for free labour movement is contained in Articles 48 and 49 of the Treaty of Rome.

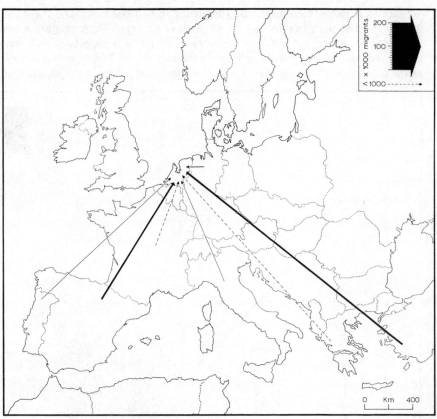

4.7 Labour migration to the Netherlands, 1970

Much of the initial drive for their inclusion came from Italy, which envisaged a solution to its acute unemployment problem in the free movement of surplus labour to its northern neighbours. Willing allies were found in the EEC Commission anxious to promote integration, and in the acute labour shortages of north-west Europe (Böhning, 1972).

Complete freedom of movement did not come all at once, but rather by stages. By 1968 all restrictions had been lifted, allowing workers and their families to cross freely the borders of member states. In addition, provision was made for the transferability of social security rights for Community migrants, thus removing a possible source of inequality.

It is difficult to measure the success of the common labour markets described above in solving imbalances in the European labour market. As all member countries have been experiencing rapid growth in their standards of living, imbalances between them have had a tendency to be ironed out, and there has thus been little incentive to migrate to another country. Where migration has taken place, especially from Italy and from Finland, it is probably fair to say that it would have happened anyway. In the case of the EEC common labour market, the integration achieved for the most part came after patterns of

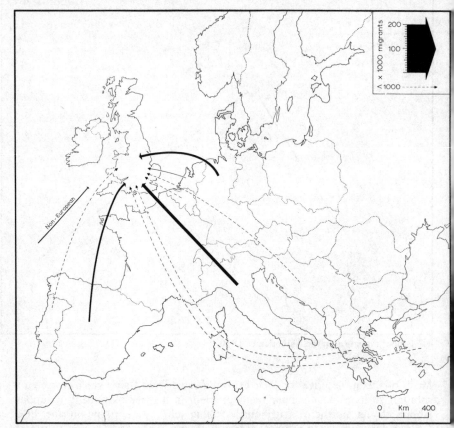

4.8 Labour migration to the United Kingdom, 1960

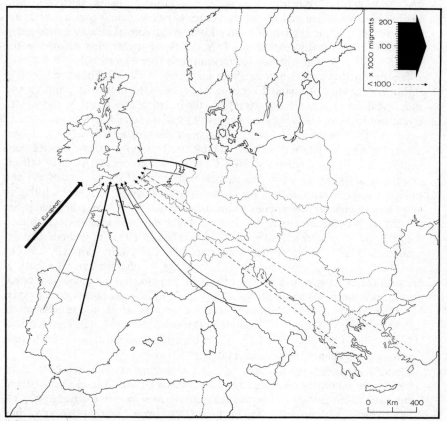

4.9 Labour migration to the United Kingdom, 1970

movement had become established and when the flows between member states were already of diminishing importance, both absolutely and relatively, in the face of much larger flows from elsewhere.

Indeed, what happened in the 1960s was that none of the common labour markets in themselves had enough workers to satisfy their labour demands. They had been set up primarily to create equilibrium, not to satisfy growth. Recruitment therefore had to be from outside the common labour markets and, as an aid to this, the system of bilateral labour agreements already developed in the 1950s was greatly extended. These bilateral agreements constitute the second major type of institution for facilitating labour migration.

The majority of contemporary labour migration in Western Europe takes place through a network of bilateral agreements between the industrial countries and those with labour surpluses. Normally the recruiting country is allowed to establish offices in the supply country which act as channels of information and organize the recruitment. West Germany's Bundesanstalt für Arbeit, for example, has established offices in the main supply countries and here applications for employment in West Germany are processed. At these offices, applicants are given aptitude and medical tests, and if they pass, transport and other formalities are arranged for them. A West German employer wishing to employ a foreign worker applies to his local labour office where he must prove he can provide accommodation. The employer pays the cost of recruitment, medical, food, and travel costs, plus a fee, raised in 1973 from about £40 per worker to £140. He also offers a contract of employment, normally for one year, written in German and in the language of the worker. The cost of recruitment is thus borne by the employer and not by the employee. Other recruiting countries operate in much the same way, though details vary. France, the other major recruiting country, also has permanent recruiting missions in some countries. These are operated through the ONI (Office National d'Immigration) and they too carry out occupational, medical, and security tests on would-be migrants and arrange transport.

Figure 4.10 shows the network of bilateral agreements in existence in 1974 between the recruiting countries and their source regions. The earliest of them were made in the middle 1950s, but the bulk of them were not signed until after 1960. There are currently 35 bilateral recruitment agreements and they emphasize the wide geographical scale on which the European labour market formally operates. They provide basic links for flows of information about employment and living conditions and both directly and indirectly act as agents of population redistribution.

France has the most agreements, sixteen in all, and there is a close relationship with former French African territories. Eight of France's agreements are with Black African states, the first ones being with Mali (1963), Mauritania (1963), and Senegal (1964), the others being signed in 1970 and 1971. France's earliest agreement was with Greece (1954), but no more were signed until 1961 (Spain); the agreement with Italy was superseded by the Treaty of Rome.

West Germany has six agreements for recruitment, plus two more with Turkey governing the reintegration of returning Turks in their own country. Because of its late start in the foreign labour recruitment field, West Germany had no agreements with non-EEC countries until 1960, when a treaty with Spain was signed. Apart from the Turkey reintegration agreements, signed in 1972, West Germany's last agreement was with Yugoslavia in 1969 following a meeting of

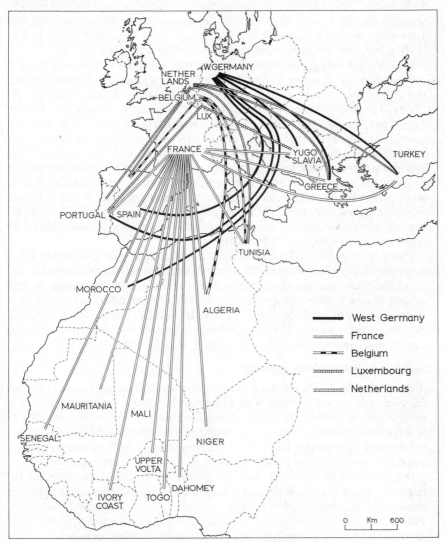

4.10 Bilateral labour recruitment agreements existing in 1974

Herr Brandt and President Tito. Unlike France, West Germany does not have strong links with Africa, the agreement with Morocco (1966) being the only one. One result of this is that West Germany has few coloured workers among its foreign immigrants.

The three Benelux countries also have wide-ranging agreements. Belgium signed a treaty with Spain in 1956 and with Tunisia and Algeria in 1969 and 1970 respectively. Luxembourg has no North African connections, but in 1970 signed agreements with Portugal and Yugoslavia. The Netherlands has had agreements since the early 1960s with Spain (1961), Portugal (1963), Turkey (1964), and, more recently, with Yugoslavia (1970) and Tunisia (1971).

It would be wrong, however, to assume that all labour migration is through official channels. A major feature has been the large amount of clandestine and illegal migration corresponding to three basic kinds of situation (McDonald, 1969). The first is where the migrant enters the country without any kind of permit and manages to obtain a job. The second type of situation is where the worker crosses a frontier legally as a tourist and subsequently takes a job without a permit. The third is where the worker, originally admitted as a seasonal worker or with an initial contract of employment for a specific period, prolongs his stay and continues to be employed without authorization after his work permit has expired. In all these cases regularization of the situation may or may not follow, but especially in France this has been relatively easy as the chronic labour shortages of the 1960s led to Nelsonian eyes being turned by employers and government to irregularities.

There is very little information on the numbers of clandestine and illegal migrants, though they do seem to be substantial. Estimates have suggested that in recent years the majority of migrants to France have not passed through official channels, with perhaps 75—80 per cent entering on tourist passports or without passports at all (McDonald, 1969). In West Germany, much more of the migration comes via the official recruitment channels, but estimates that 15 per cent of immigrants are illegal have been made (Castles and Kosack, 1973).

Social problems of labour migration

Although by the 1970s the recruitment of foreign workers had become essential for economic growth in north-west Europe, it is only in recent years that host governments have begun to turn their minds seriously to the social consequences of large flows of workers over long distances. The nature of the social problems experienced by migrants has been extensively treated in the literature already and only a brief review of the more important ones will be presented here.

Perhaps the greatest social problem is that of the living conditions of the migrants, where poor housing and overcrowding have received much publicity. Immigrants and their families occupy a range of types of housing between and within host countries. Attitudes towards immigrant housing vary according to circumstances but are primarily motivated by differences in pressure on housing resources, recency of the migratory movement and degree of assimilation, family composition of the migrants, and the availability of accommodation provided by the employer. Some of the worst housing conditions continue to be found in France. A French government survey in 1966 estimated that 75,000 migrant workers and their dependents were living in *bidonvilles*, shanty towns built of cardboard and corrugated iron, and with no sanitary facilities, on the edges of most French industrial cities, especially Paris. Later surveys suggested this figure was an underestimate, the correct one being nearer 100,000 (Granotier, 1970). Despite government attempts to reduce the *bidonville* population, this form of accommodation is still rife. Elsewhere in France migrant workers live in overcrowded hostels. Some of the hostels are government controlled and have reasonable standards; most, including the notorious *hôtels meublés*, are of extremely poor quality and are occupied especially by North Africans. In West Germany, many migrants live in hostels provided by employers. Usually the quality of these is quite acceptable, but rules are strict and the system means the foreign workers live in social and cultural isolation.

The operation of the housing market militates strongly against immigrants. In most countries migrants from abroad are not eligible for publicly owned housing. In the Netherlands, for example, migrant workers are not allowed to rent in the public sector (which contains the vast majority of that country's housing) unless accompanied by their families. But families are not allowed in unless adequate housing has been secured—very much a 'Catch 22' situation (Power, 1972). In such circumstances, many migrants have found themselves steered inexorably into the low-quality private sector, especially in inner city areas, paying high rents to live in appalling conditions. Ghettos have become commonplace as cities have developed their immigrant 'quarters', such as Porte d'Aix in Marseilles.

The poor living conditions of migrants have frequently combined with the isolation felt as a result of living in a strange country to cause medical problems (Castles and Kosack, 1973). Mental health has been a particular cause of concern, migrant workers separated from their families being especially prone to suffer.

In fairness it must be said that many migrants have been prepared to accept poor living conditions. Some, who have entered the host country illegally, feel more secure in the anonymity of the *bidonvilles*, for example. Almost all have migrated in order to acquire a sum of money to make life easier back home. Their main concern is to live as cheaply as possible in the host country, so they stay in cheap accommodation which is too often both cheap and nasty.

In this chapter so far an over-all picture has been drawn of how and why contemporary patterns of labour migration in Europe have evolved since 1945. Reference has already been made to the growing body of economic and social analyses of the problem. One of the significant features of most of the studies so far produced is the absence of a geographical perspective, most research having been carried out at the national level. Partly this is because of the paucity of data on which to base comparative local and regional analyses. Partly it is because most research into the subject has been carried out by social scientists other than geographers, especially economists and sociologists. The reality is that the situation in Europe as a whole is composed of a range of national situations; in turn national patterns are aggregations of regional and local diversities. The second part of this chapter attempts to remedy some at least of the existing deficiency in our knowledge of the detailed geography of labour migration by concentrating on one country. It must be regarded essentially as a pilot study, seeking to determine the range of spatial conditions occurring and reviewing some of the more obvious related variables, rather than providing a detailed explanation. West Germany is the optimum country to serve for such a case study. Not only has it been the leading and best-organized recruitment country, but it is also the only one with information from official government sources about migrant numbers and characteristics at regional and local levels.

Foreign workers in West Germany

Two main periods have occurred in the growth in numbers of foreign workers, before and after the recession of 1966/7. During the first half of the 1960s the total rose markedly, with annual increases ranging from 117,284 in 1962/3 to 231,000 in 1964/5. However, by 1966 the effects of the coming recession were being felt and for the first time in the decade the annual increase fell below 100,000, a prelude to the substantial fall of 322,236 in 1966/7. Recovery was dramatic, and in both 1969 and 1970 numbers increased by over 400,000 per annum. These very high levels were not maintained in the 1970s but the tide of migration continued to flow strongly between 1970 and 1973. As a result the proportion of the national labour force accounted for by foreign workers increased from 1·5 per cent in 1960 to 11·9 per cent at the end of 1973 with the actual numbers rising from about 300,000 to over 2,500,000. The statistics of net annual change hide much larger gross movements (Table 4.3). With the

TABLE 4.3 *Gross movements of labour migrants to and from West Germany*

	1966/7	1967/8	1968/9	1969/70	1970/1	1971/2
New entrants	178,578	306,477	606,086	725,121	600,259	473,172
Returnees	500,814	207,859	194,550	277,579	308,417	361,573
Total migrants	679,392	514,336	800,636	1,002,700	908,676	834,745
Returnees as % of total	74	40	24	28	34	43

Source: *Ausländische Arbeitnehmer.*

exception of the 1966/7 recession period, the majority moved to West Germany, although from 1968/9 onwards there has been a trend towards greater turn-over of migrant workers. Although many countries send workers to West Germany, over three-quarters have come from five major sources. At the beginning of 1973 the largest single group was from Turkey (528,414); next came the Yugoslavs (465,611), followed by the more long-standing source of

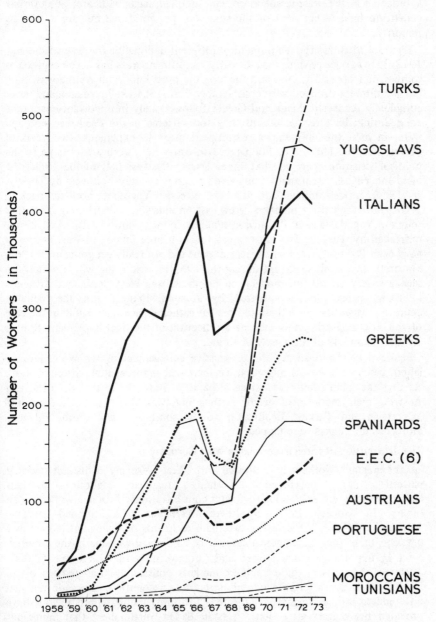

4.11 West Germany: foreign workers by nationality, 1958–1973

Italy (409,448). The recent extension of German recruitment into North Africa is reflected in the presence of Moroccans and Tunisians; with over 26,000 they constitute only 1 per cent of the total foreign workforce but are a growing minority.

Figure 4.11 shows the recruitment of different nationalities between 1958 and 1973. It is at once obvious that the early recruitment areas have been eclipsed as sources of labour. The first and for long the most important source was Italy, but recruitment dropped very considerably during the 1967 recession and never completely recovered. Spain and Greece followed Italy in importance as source areas during the early 1960s but they too suffered in the 1967 recession and were, in fact, the only major recruitment areas to experience two years of decline in 1967 and 1968. For Greece this may have been attributable to the political situation there at that time. During the first half of the 1960s the incipient Yugoslav representation started to grow steadily; followed by Turkey. By 1964, Turkish immigration numbers exceeded Yugoslavs; both fell back in 1967, but thereafter numbers grew astronomically, outstripping all other sources. Yugoslavia was the major sending country until 1972, when it was overtaken by Turkey. The latest areas to contribute labour to West Germany have been Portugal, from where recruitment did not really get going until 1968, Morocco, and Tunisia. Except during the 1967 recession, the whole period has seen a steady growth in immigration numbers from West Germany's advanced industrial neighbours, represented by Austria, France, and the Benelux countries. Migration from these sources has gathered pace since 1968; in the case of the EEC countries, this may be a reflection of the final implementation of Articles 48 and 49 of the Treaty of Rome.

Figure 4.11 demonstrates the progressive enlargement of the West German labour catchment area as migration has increased and its spatial pattern evolved. At first the main supply was close at hand, in Italy, the rest of the EEC, and Austria, then recruitment went further involving Spain and Greece, then Yugoslavia and Turkey; finally, far to the south-west and south, Portugal, Morocco and Tunisia were tapped.

The distribution of foreign workers in West Germany

As the migrant workers have flowed into West Germany a distinct regional pattern has developed. Certain regional labour markets (*Landesarbeitsamtsbezirken*) have greater concentrations of foreign workers than others. In January 1973, Nordrhein–Westfalen (679,355) and Baden–Württemberg (569,631) were the two main recipients of immigrant labour, and between them they have more than half of all foreign workers in the country. Next in importance come Hessen and Südbayern, both with over 250,000. Together these four regional labour markets contained three-quarters of all foreign workers. Differing economic structures account for the wide regional differences, and, as might be expected, the most industrialized regions have provided the biggest attractions. It is in Baden-Württemberg that immigrant workers have most importance in the regional economy, accounting for no less than 16·5 per cent of the total labour force in January 1973. Three other areas, Hessen, Südbayern and Nordrhein—Westfalen, had above the national average of 10·8 per cent. In contrast the lowest proportions were in the northern regional

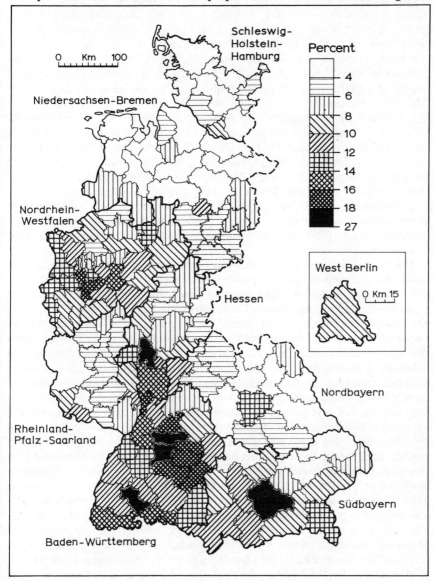

4.12 West Germany: foreign workers as proportion of total labour, January 1973

labour markets of Schleswig—Holstein—Hamburg and Niedersachsen—Bremen (6·6 per cent and 5·9 per cent). The largest concentrations of foreign workers were in the larger cities, especially Munich (156,900), Stuttgart (130,200) and Frankfurt (122,300), followed by West Berlin (82,500), Hamburg (69,500), and Cologne (63,000). In contrast, the smallest numbers were to be found in areas geographically remote from the mainstream of the West German economy and with economic structures undemanding of a large and growing labour force. However, as might be expected, the distribution has not been static and the number of local labour markets with substantial numbers of foreign workers has increased rapidly. In 1969 only 17 of the 142 local areas had over 20,000 immigrant workers, but by 1973 the number had risen to 30. An indication of local reliance upon foreign workers is provided by Figure 4.12 which shows the percentage of the total labour force in each local labour market that was accounted for by aliens in 1973. In Baden—Württemberg immigrants were very important in most local labour markets, and in only two of them was the proportion less than 10 per cent. The southern parts of Südbayern and Hessen and much of Nordrhein—Westfalen were also areas where migrant energy contributed heavily to local production. In contrast, in only a few areas of Rheinland—Pfalz—Saarland, Nordbayern, Niedersachsen—Bremen, and Schleswig—Holstein—Hamburg did migrants account for significant proportions of the work forces.

The heaviest use of foreign workers was in the large industrial cities, especially those characterized by growth industries. Stuttgart, with Mercedes and Daimler-Benz car factories and a whole range of new light industries, had the highest concentration (26·5 per cent), with neighbouring Ludwigsburg (19·2 per cent) also very reliant on foreign labour. Villingen, in the southern part of Baden—Württemberg, had the third highest concentration in the country (after Stuttgart and Frankfurt) with 22·1 per cent of its labour from abroad. Several other areas around Stuttgart—Göppingen, Heilbronn, Reutlingen, Schwäbisch—Gmünd, and Ulm—all had over 16 per cent. The central area of Baden—Württemberg, which has been a marked economic growth zone during the last two decades, has thus become very dependent indeed on foreign workers in the promotion and maintenance of its development. Further north, the area around Frankfurt has also been a centre of immigration. Here industries based on metals, engineering, and chemicals have stimulated growth. At Offenbach, for example, immigrants made up 17·6 per cent of the labour force. At Frankfurt itself the proportion was 22·6 per cent although, as will be seen later, migrants there were not concentrated in manufacturing. A third area in which migrants comprised a very substantial part of the labour force was Munich, where in 1973 18·1 per cent of the labour force was foreign. Here again light engineering industries, including motor vehicle manufacture (BMW), and public administration (the Bayern *Land*) have stimulated an employment demand that has not been matched by the traditional inmigration of indigenous workers from rural Bayern.

In contrast to the southern regional labour markets, Nordrhein–Westfalen is characterized by fewer areas of very high concentration (only Cologne, Düsseldorf, and Solingen have over 16 per cent) but in several areas there are moderate concentrations of between 10 and 15 per cent. No simple spatial pattern emerges in Nordrhein–Westfalen although it does seem that the traditional mining and heavy iron and steel areas of the northern Ruhr have slightly lower proportions than elsewhere; for example, Bochum 7·4 per cent, Gelsenkirchen 7·9 per cent, Dortmund 7·3 per cent, and Essen 7·1 per cent. On the other hand, some of the better-located heavy industrial areas and those centres of the Ruhr with more diversified employment have higher concentrations; for example, Duisberg 12·3 per cent, Hagen 11·5 per cent, Düsseldorf 16·6 per cent and the more specialized metal industry area of Solingen 17 per cent.

In Niedersachsen–Bremen and Schleswig–Holstein–Hamburg only Hanover (11·7 per cent) and Hamburg (9·5 per cent) were close to or above the national average. It is in these northern areas and in parts of the south-east, close to the East German border, where the lowest concentrations of foreign workers are to be found; for example, Emden 1·3 per cent, Heide 1·4 per cent, Leer 1·6 per cent, Verden 1·8 per cent, Schwandorf 1·5 per cent, and Deggendorf 1·8 per cent.

Regional rates of change in the foreign workforce

The distribution of foreign workers described above has evolved over the last two decades (and especially over the last 10 years) but the process has, understandably, been at different rates in different regions. Broadly the same course has been followed by each region: there was little growth before the late 1950s, then very rapid growth during the 1960s, interrupted everywhere by the 1966/7 recession. Certain regions, however, have tended to lead while others have lagged. At the start of the period Baden–Württemberg and Nordrhein–Westfalen had more foreign workers than the other regional labour markets. During the early 1960s the growth of the immigrant labour force in these two accelerated away from increases in the other regions although Hessen and Südbayern had a clear lead among the laggards. The period of growth was halted abruptly in 1967, although the effects of recession seem to have been felt least in Berlin and Schleswig–Holstein–Hamburg, the two regional labour markets with the smallest numbers of foreign workers. By 1969 numbers were again rising everywhere. The trend continued through 1970 but slowed down in 1971 and 1972. A feature of this recent deceleration was that it took effect earlier in Baden–Württemberg than in Nordrhein–Westfalen and led to the first major divergence in trend between these two since immigration began. Despite the big increase in numbers in Nordrhein–Westfalen and Baden–Württemberg after 1969, the rates of growth slowed markedly. Between 1969 and 1973, fastest rates of growth were in those regional labour markets that had lagged in their recruitment of foreign workers during the 1960s, for example Berlin (111 per

cent), Schleswig—Holstein—Hamburg (74 per cent), Niedersachsen—Bremen
(67·5 per cent), compared with 38 per cent in Baden—Württemberg and 59·5 per
cent in Nordrhein—Westfalen.

4.13 West Germany: percentage increase in number of foreign workers, 1969–1973

Figure 4.13 shows, for each local area, the rate of increase in numbers of foreign workers since 1969, the post-recession period when over-all numbers were rising very rapidly. During this time only one local labour market—Rottweil—actually experienced a decline, but there was a wide range of rates of increase. In general, the highest rates of growth took place in the northern areas. In Baden–Württemberg only two of the 24 local labour markets increased at a rate greater than the national one and in Südbayern only 7 out of 14, but elsewhere approximately two-thirds of the local areas within each regional labour market increased at a rate faster than the national one, and in Rheinland–Pfalz–Saarland 12 of the 14 local areas did so.

At the local scale variation was much more marked than for the regional labour markets and increases ranged from only 1·5 per cent at Emden to 200·5 per cent at Vechta, both within Niedersachsen–Bremen. It is not possible here to account in detail for the changes described in Figure 4.14, but certain generalizations are justified. The areas with the highest concentrations of foreign workers, for example, Stuttgart, Göppingen, Ludwigsburg, Munich, Nuremberg, and Frankfurt, did not, for the most part, have the highest rates of increase. In fact, what Figure 4.13 illustrates is a late stage in the spatial evolution of the foreign labour force in West Germany. During the early 1960s it was the main economic growth centres, especially in the south in Baden–Würtemberg and also in parts of Nordrhein–Westfalen, which experienced the labour shortages that promoted immigration. As the 1960s progressed growth in the foreign labour force tended to spread outwards from the early centres. This tendency has continued, with much recent growth in the foreign labour force occurring in rapidly developing industrial centres, such as Ingolstadt which is an oil pipeline terminus from Italy and a growing centre of the car industry. However, the period at the end of the 1960s and in the early 1970s was particularly characterized by increases in those local areas which were not the principal growth zones. Many of them experienced only slow growth in total employment but had a large proportion of jobs considered undesirable by the indigenous population. Thus, in the coalfield areas of Rheinland–Pfalz–Saarland and the northern Ruhr the flight of the German labour force from coalmining and heavy industry has led to recent increases in the foreign labour component in these industries. Bochum and Hamm in the northern Ruhr area are good examples of where these increases have occurred. It has been reported that 1 in 8 coalminers in the Ruhr are now foreigners, most of them Turks (*Guardian*, 1974). Elsewhere, foreign workers have moved into areas considered as economic problem zones, especially in the north and east. Bremerhaven, Oldenburg, and Verden in Niedersachsen–Bremen, for example, and Deggendorf in Südbayern are all government-designated growth centres which have had large increases in their foreign labour forces. Selke (1974) has claimed that increases such as these may result from a strong outmigration of indigenous workers that has exceeded total employment decline locally and therefore led to labour shortages which have been filled by foreign workers. It is perhaps significant, however, that during the period 1972–3 when the pace of the West German economy was beginning to slow, the three (out of 21) areas with the biggest declines were all in the north, at Lüneberg, Emden, and Helmstadt.

Berlin is to some extent a special case. It too has experienced a rapid increase in its foreign workforce, 111 per cent during the period 1969–73. In a large measure, this reflects the labour shortages created by the emigration of many young Berliners seeking a wider range of opportunities elsewhere in the Federal Republic.

In summary, those areas that tended to lag in terms of increase in numbers of foreign workers during the early 1960s later experienced increases at a greater rate than their former pacemakers. This illustrates in a spatial manner the continuing penetration of the foreign labour force in the West German economy. Areas that have not been ones of strong growth in total employment have, none the less, needed to import labour to balance shortages of indigenous manpower in some sectors.

The distribution of national groups

Associated with the distribution of the foreign labour force *in toto* have been spatial variations in the incidence of national groups. Figure 4.14 shows the two dominant national groups in each local labour market area. The Turks were most often the largest immigrant group (in 79 out of the 142 local areas), followed by the Yugoslavs (28 areas) and Italians (21 areas).

Regional patterns do emerge. In Baden–Württemberg, Yugoslavs and Italians are most often the dominant nationalities. Italians also tend to be concentrated in Saarland, southern Hessen, and in those parts of Nordrhein–Westfalen away from the Ruhr. Turks are widely distributed but are to be found especially in Südbayern, the Ruhr, and in most of the north. Greeks tend to be a dominant group in parts of Nordrhein–Westfalen outside the Ruhr, especially in the newer engineering industry areas, and also in Nordbayern. However, there are many detailed variations from the regional patterns which reflect local conditions. The result is that adjacent local labour markets may well have different dominant nationalities.

There are several reasons for this distribution. Many foreign workers have moved to areas of labour demand close to their own countries; the concentrations of Italians and Yugoslavs in the south are partly explained by this proximity factor. There are also temporal considerations; some nationalities were recruited earlier than others and some regional economic structures, especially in the southern employment growth areas, created an earlier demand than elsewhere. Thus workers from early sources of recruitment, such as Italy, went to early areas of demand, such as Baden–Württemberg. There are other, more local, considerations. The concentration of national groups in a city partly results from the size of the companies employing foreigners and their recruitment policies. Employers have tended to recruit from specific nationalities only because a homogeneous foreign labour force reduces costs of

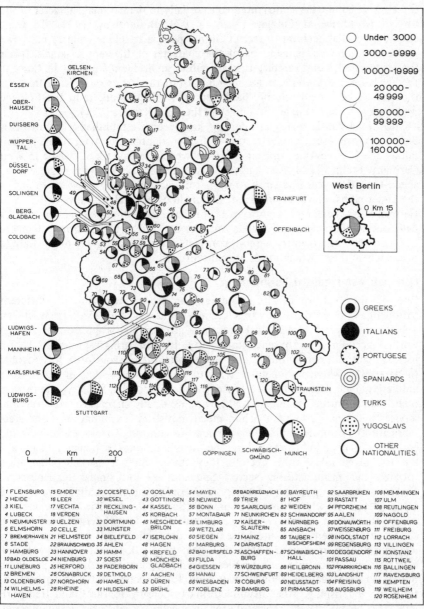

4.14 West Germany: distribution of major national groups of foreign workers, September 1972

0   Km   200

1 FLENSBURG	15 EMDEN	29 COESFELD	42 GOSLAR	54 MAYEN	68 BADKREUZNACH	80 BAYREUTH	92 SAARBRUKEN	106 MEMMINGEN
2 HEIDE	16 LEER	30 WESEL	43 GOTTINGEN	55 NEUWIED	69 TRIER	81 HOF	93 RASTATT	107 ULM
3 KIEL	17 VECHTA	31 RECKLING-	44 KASSEL	56 BONN	70 SAARLOUIS	82 WEIDEN	94 PFORZHEIM	108 REUTLINGEN
4 LUBECK	18 VERDEN	HAUSEN	45 KORBACH	57 MONTABAUR	71 NEUNKIRCHEN	83 SCHWANDORF	95 AALEN	109 NAGOLD
5 NEUMUNSTER	19 UELZEN	32 DORTMUND	46 MESCHEDE -	58 LIMBURG	72 KAISER-	84 NURNBERG	96 DONAUWORTH	110 OFFENBURG
6 ELMSHORN	20 CELLE	33 MUNSTER	BRILON	59 WETZLAR	SLAUTERN	85 ANSBACH	97 WEISSENBURG	111 FREIBURG
7 BREMERHAVEN	21 HELMSTEDT	34 BIELEFELD	47 ISERLOHN	60 SIEGEN	73 MAINZ	86 TAUBER -	98 INGOLSTADT	112 LORRACH
8 STADE	22 BRAUNSCHWEIG	35 AHLEN	48 HAGEN	61 MARBURG	74 DARMSTADT	BISCHOFSHEIM	99 REGENSBURG	113 VILLINGEN
9 HAMBURG	23 HANNOVER	36 HAMM	49 KREFELD	62 BAD HERSFELD	75 ASCHAFFEN-	87 SCHWABISCH-	100 DEGGENDORF	114 KONSTANZ
10 BAD OLDESLOE	24 NIENBURG	37 SOEST	50 MÖNCHEN	63 FULDA	BURG	HALL	101 PASSAU	115 ROTTWEIL
11 LUNEBURG	25 HERFORD	38 PADERBORN	GLADBACH	64 GIESSEN	76 WÜRZBURG	88 HEILBRONN	102 PFARRKIRCHEN	116 BALLINGEN
12 BREMEN	26 OSNABRUCK	39 DETMOLD	51 AACHEN	65 HANAU	77 SCHWEINFURT	89 HEIDELBERG	103 LANDSHUT	117 RAVENSBURG
13 OLDENBURG	27 NORDHORN	40 HAMELN	52 DÜREN	66 WIESBADEN	78 COBURG	90 NEUSSTADT	104 FREISING	118 KEMPTEN
14 WILHELMS-	28 RHEINE	41 HILDESHEIM	53 BRÜHL	67 KOBLENZ	79 BAMBURG	91 PIRMASENS	105 AUGSBURG	119 WEILHEIM
HAVEN								120 ROSENHEIM

language and job instruction. Thus the preference of the Ford Motor Company for Turkish labour has contributed substantially to the national character of the foreign workforce at Cologne (Kayser, 1971; Burtenshaw, 1974). To some extent the initial decision to recruit from a particular source country may owe much to employers' perceptions of the character of different nationals. It has been suggested, for example, that in public services employment in Cologne there has been a preference for migrants from rural sources because they are thought to be 'obedient' and 'hard-working'; foreign workers in the Cologne postal service, for example, are almost all Iberians (Kayser, 1971).

Once a substantial national minority has become established in an area it is likely to prove a source of attraction to fellow countrymen. After fulfilling their initial one-year contract, migrants are allowed to seek work elsewhere in West Germany. Steins (1974) has suggested a two-step pattern in which migrants may spend their first year in a small town or rural area and then move on to one of the larger cities. Inevitably different nationalities are likely to move within West Germany to where their countrymen are located. A similar attraction may be held out to those foreign workers not recruited through the normal channels, but who enter the country without contracts. They too are likely to gravitate to places where their own nationals are concentrated.

Nationality and industrial distribution

One of the features of the migration has been a tendency for different nationalities to gravitate towards certain industries and away from others. Table 4.4 shows, for individual industrial groups, the proportion of foreign workers accounted for by each nationality. By comparing representation of a national group in each industry and in the total foreign workforce, it is possible to determine which nationalities tend to be over-represented in the various industries. Thus, Italians tend to concentrate in agriculture, forestry, and fishing, other manufacturing (including textiles and especially chemicals), construction, services and transport, but to shun metal industries (excluding iron and steel fabrication), commerce, and social services. In contrast, Greeks are to be found especially in metal industries and in other manufacturing (particularly chemicals) but less often in all other sectors; they thus exhibit a marked polarization towards the manufacturing sector. Spaniards exhibit similar tendencies to Greeks, although agriculture, forestry, and fishing and, especially, transport are other sectors in which Spanish representation is strong. The largest national group, the Turks, have a very low representation in most services and also in construction, chemicals, and machinery production but are very heavily concentrated in mining and iron and steel production, and also in vehicles, electrical manufacturing, and textiles. The Portuguese are fairly evenly distributed between sectors, though they tend to be concentrated in agriculture, forestry, and fishing, other manufacturing (especially textiles), and transport, and have below average representation in machinery and electrical industries, construction, and commerce. Another highly polarized group are the Yugoslavs,

TABLE 4.4 Industrial sector and nationality of foreign workers in West Germany, percentages in January 1973

Sector	Nationality									
	Italians	Greeks	Spaniards	Turks	Portuguese	Yugoslavs	Moroccans	Tunisians	Others	Total
Agriculture, forestry, fishing	18·7	2·9	10·7	21·6	4·3	16·5	2·0	0·4	22·9	100·0
Mining	15·7	4·3	5·6	46·0	2·5	11·4	1·4	0·4	12·7	100·0
Metal industries	16·5	15·9	8·7	26·2	2·6	17·8	0·3	0·6	11·4	100·0
Iron and Steel production	13·2	13·7	8·4	41·4	3·3	9·7	0·9	0·5	8·9	100·0
fabrication	23·1	16·0	11·0	21·6	3·1	14·1	0·4	0·3	10·4	100·0
Machinery	15·3	13·3	9·6	21·3	2·2	21·8	0·3	0·6	15·6	100·0
Vehicles	16·7	16·1	8·7	32·2	2·7	13·5	0·4	0·9	8·8	100·0
Electrical engineering	12·9	19·6	6·7	23·3	1·2	20·9	0·1	0·4	14·9	100·0
Other manufacturing	19·1	15·8	9·6	24·1	4·5	14·5	0·3	0·3	11·8	100·0
Chemicals	21·2	19·7	10·3	15·2	2·4	9·6	0·5	0·3	20·8	100·0
Textiles	19·7	15·3	7·5	29·0	7·7	12·9	0·1	0·2	7·6	100·0
Construction	20·5	2·8	3·6	19·3	1·8	35·0	1·3	0·3	15·4	100·0
Commerce	14·7	7·6	5·9	11·7	1·6	16·1	0·5	0·5	41·4	100·0
Private services	19·2	6·7	6·4	11·2	3·0	24·2	0·7	1·0	27·6	100·0
Transport	20·4	4·6	15·2	22·4	5·3	11·9	2·6	0·2	17·4	100·0
Social services	8·8	6·9	5·9	12·9	2·8	19·5	1·1	0·4	41·7	100·0
TOTAL	17·5	11·4	7·6	22·5	2·9	20·0	0·6	0·5	17·0	100·0

Source: Ausländische Arbeitnehmer.

who account for 35 per cent of the foreign construction workers, but only 20 per cent of the total foreign workforce. Yugoslavs also have above average representation in machinery production, electrical industries, and services, but tend to be below average in agriculture, forestry, and fishing, mining, most manufacturing, commerce, and transport. The most recent entrants, Moroccans and Tunisians, are poorly represented in the manufacturing sector, and are more likely to be in agriculture, forestry and fishing, mining, and all services. Although the national groups listed in Table 4.4 include most of West Germany's foreign workers, in certain sectors there are substantial groups from other countries. This is particularly true of the commerce and social (public) services sectors which contain many 'white-collar' occupations held by nationals of West Germany's EEC partners (excluding Italy).

Towards a general model

On the evidence so far presented it is possible to postulate a simple and very generalized model to account for the broad spatial patterns of foreign worker immigration within West Germany. The main variables are the economic structures of the regions within the host country (which in turn have determined the timing of the recruitment), the national origin of the immigrants, and the tendency for particular groups to be recruited into certain sectors of the economy.

Table 4.5 shows the proportions of different nationalities in the nine regional labour markets; by comparing these with the proportion of the total immigrant workforce contained in each regional labour market of West Germany, it is possible to calculate whether or not that regional labour market has more than its share of each nationality. For example, Schleswig—Holstein—Hamburg has only 4·3 per cent of all foreign workers but has considerably more than its share of Portuguese (11 per cent) and less of Italians (1·7 per cent). In Baden—Württemberg, Greeks and especially Italians and Yugoslavs are well represented, but the region has less than its share of Turks and especially Spaniards, Portuguese, Tunisians, and Moroccans. The same principle is adopted in Table 4.6 which shows the tendency for labour migrants in different regional labour markets to concentrate in specific industrial groups. Where there is regional specialization the migrant labour force tends to be well represented in those specialisms: for example, in metal industries and chemicals in Nordrhein—Westfalen, and in textiles in Baden—Württemberg. Elsewhere, for example in Schleswig—Holstein—Hamburg and in Berlin, foreign workers are concentrated in those branches of the economy most characterized by jobs regarded as undesirable by the indigenous labour force such as many of those occurring in agriculture and services.

It was observed above that migrants of different nationalities tend to gravitate towards particular sectors. It has now been shown that different nationalities and the sectors of the economy are not proportionately distributed between regional labour markets. What thus emerges is a regional pattern in which the

TABLE 4.5 *Percentages of national groups in each regional labour market January 1973*

	Schleswig—Holstein—Hamburg	Niedersachsen—Bremen	Nordrhein—Westfalen	Hessen	Rheinland—Pfalz—Saarland	Baden Württemberg	Nordbayern	Südbayern	West Berlin	TOTAL
Italians	1·7	4·4	27·1	13·0	5·9	34·4	4·0	8·7	0·8	100·0
Greeks	2·8	5·5	34·7	9·5	2·0	25·8	7·2	10·4	2·1	100·0
Spaniards	4·0	12·1	34·9	19·3	3·5	18·0	4·1	3·5	0·6	100·0
Turks	5·1	8·1	29·1	10·1	4·1	20·0	6·5	10·0	7·0	100·0
Portuguese	11·0	8·0	41·9	11·9	4·3	18·5	2·0	2·0	0·4	100·0
Yugoslavs	3·9	5·3	20·7	12·2	3·1	30·8	4·5	15·4	4·1	100·0
Moroccans	1·3	1·9	50·3	36·5	3·7	3·3	0·5	1·3	1·2	100·0
Tunisians	8·7	13·7	32·8	9·5	6·0	12·4	3·6	8·5	4·8	100·0
TOTAL (all foreign groups)	4·3	6·5	29·0	11·7	4·5	24·3	4·8	11·4	3·5	100·0

Source: *Ausländische Arbeitnehmer.*

TABLE 4.6 *Regional percentages of foreign workers in each industrial sector, January 1973*

	Schleswig-Holstein-Hamburg	Niedersachsen-Bremen	Nordrhein-Westfalen	Hessen	Rheinland-Pfalz-Saarland	Baden-Württemberg	Nordbayern	Südbayern	West Berlin	TOTAL
Agriculture	5·6	9·4	24·2	12·0	6·8	21·4	3·7	9·4	7·5	100·0
Mining	1·6	6·6	52·5	7·2	6·8	14·6	3·8	5·7	1·2	100·0
Metal industries	3·4	6·9	32·0	9·6	3·5	26·6	5·3	9·3	3·7	100·0
Iron & steel production	0·8	6·7	78·5	3·1	6·3	3·2	0·5	0·8	0·1	100·0
fabrication	1·8	3·4	49·5	9·1	3·7	23·8	4·2	3·1	1·5	100·0
Machinery	3·9	4·5	27·1	11·3	2·9	31·2	5·1	10·5	3·3	100·0
Vehicles	1·5	12·0	24·1	10·9	3·7	32·0	3·0	11·7	1·2	100·0
Electrical engineering	2·5	6·3	17·2	7·0	2·4	30·8	10·3	13·4	10·2	100·0
Other manufacturing	4·0	7·6	27·8	11·0	6·0	24·5	6·2	10·0	2·8	100·0
Chemicals	4·7	3·8	33·8	20·4	11·0	13·4	1·9	9·6	1·4	100·0
Textiles	1·3	6·8	28·4	3·2	1·5	37·7	5·3	12·4	3·7	100·0
Construction	3·4	5·5	24·5	13·4	4·4	26·6	3·8	16·2	2·1	100·0
Commerce	8·4	5·2	25·3	16·2	3·4	19·0	3·8	14·4	4·2	100·0
Private services	7·0	5·5	21·7	14·4	4·8	18·4	3·5	17·6	7·0	100·0
Transport	12·1	7·8	27·8	18·9	2·0	17·3	1·5	10·5	2·0	100·0
Social services	5·2	6·4	26·6	14·6	5·9	21·0	3·3	10·3	6·9	100·0
TOTAL	4·3	6·5	29·0	11·7	4·5	24·3	4·8	11·4	3·5	100·0

Source: *Ausländische Arbeitnehmer.*

presence of particular national groups in individual regional labour markets is related to the degree to which the foreign labour force is concentrated in certain sectors of the regional economy. This can be seen by observing individual regional labour markets. Baden—Württemberg, for example, has more than its share of Italians, Greeks, and Yugoslavs. It was also a region of early recruitment for its growth industries. The sectors in which Baden—Württemberg has more than its share of foreign workers include metal industries (especially machinery production, vehicles, and electrical goods) other manufacturing (especially textiles), and construction. These are all sectors in which, at the West German level, those national groups that are particularly well represented in Baden—Württemberg are seen to specialize. Nordrhein—Westfalen has more than its share of Greeks, Spaniards, Portuguese, Moroccans, and Tunisians, and of metal industries, mining, and chemicals, all sectors in which all or some of the nationalities mentioned are particularly concentrated at a national level. Nordbayern provides a third example. It has more than its share of Greeks and Turks and its foreign workers are especially concentrated in the metal industry and other manufacturing sectors. These are sectors in which both Greeks and Turks are particularly well represented. Similar relationships may be observed in each of the regional labour markets, demonstrating at this aggregate level the association of regional economic structure within West Germany with the occupational characteristics of individual national groups.

Local labour markets

Although much of the foregoing analysis of the West German situation has been at the national or regional labour market level, enough has been said to indicate the existence of substantial variations in migrant numbers and characteristics between local labour markets. Indeed, as pointed out in Chapter 3, it is at this spatial scale that the phenomenon of labour migration, international or internal, needs to be studied. For the most part we can only speculate about the details of labour migration at the local level. However, the 1972 survey of the Bundesanstalt für Arbeit provided some information on selected social and economic characteristics of male migrants, and this provides at least a starting-point for analysis. For the 10 local areas with the highest densities of immigrants separate results were published. In some cases information was available for individual cities, in others, for groups of adjacent cities (Bundesantalt für Arbeit, 1973).

Because of the numbers and densities of the immigrant labour force contained within them, these 10 areas may well be atypical. None the less, it was thought valuable to describe their distinctiveness simply to determine the range of local conditions existing. In what follows, an attempt is made for each of the local areas to distinguish the ways in which its migrant characteristics differ from the average for the 10 areas. The characteristics analysed were personal (including whether the migrant was married or single, whether or not the family was in Germany, and the migrant's knowledge of the German language), industrial (sector of the economy in which the migrant worked, and whether with a large or small employer), stability (length of time with employer, intentions regarding length of stay), occupational (manual or white-collar worker, skill level attained, and any change in skill level occurring since entering Germany), and pay.

(a) *Rhein–Ruhr*

The Rhein–Ruhr area was the largest and most diffuse of the ten, containing 11 local labour markets. As a result there was some averaging-out of conditions. In all, the area had 286,000 foreign workers, the main national groups being Turks (24 per cent), Italians (19 per cent) and Yugoslavs (16 per cent). What emerged clearly in this area was a higher-than-average proportion of manual, and especially of unskilled workers, and a low representation of the skilled. Not surprisingly, mining and the metal industries were over-represented among the foreign workers while construction and commerce and services had lower-than-average proportions. More foreign labour than the average was employed in large establishments (those with more than 1,000 employees). The over-all picture for the migrants of the Rhein–Ruhr area is thus one in which unskilled manual labour is concentrated in large establishments in the metal and mining industries.

(b) *Munich*

In 1972 Munich had 150,000 foreign workers. The Yugoslavs were easily the leading national group with 30 per cent of the total, followed by the Turks (15 per cent), Italians (14 per cent), and Greeks (13 per cent). There was a greater concentration of single migrants than in some of the other areas, and the proportions of married workers and of those accompanied by their wives were lower than the average. However, a higher-than-average proportion had a good knowledge of German, mostly learnt before arrival. The effect of the construction industry was notable. It occupied a much higher proportion than average and was in turn reflected in the considerable dominance of the Yugoslavs among the national groups. Other sectors had average representation except for 'other manufacturing' in which representation was lower-than-average. There was also a lack of stability among Munich's immigrants. A higher proportion than average had been with the same employer for less than a year, while, conversely, a lower-than-average proportion had not changed jobs during the last three years. There was a higher proportion of skilled workers and unskilled workers were comparatively poorly represented; a low proportion only had bettered their skill status since entering West Germany. The over-all picture at Munich was thus one of lack of stability among the immigrants with more single people, more job changing, and a concentration in the construction industry, notorious for its fluctuations in activity. While there were many skilled foreign workers, over-all there had been little improvement in skill status.

(c) *Stuttgart*

At the time of the survey, Stuttgart had 130,000 foreign workers with Yugoslavs (30 per cent), Italians (26 per cent), and Greeks (17 per cent) being the main groups. The city was about average in terms of the proportion of male migrants who were married and who had spouses with them. A lower-than-average proportion had a good knowledge of German and a high proportion had no knowledge at all, indicating the possibility of the migrants being cut off from the indigenous community by a language barrier. However, in contrast to Munich, there was evidence of stability among Stuttgart's migrants. A high proportion intended a long stay and had been with the same employer for over three years, while the proportion with the same employer for less than a year was lower than average. Despite the high proportion working in metal industries (a sector characterized by large employers) the proportion working in large establishments of over 1,000 employees was lower than average. This seeming anomaly may result from the concentration of migrants also in construction where numbers of employees per establishment tend to be lower than in manufacturing. The proportion in 'other manufacturing' was low, perhaps as a reflection of the economic structure of Stuttgart, which has developed as an engineering centre. Higher-than-average proportions of the foreign labour force were manual workers and were skilled and a lower-than-average proportion was unskilled. More than average had bettered their skill status since entering West Germany, probably reflecting the semi-skill needs of the engineering industries and the demand by the construction industry for skilled craftsmen. Stuttgart was also an area of higher-than-average pay rates, especially in the construction industry.

(d) *Frankfurt*

Frankfurt had 118,000 foreign workers with Yugoslavs (27 per cent) and Italians (21 per cent) being the major national groups, followed by Spaniards (13 per cent) and Turks (12 per cent). Frankfurt was characterized by a high proportion of married migrants having their wives with them, and a high proportion having a good knowledge of the German language. Higher-than-average proportions worked in construction, commerce, and services (sectors in which Yugoslavs and Italians tend to be concentrated), with lower-than-average proportions in manufacturing. There was also a higher-than-average proportion of white-collar workers, but fewer manual (especially skilled manual) workers than might have been expected. A lower-than-average proportion of migrants had bettered their skill status since entering West Germany. Fewer migrants in Frankfurt tended to work in large establishments, probably the result of a lower-than-average representation in manufacturing. However, a high proportion had worked for over three years for the same employer. Like Stuttgart's, therefore, Frankfurt's immigrant group seemed more settled although the economic structures were very different.

(e) *Berlin*

Berlin had 67,000 foreign workers, the dominant nationalities being Turks (43 per cent) and Yugoslavs (26 per cent). A comparatively low proportion of the men were married (although a high proportion of these had their wives with them) and a lower-than-average proportion had been with the same employer for over three years. In contrast, the proportion who had changed job within the last year was comparatively high. Thus Berlin was characterized by a relatively unstable immigrant workforce. A higher-than-average proportion worked in metal industries and in large establishments, but, surprisingly, pay rates were comparatively low, especially in manufacturing. It seems that despite its continual loss of indigenous population through emigration Berlin does not have to offer high rates of pay to attract foreign labour and this may, of course, explain the unsettled nature of its immigrant group.

(f) *Hamburg*

Hamburg had 52,000 foreign workers, of whom 22 per cent were Turks and 20 per cent Yugoslavs; Italians, Greeks, and Portuguese each accounted for 8 per cent. Like Munich and Berlin, Hamburg had a preponderance of single migrants. A higher-than-average proportion had been with the same employer for less than a year and a low proportion had not changed employer for over three years. However, this may reflect the recency of large-scale immigration into Hamburg which had a higher-than-average proportion intending a long stay, perhaps because of the high pay rates there. Befitting a major port, migrants were comparatively more likely to be working in the 'other manufacturing' sector (which includes port industries), while metal industries were less well represented. Although in general the balance of skill levels at Hamburg was about average, there was a tendency for migrants to better their skill status after arrival.

(g) *Nuremberg*

At the time of the survey, Nuremberg had 51,000 foreign workers, dominated by three major national groups; Greeks (23 per cent), Yugoslavs (22 per cent), and Turks (20 per cent). A high proportion of the male migrants were married and had their wives with them, although only average numbers intended a long stay. As at Stuttgart, a low proportion had a good knowledge of the German language but a high proportion of those knowing German had learnt it at work. The picture then, is one of family settlement but of possible alienation from the indigenous population, as a result of a language barrier. A higher-than-average proportion of the migrants were employed in the metal industries and worked in large establishments of over 1,000 employees. Manual workers, especially semi-skilled, were better represented than average, but despite Nuremberg's speciality in the more skilled branches of engineering, skilled workers were not well represented. A higher-than-average proportion, however, had bettered their skill status, probably reflecting the semi-skilled needs of the engineering industries. Pay rates at Nuremberg were considerably lower than average.

(h) *Rhein—Neckar*

This comprised the Mannheim and Ludwigsburg areas and had about 65,000 foreign workers with three major groups, Italians (24 per cent), Turks (22 per cent), and Yugoslavs (18 per cent). For the most part, conditions were fairly average, but as at Stuttgart, Frankfurt, and Nuremberg, a feature of the immigrant group was its stability. More migrants than average had worked for the same employer for over three years and fewer for less than one year. In addition a higher-than-average proportion intended a long stay. As at Hanover, the 'other manufacturing' sector was very strongly represented, largely owing to the chemicals industry, while metal industries occupied fewer than average. Also in common with Hanover, and with the Rhein—Ruhr area, there was a predominance of unskilled workers and a low proportion of skilled.

(i) *Hanover*

Hanover had about 27,000 foreign workers at the time of the survey, 28 per cent of whom were Spaniards, 20 per cent Yugoslavs, 17 per cent Turks, and 15 per cent Greeks. As at Nuremberg, many of the immigrants were married. A lower-than-average proportion were intending a long stay and a notable feature was the high proportion who were uncertain of their length of stay. However, the proportion with the same employer for less than one year was below average. Fewer than average had a good knowledge of German and of those who had, a high proportion had gained their knowledge at work. As in Rhein—Neckar, the 'other manufacturing' sector employed more migrants than average; there was also a tendency for migrants to be employed in large establishments. Manual workers as a whole were over-represented compared with the average, as were unskilled, and there were fewer skilled workers. Pay rates tended to be lower in Hanover than the average for the other nine areas, though they were at about the same level as for all migrant workers in West Germany.

(j) *Bremen*

Bremen was the smallest of the local labour markets surveyed, having only 14,000 foreign workers. The Turks were easily the leading group (36 per cent), followed by the Yugoslavs (17 per cent) and Portuguese (17 per cent). The sample was too small for a detailed breakdown of its migrant characteristics, especially those of industrial sector and skills. As at Hamburg, immigrants to Bremen seemed to intend a long stay, but, in contrast to Hamburg, monthly pay rates were below par.

This description of conditions in the ten areas has considered especially those migrant characteristics in which the individual areas diverged from the average for the group as a whole. As a result attention has been focused on differences rather than similarities between them. However, certain general points emerge. There does seem to be some polarization as far as maturity of the migration pattern is concerned and this can be related, in part, to the maturing of migration streams discussed in Chapter 5. Some of the areas show a maturity that is characterized by higher-than-average proportions of married migrants, many having families with them, and a low turnover of jobs in recent years. Others show a reverse situation. It is also clear that in many areas, for example, at Bremen, Stuttgart, Hanover, and Nuremberg, very considerable language barriers exist between the migrants and the indigenous population. Elsewhere, for example, at Frankfurt and Munich, the language barrier was lower. Very frequently, however, the German that was known had been learned at work.

Perhaps the salient point emerging for studies attempting to produce both descriptive and explanatory models of labour immigration is the wide range of local conditions that occurred. Some of the local areas were quite distinct; Frankfurt, with its more mature pattern and low representation in manufacturing, is a good example. What is especially striking, however, is the absence of obvious systematic associations of migrant characteristics with respect to economic structure at this local level. For instance, in Berlin, Rhein—Ruhr, and Nuremberg, higher-than-average proportions in metal industries and in large establishments occurred together, whereas at Stuttgart, a higher-than-average proportion in metal industries was associated with a lower-than-average proportion in large establishments. Similarly, in cases such as those of Nuremberg and Stuttgart, a comparatively high proportion improving their skill status was associated with a high proportion in metal industries, whereas at Hamburg improvement in skill status was associated with a lower-than-average proportion in metal industries. Such variation between places suggests that much research remains to be done at this spatial level before satisfactory explanatory models can be developed. Quite clearly, there are many local demand factors at work which combine in different ways with the supply factors to contribute to the local immigration character. The result of this interplay is that no simple model can explain the immigration pattern for local labour markets in West Germany. The same can probably be said for the other countries of immigration also.

Conclusion

This chapter has concentrated on certain aspects only of the migration of labour in Western Europe, and has viewed the subject primarily from the point of view of the destination countries. Many relevant themes have, of necessity, been omitted or else given scant recognition. While it is clear that, in broad terms, the movement conforms to classical and neo-classical economic theory, which emphasizes differences between areas in job availability and levels of earnings, at the same time the relationship between the countries of demand and those of supply has not been a static one. The last two decades have witnessed a steady evolution of the basic geographical pattern that is summarized in the maps of migration flows for different dates. This spatial evolution has been paralleled by changes in organization as various national institutions have been established to deal with the migrants. It has also been associated with other changes in the demand countries. In particular, it cannot be divorced from the steady penetration of migrants into virtually all sectors of the indigenous economies which, in turn, has influenced the detailed pattern of immigration. As the initial partial labour shortages became general, so there was a geographical spread of the demand for, and use of, migrant labour. This was amply demonstrated in the West German case.

As immigrants have become more rooted in the European economy, so the economic costs and benefits of labour migration have become increasingly a source of debate, particularly in the recent conditions of inflation and recession. Quantitative determination of the economic effects of migration remains largely theoretical because of the absence of empirical data (Lutz, 1963; Kindleberger, 1967; Mishan and Needleman, 1966; Castles and Kosack, 1973; Böhning and Maillat, 1974). It does seem, however, that over all the destination countries have gained a distinct economic advantage from the migrants who have provided an industrial labour reserve and slowed down the rate of wage increases at a time of economic expansion and low population growth rates. Their recruitment from year to year is likely to remain prey to short-term fluctuations and crises. In late 1973 and 1974 several of the major immigration countries, especially West Germany and France, prohibited new immigration. But it is undoubtedly true that the migrants have become such an integral part of economic growth in north-west Europe that their long-term presence seems assured. (See Postscript).

This growing reliance on migrant labour has meant that host countries have needed to come to terms with a large floating population. Inevitably there has been some more or less permanent settlement of migrants and their families. In recognition partly of this but also of the need for greater social justice for the temporary population, governments have been forced to consider and introduce social legislation to provide some protection for their new-found workforce. This has become increasingly important with the realization that the temporary palliative of labour migration has become a permanent feature. Much still remains to be done in this field, especially in respect of the assimilation of migrants in areas of greatest pressure.

As the scale and permanency of the migration has increased, the governments of host countries have had to think hard about political relationships with their sources of supply. Long term agreements have been drawn up, *ad hoc* situations institutionalized in bilateral treaties, and care taken to cultivate new sources as necessary. These more permanent arrangements between governments ultimately have their expression in better organization of the international labour market, more serious efforts at improving migrants' social conditions, and less cavalier treatment of migrants at times of recession—especially summary redundancy and expulsion.

The political, economic, and social issues of Europe's labour migrations have been reverberating for some time and have attracted a good deal of attention. For geographers the task has hardly begun. The geographical variations that characterize immigration—especially in the associations of economic structure, migrant characteristics, and social conditions in local labour markets—present a potentially fruitful but yet little tilled field of analysis. Further research on Europe's labour immigration ought now to be poised to explain its lack of spatial homogeneity.

In this chapter, attention has been focused on the demand for foreign workers. However, geographical variations in the incidence and character of labour immigration in individual host countries are not due solely to demand factors; there are also local supply factors at work. The tendency for individual employers to continue to recruit from an established source area has already been referred to and it is also known that the characteristics of migrants vary from source to source, even within individual origin countries. One consequence of this is a flow to individual local labour markets of migrants with particular social and economic characteristics.

What emerges from this chapter is a contrast between, on the one hand, the generalities of labour supply and demand at the aggregate level of north-west Europe's industrial economies and, on the other, the very great spatial, social, economic, and institutional complexities that affect individual countries and their regions. A comparable picture occurs in the case of the supply countries. Whereas, in general, similar reasons for labour emigration apply throughout the Mediterranean Basin, they vary in detail not only between supply countries but also between regions within individual supply countries. And as reasons for migration vary, so do reactions to them, particularly in the case of direction of migrant flow. It is, therefore, appropriate now to consider the geography of labour migration from the point of view of the countries which act as source areas.

References

Böhning, W. R. (1972) *The Migration of Workers in the United Kingdom and the European Community*, Oxford University Press, London.

Böhning, W. R., and Maillat, D. (1974) *The Effects of the Employment of Foreign Workers*, OECD, Paris.

Böhning, W. R., and Stephen, D. (1971) *The European Economic Community and the Migration of Workers*, Runnymede Trust, London.

Bouscaren, A. T. (1969) *European Economic Community Migrations*, Martinus Nijhoff, The Hague.

Bundesanstalt für Arbeit (1973) *Repräsentatur-untersuchung 1972, Beschäftigung Ausländischer Arbeitnehmer*, Bundesanstalt für Arbeit, Nuremberg.

Bundesanstalt für Arbeit (1974) *Ausländische Arbeitnehmer* (annual), Bundesanstalt für Arbeit, Nuremberg.

Burtenshaw, D. (1974) *Economic Geography of West Germany*, Macmillan, London.

Castles, S. and Kosack, G. (1973) *Immigrant Workers and Class Structure in Western Europe*, Oxford University Press, London.

Feldstein, H. S. (1967) 'A study of transaction and political integration: transnational labour flow within the EEC', *Journal of Common Market Studies*, 6, 24–55.

Granotier, B. (1970) *Les Travailleurs immigrés en France*, François Maspero, Paris.

Guardian (1974) 'The rise of Ruhr coalmining', *Guardian* 21 Nov., London.

Hogarth, J. and Salt, J. (1973) *Postwar Labour Migration in Western Europe: a Preliminary Working Bibliography*, University College London (mimeographed).

Hume, I. M. (1973) 'Migrant workers in Europe', *Finance and Development*, 10, 2—6.
Hunter, L. C., and Reid G. L. (1970) *European Economic Integration and the Movement of Labour*, Industrial Relations Centre, Queen's University, Kingston.
International Labour Office (1973) *Some Growing Employment Problems in Europe*, ILO, Geneva.
Kayser, B. (1971) *Manpower Movements and Labour Markets*, OECD, Paris.
Kindleberger, C. P. (1967) *Europe's Postwar Growth—the Role of Labour Supply*, Harvard University Press, Cambridge, Mass.
Lutz, V. (1963) 'Foreign workers and domestic wage levels with an illustration from the Swiss case', *Banca Nazionale del Lavoro, Quarterly Review*, 16, 34—68.
Mayer, K. B. (1965) 'Post-war migration to Switzerland', *International Migration*, 3, 122—37.
McDonald, J. R. (1969) 'Labour immigration in France, 1946—1965', *Annals of the Association of American Geographers*, 59, 116—34.
Mishan, E. J., and Needleman, L. (1966) 'Immigration: some economic effects', *Lloyds Bank Review*, 86.
Power, J. (1972) *The New Proletarians*, British Council of Churches, London.
Rose, A. M. (1969) *Migrants in Europe: Problems of Acceptance and Adjustment*, University of Minnesota Press, Minneapolis.
Selke, W. (1974) 'Regionale Prognosen der Ausländernwanderung in der Bundesrepublik Deutschland und Möglichkeiten ihrer Steuerung', *Informationen zur Raumentwicklung*, 2, 39—48.
Steins, G. (1974) 'Zur infrastrukturomentierten Plafondierung des Ausländerbeschäftigung', *Informationen zur Raumentwicklung*, 2, 49—57.
Time (1973) 'Europe's other energy source', *Time*, 3 Dec., 12—19.

5. INTERNATIONAL LABOUR MIGRATION: THE SOURCES OF SUPPLY

JOHN SALT AND HUGH CLOUT

General Survey

It is clear from the preceding chapter that a large amount of migration has taken place in recent decades between the countries of the Mediterranean Basin and those of north-west Europe, and that the southern countries have been net losers of population. Emigration is not a new phenomenon for the Mediterranean countries which, having considerable diversity within and between themselves, none the less share common characteristics of relative underdevelopment. With the exception of Italy, their living standards are generally well below those of their northern neighbours. Traditionally, emigration has been a means of escape from poverty and unemployment; the present labour migrations can thus be seen as a continuation of a long-established trend. For some countries, such as Portugal, recent migrations to north-west Europe represent a diversion of time-honoured flows overseas, especially to Latin America and Africa. In other cases, such as Italy and Algeria, they are an intensification of already existing patterns of movement. Turkey is an exception, since emigration has not been a customary antidote to hardship, and movement of labour to north-west Europe represents a completely new departure.

A number of general statements about the departure countries may be made which provide an over-all picture of the reasons for and the nature of emigration. When individual countries are examined, however, reality is seen to be complicated. The level of economic and social development, political attitudes, chronology of migration, types of migrants, spatial impact of emigration in particular regions, and direction of movement—even the degree to which individual departure areas have been studied—all vary in detail from country to country. Accordingly, the first part of this chapter will look in general terms at the reasons for the northward tide of migration and at the social and economic problems created in the countries of origin. Later, the cases of individual supply countries will be examined in more detail. Italy, the oldest major source country, will be the first one considered. Then there will be a review of the situation in Iberia where, in post-war years, Spain and Portugal have displayed many economic and social similarities, but not always with parallel demographic features. Yugoslavia, with its special political interest as the only major Communist source of migrants to Western Europe, will be a third case study. Attention will then switch to North Africa and Turkey, sources having a lower level of economic development and experiencing rapid population growth.

Reasons for labour emigration

The basic causes of emigration have been economic. In much of the Mediterranean area incomes are low by Western European standards and job opportunities are either lacking or confined to only a few sectors of the economy. Unemployment and especially under-employment are rife; and providing enough work for all constitutes perhaps the biggest economic and social problem facing governments of the supply countries. There are several reasons for this. One of the principal ones has been the slow pace of economic development in countries to which the 'Industrial Revolution' came late, and which lack sources of raw material for the sort of large-scale industrial development achieved by their northern neighbours. Hence in most labour supply countries the structure of employment remains strongly agricultural, but farming systems are often backward by modern standards. Overpopulation with associated under-employment in rural areas is one result. Release of labour from agriculture has not been accompanied by adequate growth of non-agricultural employment, and emigration has become a natural corollary.

In many cases political considerations are of fundamental importance in fashioning labour migration. The aftermath of Civil War in Spain, the drain on the Portuguese economy of colonial wars, the French withdrawal from North Africa, and the 1965 economic 'reforms' in Yugoslavia have all left their mark on patterns of domestic economic development, usually in the form of slow growth or even decline in total employment availability. All the time an underlying factor has been natural increase of population, moderated in some countries by emigration of the fertile age groups but elsewhere exerting further pressure on employment-creating mechanisms. The nine Mediterranean countries which supply most of north-west Europe's migrant workers constitute a large and growing reserve of population. In 1930 they had 118,000,000 inhabitants but by 1972 this figure had increased by 70 per cent to 200,000,000. Table 5.1 shows that demographically the supply countries fall into two groups. The three

TABLE 5.1 *Population characteristics of nine Mediterranean countries*

	1930	1972	Increase	Crude birth rate	Crude death rate	Natural increase
	(thousands)		1930–72	(per thousand)	(per thousand)	(per thousand)
			(%)	1970	1970	
Algeria	6,553	15,270	133	50·0	16·0	34·0
Morocco	6,300	15,830	151	50·0	18·0	32·0
Tunisia	2,410	5,380	123	36·2	16·0	20·2
Turkey	11,500	37,010	232	40·0	15·0	25·0
Spain	23,564	34,360	46	19·6	8·5	11·1
Italy	41,069	54,350	32	16·8	9·7	7·1
Portugal	6,826	8,830	29	19·3	10·4	9·9
Greece	6,350	8,850	39	16·5	8·4	8·1
Yugoslavia	13,780	20,770	50	17·8	8·9	8·9
	118,352	200,650	70			

Maghreb states and Turkey form the first of these, with crude birth rates and rates of natural increase between two and three times as large as those in the second group, which comprises Greece, Italy, Portugal, Spain, and Yugoslavia.

In the first group the demographic transition is still in train and a case for labour migration as a demographic safety valve may certainly be made. The consequences for the labour force of such a rapid increase in population may be illustrated by reference to Turkey. Between 1960 and 1970, the Turkish labour force grew at 1·9 per cent per annum, posing formidable problems of job provision. The country's recent five-year development plan estimated that out of 480,000 joining the labour force annually, only 160,000 enter productive activity. Current trends suggest that unemployment is likely to continue rising until 1987 and that between 1973 and 1995, an extra 13–14,000,000 jobs will be needed (ILO, 1973). In these circumstances, the very rapid growth in emigration to north-west Europe during recent years can easily be understood, along with the Turkish government's willingness to assist the agencies of recruiting countries.

In the second group of countries birth rates and rates of natural increase are much lower than those in the Maghreb and Turkey, but, with the exception of Italy, they are still higher than those in the rest of Europe. The countries of the second group experienced the demographic transition after their northern neighbours but before the countries further to the south and east. The transition has, however, been accomplished with the help of a long-established tradition of emigration. Not only has this reduced population pressure directly but its selective nature has meant that the majority of emigrants were in the fertile age groups. Thus, the birth rate has been reduced and natural increase curtailed. As a result of this migration 'safety valve' recent labour-force growth in these five countries has been low. Between 1960 and 1970, for example, annual rates were Yugoslavia 1 per cent, Greece and Spain 0·5 per cent, Portugal and Italy 0·1 per cent. Employment strategies in these countries have thus been less concerned with providing jobs for new entrants to the labour force and more concerned with changing the existing employment structure, particularly in the more backward regions which have large-scale under-employment.

Individual countries have tried to tackle the disparity between population and economic growth in different ways. Schemes for birth control have been introduced in those Mediterranean countries (for example the Maghreb and Turkey) where religious beliefs permit. Elsewhere, programmes for industrial and regional development have been instituted, perhaps the best-known example being that of the Italian Mezzogiorno. By themselves, these programmes have proved inadequate in dealing with the twin problems of population growth and rural under-employment, and the task of providing enough work for all who want it has proved formidable. Indeed in some cases one effect of these schemes seems to have been to stimulate emigration (Censis, 1968). In other countries, manpower mobilization projects have simply aimed at measures to create employment; for example the land development and public works programmes established by the governments of Morocco and Tunisia. As with regional industrialization, manpower mobilization projects have proved expensive to institute and have only partially alleviated problems of unemployment and under-employment. One estimate of the success of the Moroccan and Tunisian schemes suggested that they had absorbed only 5–6 per cent of the mass of under-employed workers (Tiano, 1963), whilst another indicated that rural under-employment had been reduced by one-quarter (Arles, 1966).

For the most part, governments in the supply countries have been willing to foster the aspirations of their citizens wishing to emigrate and, as was seen in the last chapter, frequently entered into recruitment agreements with governments of labour-importing countries. Both short- and long-term benefits from what was assumed would be temporary migration were hoped for in the supply countries. In the short term, miseries of endemic poverty and unemployment could be assuaged and a breathing space won from the pressure of a rising population on a sluggish economy. Remittances to families staying behind would bring an immediate rise in their living standards and add valuable spending power to fuel the economy. In the long term, the savings of returning migrants would be invested fruitfully and the industrial training received abroad would provide much needed skills at no cost to the home country.

The task of providing work in their home countries for all of the migrant workers would clearly have been impossible without massive outside aid. One estimate has suggested that to employ at home the 8,000,000 workers who have emigrated would have required, on plausible assumptions about the cost of creating each job, an amount of capital similar to the total flow of aid from the West plus Japan to the entire developing world during the 1960s (Hume, 1973). Indeed, if one were to base estimates on the cost of job creation in British development areas (about £10,000 per job), the figure would be much higher. Such immense amounts of capital have not been available and, therefore, the absorption of so much of their labour by the industrial economies has almost certainly led to substantial reductions in unemployment in the supply countries.

Unfortunately, assessing the true dimensions of unemployment in the supply countries is a virtually impossible task. The concepts of unemployment applied and, more especially, the techniques of measurement used by individual countries in producing statistics of registered unemployed vary considerably, and thus prevent meaningful comparisons being made between countries. However, a more fundamental problem is the existence of habitual under-employment that seldom finds its way into official statistics. This may take many forms, among the most common of which are seasonal under-employment in agriculture or involvement in unproductive services in towns. Low activity rates, caused by the withdrawal from the labour force of those who cannot obtain jobs, are frequent manifestations of unemployment and under-employment. In Italy, for example, the active population in 1966 constituted only 38 per cent of the total compared with 40 per cent in France and 56 per cent in the United Kingdom (Censis, 1968).

Some indications of the scale of the problem are available. In Yugoslavia in 1971, there were 320,000 registered unemployed and an estimated 100,000 unregistered, out of a total labour force of 4,250,000. In addition, it was estimated that there were 2,200,000 surplus rural workers and a further 3,200,000 non-employed women of working age (Roux, 1972). In 1973, the ILO recorded 354,000 unemployed in Yugoslavia, about 7·5 per cent of the national labour force (ILO, 1974). This situation, in which a large volume of under-employment exists but does not appear in official statistics relating to unemployment, occurs widely. A report in 1971 suggested that in Italy there were between 2,500,000 and 3,000,000 hidden unemployed, in addition to 900,000 registered unemployed (EEC, 1971). In Turkey there seems to be an even worse ratio. Official Turkish figures for 1969 showed 1,100,000 unemployed out of a total labour force of 14,900,000, but one researcher suggested there were actually 7,000,000 real and concealed unemployed, including 2,400,000 completely out of work, 3,300,000 under-employed farmers, and 800,000 marginal workers in the tertiary sector (Kayser, 1972). A similar situation has been reported in Portugal (Poinard, 1972a).

National unemployment figures often hide great differences between rural and urban areas. Frequently urban areas display higher rates of overt unemployment which is recorded in official statistics because of better registration facilities; while rural areas have more under-employment owing to the tendency for marginal workers to gravitate to agriculture as 'the employment of last resort'. Differences in unemployment rates between rural and urban areas may be illustrated from Morocco and Tunisia. In Morocco, surveys in Casablanca and other towns in 1958 and 1960 showed an urban unemployment rate of 18–20 per cent compared with a rural rate in 1963 of 50 per cent (Dubois, 1959; Haut Commissariat à la Jeunesse et aux Sports, Maroc, 1962; Tiano, 1963). For Tunisia in the early 1960s national unemployment rate was estimated to be 20–25 per cent, but 40 per cent for rural areas (ILO, 1963; Silberzahn, 1964).

The relationship between unemployment rate and emigration rate is a vexed question. Most evidence suggests that only a minority of migrants are unemployed. For example, surveys in Yugoslavia in 1970 found that only 26·7 per cent of emigrants were unemployed on departure (Roux, 1972). Böhning (1972) suggested a lower proportion—10 per cent—for Italy; other evidence from Italy also suggests that most migrants had jobs before going abroad (Censis, 1968). That the unemployed should be a small minority of emigrants is what might be expected; it is usually the better educated and more skilled elements in the labour force that migrate, and they are less likely to be unemployed. But undoubtedly a substantial number of emigrants are under-employed upon moving, especially those from rural areas.

Enough has already been said to infer a strong relationship between under-employment and an employment structure dominated by an over-populated agricultural sector that is characterized by inefficient production. As economic development has proceeded in recent years, agriculture has become more efficient and the rural population has fallen. The agricultural labour force of Spain, for example, continued to increase until 1960 but thereafter it declined from 4,700,000 (40 per cent of the workforce) to 3,600,000 (28·6 per cent) in 1970. Some 105,000 workers left farming for alternative employment each year during that decade, but even so much of the Spanish interior was still employing more than 60 per cent of its workforce in agriculture during the early 1960s. Turkey still has an essentially agricultural economy and farm products represent three-quarters of total exports. About 68 per cent of the workforce is engaged in agriculture, forestry, and fishing (with 12 per cent in manufacturing, 4 per cent in construction, and 16 per cent in services). Over most of the country in 1965 farming occupied over 80 per cent of the working population, falling below 50 per cent only in the provinces of Ankara, Istanbul, and Izmir (Dewdney, 1972). In Yugoslavia the agricultural population declined from 67·2 per cent to 36·4 per cent of the total between 1948 and 1973. Over the same period the proportion of farmers among the total employed fell from 74·2 per cent to 38·5 per cent. During the last ten years most of this fall in agricultural population has been because of migration abroad (Baucic, 1974).

Such falls in agricultural population have resulted from increasing difficulties faced by many small farmers and landless labourers in gaining a living from the soil. Often property fragmentation has meant that units are uneconomic to manage, for example in north-west Spain and in north Portugal (Daumas, 1971; Piel, 1966). Elsewhere, the continuation of the *latifundium* system, with its built-in tendency to under-employment, has encouraged emigration, for example from southern Portugal. In many countries the difficulties of the physical environment, which restrict the amount of land that may be cultivated, have led to high agricultural densities in some areas, which have encouraged outmigration. In Yugoslavia, for example, in 1961, each farmer cultivated an average of only 2·2 hectares of arable land. It is therefore not surprising to find that although farmers then accounted for 56·3 per cent of Yugoslavia's total population, they realized only 23·2 per cent of the national income (Baucic, 1971). The decline in the agricultural population has not only affected the more difficult areas. In Greece, for example, rural outmigration is affecting all parts of the country. Losses have not only occurred in upland territory with limited resources, which have been losing migrants for decades. Fertile lowland farming plains, such as those of west Thessaly, have all lost population.

The changing pattern of emigration

With the development of migration streams over the years and the consequent spread of information, people in remoter areas of the supply countries have become aware of the advantages of working abroad, where jobs are plentiful and pay is good. As a result, the origin areas of migrants have been extended from the main urban centres, which were the earliest migrant sources. This has been accompanied by a slow change in the types of migrant becoming available for foreign recruitment. The basic pattern has been for the earliest emigrants to come predominantly from urbanized areas and to be among the more skilled and educated. Later migrants have tended to come from rural regions (although not necessarily from farms) and to have few skills and little education. For example, migrants from Italy were initially from the urbanized north rather than the more rural south, whereas in recent years more have come from the south. Since the mid-1960s there has been a change in the composition of Italians wanting to go abroad. In 1965 the Italian government estimated that of *c*. 300,000 available for employment in EEC countries about one-third were skilled or semi-skilled, one-third 'experienced' (mostly unskilled), and one-third completely unskilled. By 1971 the over-all number of potential migrants was estimated to be down to 80,000 but the proportion of skilled and semi-skilled had fallen to 20 per cent, while the completely unskilled had increased to 55 per cent (EEC Commission, 1966, 1971).

A similar trend is found in Yugoslavia. The more urbanized areas, especially in Croatia and Slovenia, were the first sources of migrants but emigration in recent years has been increasingly from less developed areas especially to the east and south (Baucic, 1971). Yugoslavia, especially in the early years of emigration, has also been characterized by loss of skilled and educated labour (Nikolic, 1972). In recent years an increasing proportion of migrants have been less well educated. North Africa is also characterized by a spread of migrant origins away from the more urbanized areas—usually coastal—to more isolated interior regions (Simon and Noin, 1972).

In part, this extension of migrant origins into remoter areas is a natural result of the spread of information about opportunities arising from emigration. It is a trend reinforced by the unskilled nature of the labour demand in destination countries, which has meant that lack of skill or education has not been a drawback in recruitment of workers from remote rural areas and small towns. As mentioned in chapter 4, such people can easily be trained and the so-called 'docility' of peasants in an industrial environment makes them an attractive proposition for recruitment.

The phenomenon of rural outmigration has already been explored in Chapter 2. From what was said there, and from the evidence here, there is a clear link between migration out of rural areas and migration abroad. It would be wrong to assume that most of the migration abroad from rural areas takes place directly from the land. A distinction has to be made between migrants who move abroad straight from the countryside—probably a minority of migrants from rural areas—and those who first migrate to a nearby town. It seems that for many migrants going abroad is an extension of the rural—urban migration process, and this will be a recurring theme in this chapter. The poverty of agriculture, with poor prospects of a better standard of living, is the initial and all-important unsettling factor in the creation of a mass of potential migrants. It pushes them from farms into towns and cities, where often growth of employment is slow, unemployment high, pay low, and living conditions overcrowded and poor. Having taken the psychological step of making the first move, the next—abroad—is less difficult. Often the migration is stimulated by governmental attempts to create employment in poorer, predominantly rural regions. In Italy, for example, investment by the government in parts of the Mezzogiorno in the 1950s and 1960s provided urban employment which encouraged an exodus from surrounding rural areas. Much of this investment was in public works programmes, and a study in the Bari—Brindisi—Taranto area showed that upon completion of major construction projects there was a wave of migration abroad. Most of the emigrants were not first-job seekers but already had employment experience, especially in the construction industry (Censis, 1968).

For the individual, migration provides a means of escape from poverty, low pay, and unemployment. It is a social process as much as an economic one, in which geographical mobility is seen as a means to upward social mobility. There is good reason to believe that at the outset the migrant sees himself as a 'target worker'. The target is to earn as much money as quickly as possible and then return home. Many migrants do intend returning home as soon as possible, but many others have no definite time horizon, and some evidence suggests the latter constitute the larger group (Braun, 1970; Kuhne, 1971). Böhning (1972) has pointed out that this attitude on the part of the migrant coincides very nicely with the attitudes of most of the labour-importing countries that have continued to see the migrants as a short-term, rapid-turnover labour source. Both attitudes, however, ignore the changing values and feelings of the migrant who may spend several years in the host country or repeatedly return on new work contracts. In time, the migrant will absorb the norms and values of the host society, realizing that the standard of living he now seeks cannot be attained in one or two short years abroad. Böhning (1972) suggests that labour migration matures by stages as migrant attitudes change. Initially, single migrants move for a short time; ultimately, the movement is of family groups settling permanently in a new country. Four main stages may be recognized. They are difficult to disentangle empirically and are debatable in part, but in broad outline they are supported by available evidence.

In the first stage, most migrants are young, single, and male. They are mainly from the more industrialized and urbanized regions of the sending countries, namely those areas with the best access to information about opportunities overseas. The migrants are also likely to be more skilled than the non-migrant population. In the early days of the migration stream, when the host countries have only recently begun importing labour, the duration of stay is likely to be short, for two main reasons. Firstly, the migrants will tend to be employed in marginal jobs which have high turnovers; and secondly, the migration stream will not have had time to mature so the migrant will expect only a short stay.

The second stage is characterized by more information about opportunities resulting from migration becoming available in supply countries as first-stage migrants report back. Migrants are by now slightly older; more of them may be married but families are left behind. The duration of stay may increase because migrant labour is now a more permanent feature in the host country and the migrant himself realizes that his target is not immediately attainable. Since in this stage the volume of migration is likely to have increased, more information finds its way back to the sending country and there it spreads to more remote, especially agricultural, areas. A wider range of people is now being attracted to emigration and those involved are often more unskilled and of a lower socio-economic status than their predecessors, especially when they come from rural areas.

In the third stage, the stream continues its ageing process and there is more emphasis on family reunion. The single migrant either finds his target is being met more slowly than he hoped or he becomes enmeshed in the social values of the host community, with its emphasis on consumption. In either case the migrant prolongs his length of stay and may well send for his wife to help him achieve his goals. Thus by stage three the migration is becoming more permanent; the migrant may still intend to return home one day, but in the meanwhile he and perhaps his family are becoming more settled in the host country.

The fourth stage is a natural continuation. The psychological costs of separation from home become less important in the face of the material opportunities presented by the new environment. Stays become longer; returns may be postponed indefinitely; more family reunions take place; children who had been left with relatives join their parents; immigrant minorities with their own ethnic institutions have become an established feature in the host countries. Effectively, the migration becomes for permanent settlement, rather than a mere short-term expedient.

There is plenty of evidence to suggest that labour migration streams are tending to mature in this manner. It is certainly true that a majority of migrants are male and young; one estimate is that males constitute between 55 per cent and 80 per cent of the migrants, depending on the country (Hume, 1973). Italy, for example, has more female migrants than most supply countries and Turkey has the least. Hume (1973) has also suggested that about 60 per cent of all labour migrants are aged 18 to 35 and a further 10 per cent between 35 and 40, although few women are in the older age group. It must not be imagined, however, that all emigrants eventually settle with their families in the host countries. In fact, only a minority do so, although as the number of migrants has increased the volume of permanent settlement has grown likewise. But while a majority of the migrants do not reach the fourth stage, many do stay abroad for far longer than their original intentions demanded.

The situation varies from country to country. Turkey, which has only recently become a labour-exporting country, is the origin of a migration stream still at the youthful stage. By far the majority of migrants from Turkey are men, mainly in their 20s and 30s; for example in 1971, 28 per cent of Turks entering France were aged between 21 and 25, 27 per cent were between 26 and 30 and 21 per cent between 31 and 35. Only 1·5 per cent were women. Over four-fifths of

Turkish labour migrants were married, but fewer than 1 in 20 workers had been joined in France by their families (Gokalp, 1973).

The migration stream from the Maghreb is more advanced. As in Turkey, the majority of migrants are male and the tendency has been for those under 25 years of age to become increasingly important in recent flows. However, since 1968 there has also been a trend for family members to migrate and regroup in Western Europe; for example, in 1954 there were only 7,000 Algerian families in France but by 1966 this number had risen to 40,000 (Sutton, 1972). Nevertheless, the age/sex pyramid for North Africans in Europe is still heavily distorted towards males between 20 and 45 years of age. This is unlike more established migrant groups which tend to display rather more 'normal' age/sex pyramids in their reception countries.

A similar trend has been recorded in Portugal. Young, single adults have formed the bulk of migrants; in 1970 about 10 per cent of the country's 25–30-year age group emigrated. Leloup (1972) reports the fact that priests have to mail their parish newsletters 'to the four corners of the earth' and visit their parishioners in France to celebrate marriages and baptisms (p. 71). Whilst the early flows of labour migrants mainly involved males, there has been a marked tendency for wives and children to join their menfolk in France in recent years (Poinard, 1971, 1972a and b).

In the case of more established sources like Italy and Spain, which are no longer the chief source of fresh labour supplies, the inflow of dependants to France and West Germany has not been falling as rapidly in recent years as that of new workers, indicating that families have been 'catching up' with fathers who migrated earlier (Hume, 1973).

Evidence from demand countries provides a clear indication that the migration streams have been maturing in the direction of permanent family settlement. A first indication is the increasing importance of women in the foreign labour force; in West Germany, women accounted for 18 per cent in 1962 but 29 per cent in 1972. Of course not all of the women are married, but a majority are, the proportion being 68 per cent in West Germany in 1972 (Bundesanstalt für Arbeit, 1973). In the Rhône *département* of France, the number of foreign families settling between the mid-1950s and the mid-1960s increased tenfold (Kayser, 1971, p. 171). Differences existed in the mid-1960s between the family structures of recently arrived national groups and those that were longer established. The more recently arrived Portuguese group contained fewer women and children than the other nationalities.

Confirmatory evidence comes from West Germany. Between 1968 and 1972 the proportion of married male migrants having their wives with them increased from 58 per cent to 62 per cent. At the same time, the proportion of women married to immigrant males, and who were themselves working, fell from 71 per cent to 64 per cent. Thus more male immigrants had their wives with them in 1972, but fewer of the wives were working; hence there were more women dependants in 1972 than in 1968 (Bundesanstalt für Arbeit, 1973).

Another indication that migration is tending to become more permanent than originally envisaged by the migrants comes from a study of their intentions. The bulk of evidence suggests that the intended stay abroad becomes longer after the initial move is made. A survey of emigrants from Yugoslavia, for example, found that when they were leaving the country for the first time most of them wanted to stay abroad for only 1 or 2 years. However, another survey, of migrants coming home for the Christmas/New Year holiday in 1970/1, found that only 3 per cent did not intend returning abroad; only 14 per cent of them would return home immediately if they could find suitable jobs; and 16 per cent wanted to stay abroad for over three years (Baucic, 1971). A study in West Germany of the staying intentions of migrants found in 1972 that 68 per cent definitely intended staying for over one year; 4 per cent would definitely stay one year or less, the remainder (28 per cent) did not know how long they would stay (Bundesanstalt für Arbeit, 1973). The existence of this sizeable minority expressing uncertainty may reflect the feeling on the part of the migrants that the move had become so permanent a feature that no return to the home country was contemplated. Alternatively, it may reflect the genuine uncertainty as to what the future might hold, with the possibility of returning at any time. In any case, the evidence from West Germany does suggest a growing uncertainty among immigrants over recent years; in 1968, only 5 per cent did not know how long they would stay and 90 per cent intended staying more than a year.

Advantages and disadvantages of emigration

Perhaps the principal advantage the sending countries wish to receive from emigration is financial. They hope that the remittances and savings of their workers abroad will improve the living standards of families left behind, and will also provide valuable foreign exchange and investment capital in the drive for economic development. Experience has shown, however, that some of these hopes are largely illusory.

There is no hard and fast information on the total amount of money transferred by migrants from host to sending countries, but undoubtedly the sum is vast. Hume (1973) estimated that for 1972 the annual flow of remittances from all migrants in Europe to their home countries was over $2,500,000,000. This figure has been accepted elsewhere (ILO, 1973; *Time*, 1973) but it is almost certainly an underestimate. West Germany is a major source of remittances and is the only host country for which reasonably comprehensive information is available. In 1973 8,450,000,000 DM—an increase of 1,000,000,000 DM on the previous year—were sent or taken home by migrant workers (see Table 5.2). Clearly, for the whole of Western Europe the figure may probably be doubled. Turkey and Yugoslavia were the main beneficiaries, and what is especially noticeable is the dramatic increase in remittances to these countries in recent years. As migrants have flowed towards West Germany so the money has streamed back.

These sums are very significant for the receiving countries. Between 1954 and

TABLE 5.2 *Remittances from foreign workers in West Germany, 1960–1973 (million DM)*

Nationality of Workers

Year	Italians	Spanish	Greeks	Yugoslavs	Turks	Portu- guese	All Med- iterranean countries	Other count- ries	Total remitt- ances
1960	200	50	50	0	0	0	300	–	300
1961	350	100	50	50	0	0	550	–	550
1962	500	200	100	50	50	0	900	–	900
1963	600	250	200	100	100	0	1,250	–	1,250
1964	700	350	250	100	150	0	1,550	–	1,550
1965	850	450	350	150	300	50	2,150	–	2,150
1966	1,000	500	400	200	350	50	2,500	–	2,500
1967	850	350	350	200	300	50	2,110	40	2,150
1968	850	300	300	250	350	50	2,110	40	2,150
1969	950	400	400	600	700	100	3,175	125	3,300
1970	1,100	550	600	1,150	1,250	150	4,850	150	5,000
1971	1,150	650	750	1,600	1,800	200	6,215	235	6,450
1972	1,300	750	850	1,900	2,100	200	7,180	270	7,450
1973	1,350	850	900	2,200	2,500	250	8,145	305	8,450

Source: Bundesanstalt für arbeit (1974), *Ausländische Arbeitnehmer* 1972/3.

1970 the volume of remittances to Spain rose more than tenfold, to $480,000,000, and migrant remittances are now Spain's second source of foreign exchange after tourism (Anon., 1972a). In 1963 Yugoslavia received an estimated $15,500,000 in remittances, representing 4·4 per cent of total foreign currency earnings; in 1972 the amount had soared to $868,000,000, 22 per cent of foreign currency earnings. Indeed, earnings sent home to Yugoslavia have turned a balance of payments deficit into a surplus. One estimate in 1972 suggested that remittances account for over one-tenth of the personal expenditure of the whole Yugoslav population (Baucic, 1974).

The importance of this money to the individual supply countries varies. An article in *Time* (1973) showed the value of remittances as a percentage of total imports for Mediterranean countries, with values ranging from 9 per cent for Spain, 14 per cent for Italy, 24 per cent for Greece, 37 per cent for Portugal, to 47 per cent for Turkey. A comment on Portugal in 1971 could clearly be echoed for the other supply countries.'If France or Federal Germany were to block the flow of cash transactions a large number of families in Portugal would suddenly be reduced to poverty. The country's economy is thus very vulnerable and, after a century of intense emigration, depends on economies that have received her migrants and profit from their labour' (Anon., 1971, p. 1160). Within the supply countries, those regions which have lost many migrants tend to be very heavily dependent on money sent home. Remittances are estimated to account for three-quarters, four-fifths, or even more, of the cash resources of some villages in the eastern Rif and the Kabylie in Algeria (Simon and Noin, 1972). In 1971

Tunisian workers abroad sent home 18,000,000 dinars, making remittances the third major source of income to the national economy after tourism (32m) and oil (25m) (Simon, 1973).

Despite these large amounts of money flowing to the supply countries, and the reliance of many families on them, there is clear evidence that they are not invested as productively as they might be. For individual families remittances are used to cater for daily needs—to buy food, clothing, and consumer goods. One Spanish study found that 22 per cent of migrants used their savings to pay their debts to their grocer (Kayser, 1971). There is plenty of evidence of improvement in the well-being of communities that have bread-winners abroad (e.g. Russo, 1964). Often, however, the consumer goods are imported anyway and the remittances go straight back whence they came. A Greek study suggested that for this reason remittances seemed to worsen rather than improve the underlying balance of payments problem (Nikolinakos, 1971).

Of course, if migrants decide to stay abroad and bring their families to join them, the remittances cease. But when migrants return, their savings are usually invested in only a marginally productive fashion. The bulk of investment is in housing, either repairs or building anew. Abadan's (1972) survey of Turkish returnees found that half of them used their savings in this way. A survey of emigrants returning to Croatia found that of those spending their savings, over two-thirds used them for housing, furnishing, or the purchase of a house site (Baucic, 1971). In some southern Italian towns demand for houses is largely maintained by returning emigrants (Censis, 1968). Besides housing, the other major uses of savings from abroad are purchase of motor cars (18 per cent in the Croatian survey), to be used either as a symbol of success or as a taxi business, the opening of a retail shop or small craft workshop (23 per cent in the Turkish survey), the purchase of land, or of farm machinery.

While many of these investments are laudable in themselves, they are frequently inefficient by macro-economic standards. Many migrants, having achieved their target, return to their home area and invest their savings there. This has resulted in investment in housing, land, and transport in hopelessly uneconomic locations. In areas of small-scale agriculture purchase of expensive machinery for which there is not enough work has proved wasteful, and many parts of the Mediterranean lands are now over-mechanized in their farming.

One of the problems has been the lack of investment assistance by governments. In Yugoslavia, for example, private investment is difficult anyway and the range of investment alternatives for individual migrants is limited. One result has been an excess of haulage capacity in many areas, especially the north-west, since transport is one sector in which private investment can be made. Baucic (1971) has argued that the provision of 'organized assistance' for migrants regarding investment is essential (p. 52). Elsewhere, government proposals for investment assistance seem to have been still-born. In 1966 the Turkish government announced the setting up of an Industrial and Commercial Corporation which would have allowed migrants to invest their savings in return for jobs when they came home; but the scheme never got off the ground (Abadan, 1972). However, one group of Turkish migrant workers, with German co-operation, did succeed in establishing a factory on their return (Kayser, 1972).

One of the important long-term benefits that the supply countries hope to receive from emigration is vocational training. All too often these hopes have not materialized. It has already been pointed out in Chapter 4 that most migrants learn no skills to speak of while abroad; certainly the numbers gaining craft skill status are few. Indeed, it seems that the supply countries may even experience a net loss of skilled workers as a result of emigration, since skilled workers are those most in demand in the destination countries. They are the first to emigrate and often the high pay they receive makes them reluctant to return.

It seems that there may, in fact, be an over-all weakening of the labour force in the supply countries as emigration continues. The better and keener workers are usually those most aware of the opportunities for migration and among the first to go abroad. This natural selection process is taken further by the recruitment agencies which choose only the best workers from those who apply for migration. This results in the poorer elements being left behind, a tendency already mentioned in Chapter 2 in connection with rural—urban movement. A further selection takes place at the conclusion of the first contract, when poorer workers do not have their contracts renewed, and return home (Baucic, 1971). Gradually, therefore, a dilution may take place in the labour force at home.

For those who do receive vocational training in the destination countries, there is no guarantee of a suitable job on their return. It has been pointed out, for example, that twice as many Algerians in France are being trained in building and metal-working as Algeria is likely to need, whilst in the chemical and textile industries the disparities are reversed (Trebous, 1970). A similar situation has been reported in parts of Italy (Zingaro, 1969; Castles and Kosack, 1973; Censis, 1968). The type of factory training received in the industrial countries may also be unsatisfactory for the supply countries. The latter tend to require each worker to have a wide range of experience, but the vertical specialization of European industry means that the training received is becoming more and more narrow. Finally, there is little evidence that many migrants wish to undertake industrial employment upon their return anyway. For some, industrial work is of low social status, and, as was shown above, migrants prefer to invest their hard-won savings in small independent businesses, or return to their home villages and continue farming the family land (Vigorelli, 1969; Zingaro, 1969; Censis, 1968; Kayser, 1971). Hence the contribution to economic development made by the skills and experience of returning migrants is, like that of their remittances, low.

From the analysis so far a number of general points emerge. The basic reasons for immigration are related to rapid population increase and/or to under-employment and to the need to change employment structures dominated by inefficient and low-income agriculture. There is also evidence that emigration countries have found a tendency for migration streams to 'mature', as short-term moves abroad of single people became semi-permanent or permanent stays of families. Finally, the almost universal hopes of gains from migration have at best only been partly fulfilled.

Such generalizations are not equally applicable to all supply countries, which display a wide range of geographical conditions and which have links of varying types and strengths with destination areas. The remainder of this chapter will focus on individual countries of emigration. The main considerations will be geographical, with special attention paid to distinctive origin areas within countries, and to their links with destinations abroad. In addition, appropriate emphasis will be placed on those aspects of labour emigration that are either particularly distinctive in the country under consideration, or have notable repercussions for its development. However, to some extent the choice and the attention paid to each country will inevitably reflect the available literature. Italy, the main source area in the early post-war years, will be examined first.

Italy

Italy has traditionally been a country of emigration, but recent years have seen a slowing-down of out-movement. During the 1950s Italy was the main source of migrant labour for north-west Europe, and still remains important, but its migration stream is now waning. In aggregate, of course, the country has long been 'developed', along with its northern neighbours, but in economic circumstances there is still a division between north and south, which is critical in understanding the course and patterns of emigration. Since the mid-1950s this division has become increasingly blurred. Economic growth in the industrial north has attracted and absorbed millions of southerners, while at the same time, the steady establishment of industrial centres in the Mezzogiorno has curbed the need to migrate (Rodgers, 1970).

During the post-war period southern Italy and the Islands especially, have in varying degree suffered from poverty, unemployment, and under-employment. These problems have initiated a process of rural decongestion that, as in other Mediterranean countries, has been partially translated into foreign migration. In northern Italy, the same process has also been under way, although in more muted form. There the attraction for migrants has particularly been the Genoa–Milan–Turin triangle, although the higher pay offered abroad has continued to divert even some of this stream.

Post-war labour migrations are the culmination of a long-established tradition, and for over a century the theme of emigration has been crucial in Italy's population geography. Since 1861 about 26,000,000 Italians have emigrated (Monticelli, 1967), but both the volume of movement and the balance of destinations have fluctuated. During the second half of the nineteenth century about 7,000,000 Italians emigrated, mainly from the north and particularly to other European countries. By the turn of the century, not only did the pace of emigration quicken, (9,000,000 emigrants between 1900 and 1915), but the origins and destinations changed. In the decades leading to World War I, southern Italy provided more emigrants than the north and there was more trans-oceanic migration, especially to the United States, than to destinations elsewhere in Europe. The interwar period saw a very reduced amount of migration, and also a swing back to a situation in which most emigration was again from the industrial north and was mainly to elsewhere in Europe. It was at this time that what Perotti (1967) has called a 'demographic reservoir' was created in southern Italy. This resulted from a combination of a high rate of natural increase, anti-immigration regulations in reception countries, anti-emigration measures in Italy (imposed by the Fascist government), and, ultimately, restrictions on movement imposed by wartime conditions.

Although the post-war period has seen a continuation of trans-oceanic Italian emigration, this flow has been transcended by movement to industrial Europe. Between 1946 and 1965 there were 5,600,000 emigrants, initially mostly from northern Italy but later mainly from the centre and south. A majority of these people moved to the industrial countries of north-west Europe. From the late 1940s to the early 1960s, the proportion of Italian emigrants moving to other European destinations increased from 55 per cent to 84 per cent. More of these migrants returned home than traditionally and by the mid-1960s those coming home from European migrations accounted for 93 per cent of returnees (Monticelli, 1967). By this time migration to north-west Europe represented over 80 per cent of exits, over 90 per cent of returns, and 65 per cent of net migration. In 1966, 2,500,000 of the 3,000,000 Italians working outside Italy were elsewhere in Europe (Bouscaren, 1969).

The post-war period has seen the level of emigration fluctuate markedly. For most of the 1950s, there was a steady increase in Italian emigration, especially to France and Switzerland, with net emigration reaching a peak in 1960 when 192,000 left (Bouscaren, 1969). During the 1960s, numbers of emigrants continued to fall, especially as economic conditions at home improved, although in the middle of the decade there was some increase again as the Italian boom slackened. From 1967 to 1970, the diminution in emigration continued and then there was another increase, owing to the very strong German demand for labour and to internal conditions within Italy (Anon., 1974). During this time, total net emigration fell from 60,000 to only 9,000, and total emigrants from 229,000 to 151,000 (Istituto Centrale di Statistica, 1972). In 1971 however, emigration increased again, owing both to failing conditions at home and to the powerful demand from West Germany.

Fluctuations in labour emigration since the last war reflect economic conditions both at home and abroad. The general downward trend since the early 1960s reflects the pace of the exodus from Italy's rural areas, particularly in the south. This process of rural decongestion seems to have reached its greatest intensity around the years 1960—4 and, as pressure in the rural areas decreased, the forces pushing migrants away became less acute (Perotti, 1967).

In 1971, Italy's agriculture was still estimated to be 15 years behind that of West Germany and 7 or 8 behind France, in terms of the surplus of manpower, with nearly 3,500,000 workers (18 per cent of the labour force) on the land (Böhning, 1972).

It is the continuing existence of rural labour surpluses in southern Italy, and the growth of industry in the north with resultant labour shortages over the last 10–15 years, that has been responsible for the increasing emergence of southern Italy and the Islands as the dominant source area for foreign labour migrants. By

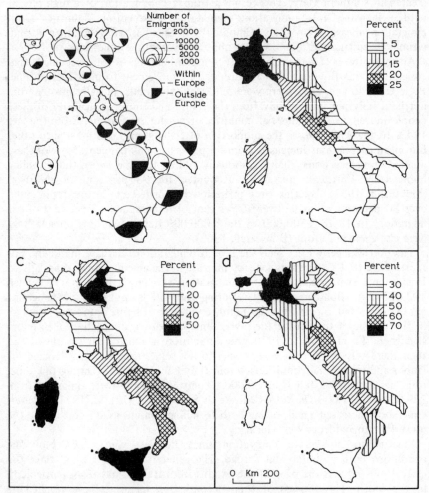

5.1 Italy: (a) emigration, 1970; proportions of emigrants within Europe going (b) to France; (c) to West Germany; (d) to Switzerland

1970, the southern provinces of Puglia (24,000 emigrants), Campania (21,000), Sicilia (19,000), and Calabria (17,000) were the main sending regions in the country (Fig. 5.1a). The vast majority of emigrants from all regions were towards Europe, with only a handful of exceptions; Sicilia, for example, still sends a substantial proportion of its people to the United States, while Lazio, containing Rome and the Vatican City, distributes emigrants world-wide.

Italy also demonstrates very well the association of regions of emigration with specific destinations, reflecting a variety of cultural proximity and temporal factors. Although in 1970 France received only 7·7 per cent of Italian emigrants moving within Europe, the proportions varied very considerably between regions (Fig. 5.1b). Almost a third of Liguria's emigrants and over a quarter of those from Piemonte went to France, whereas from Trentino and Basilicata the proportions were under 3 per cent. On the whole, France tended to recruit from the north-west and centre of Italy. In part, this reflects France's early recruitment of Italian labour in the 1950s, when northern Italy was a major emigration source. It also reflects cultural ties between north-west Italy and France, as well as the proximity of the area to France's Mediterranean coast with its well-established demand for labour from the tourist industry and, more recently, from large-scale industrial development in the Marseilles region.

By 1970, France's recruitment of Italians was easily exceeded by that of West Germany which took 38·3 per cent of all Italians emigrating elsewhere in Europe. Again, there were wide variations between regions; Sicilia, Sardinia, and Veneto sent over half their migrants to West Germany, while Val d'Aosta sent less than 2 per cent. The geographical pattern of migrant origins to West Germany was very different from that of those going to France and Switzerland (Fig. 5.1c). In particular, West Germany took most of its migrants from southern Italy, a result of being a late-comer in the recruitment of Italians. Hence West German employers have recruited more heavily from the rural parts of Italy rather than the industrial areas. This explains the considerable West German recruitment from Veneto, a predominantly agricultural and relatively poor farming area in the north.

The spatial pattern of recruitment to Switzerland contained elements of those described above for France and West Germany (Fig. 5.1d). In 1970 Switzerland received more Italian migrants than either France or West Germany. None of the italian regions sent less than 20 per cent of its European migrants to Switzerland and the figure for Lombardia was 79 per cent, well above the national average going to Switzerland of 46·5 per cent. The heavy emigration to Switzerland from northern Italy reflects both proximity and early post-war establishment of labour migration links with Switzerland from this most heavily populated part of the country. This movement has persisted, being helped by the sharp wages gradient across the Swiss—Italian border. Since the mid-1960s the Swiss recruitment effort has been slowed for political reasons at home and so Switzerland had little incentive to compete with West Germany in recruitment from southern Italy.

Italy has been lessening its dependence on labour emigration as a safety valve for over a decade, although there will still be a need for it for some time. On the basis of estimates of unemployment and under-employment in 1971, Böhning (1972) suggested than an intra-European migration potential of 400,000 workers still existed. Whether or not this potential materializes depends on many factors, not least the economic situation in destination countries. It is clear, however, that the days when Italians were the main migrant labour force in Europe are past. As was noted in the last chapter, when competition for labour increased in the late 1950s other sources in addition to Italy were drawn upon. The first of these was Iberia, which has many economic and social parallels with the south of Italy especially. It is therefore appropriate now to survey the situations in Spain and Portugal that have engendered and maintained the flow of workers abroad.

Iberia

In spite of striking political contrasts now, the population history and contemporary geography of Portugal and Spain display many similarities. In recent decades, both have experienced large-scale emigration from backward (usually interior) rural areas to centres of industrial and commercial development, usually on the coast but also to Madrid in the case of Spain. Recent labour migrations to north-west Europe are usually either a diversion of this internal rural—urban movement, or a second stage after the initial move to the city.

Both countries have a long tradition of emigration. Many Portuguese have moved in recent decades to their former colony of Brazil; of 272,000 emigrants between 1951 and 1960, 76·3 per cent went to Brazil. There were also important flows to the United States, Canada, Venezuela, and Argentina (Garnier, 1971). But since the mid-1950s there have been marked changes in destination, with north-west Europe, especially France, rising to a leading position. This change in destination was in response to a slackening in the economic growth of Brazil and to that country's bar on unqualified immigrants from 1964. At the same time the demand for labour in industrial Western Europe was growing rapidly. Of the 215,000 emigrants between 1961 and 1965, only 20·4 per cent went to Brazil, with the majority (66·2 per cent) going to north-west Europe, most notably (55·4 per cent) to France (Anon., 1971). Already at the end of World War II, 1,000 Portuguese migrants were installed in Paris, working especially in the building trade and representing points of contact for later migrants. However, it was not until 10 years later that the annual flow of Portuguese to France exceeded 1,000 people. Thereafter, numbers grew rapidly to over 70,000 in 1966 (Battesti, 1968).

Like Portugal, Spain has a long history of outmigration with, for example, flows directed to Latin America, southern Italy, the Philippines, and the Oran region, from the seventeenth century onwards. Spanish emigration for settlement purposes declined in importance in the 1960s and there has been an increasing emphasis on labour migration to countries in north-west Europe (Anon., 1972a). In 1969 some 617,000 Spaniards were living in France, 207,000 in West Germany, 102,000 in Switzerland and 50,000 in Belgium (Anon.,

1972a). Such flows are additional to temporary movements of Spanish agricultural workers to the vineyards, rice fields, and orchards of France, which account for more than 90 per cent of all seasonal workers employed in France (Battesti, 1966).

In recent decades, the demographic histories of Spain and Portugal seem to have diverged somewhat, with Portugal continuing to have population growth limited by emigration, while increases in Spain have recently gone ahead much more quickly than in the past. Both countries share common characteristics of very rapid growth in labour migration within Europe during the 1960s, easily surpassing in volume all their other emigration flows. Although Portugal displays a high rate of natural increase by European standards, it had an increase in population of only 29 per cent between 1930 and 1972, largely owing to emigration. The direct result of emigration and the indirect result of reducing rates of natural increase actually caused Portugal's resident population to decline by 114,000 (1·4 per cent) during the 1960s to reach 8,100,000 in 1970 (Poinard, 1972b). Nationwide, natural increase declined from 123,000 in 1962 to 88,000 in 1969, with the rate of emigration increasing over the same period. Many interior areas underwent serious declines in natural increase during the 1960s and some villages lost more than half their residents.

In Spain, during the 1960s, the population increased by 11 per cent to reach 33,800,000 at the end of 1970 (Courtot, 1971). This represented a faster rate of growth than for any earlier decade in the twentieth century, and was substantially greater than the 8·7 per cent growth in the 1950s. It was achieved in spite of the fact that roughly 500,000 people left to settle abroad during the decade. In addition, an estimated 1,000,000 Spaniards were living in other parts of western Europe in 1965, but in many cases this simply represented a temporary expatriation for a few years.

There is no doubt that demographic pressures in both Portugal and Spain have been eased by emigration, but the familiar themes of a relatively backward agrarian economy and inadequate industrial development have stimulated migration in recent years. For the most part, the factors that account for outmigration from rural areas are those that encourage overseas migration, and within both countries there are distinctive regional patterns of population loss. In Portugal, outmigration involves not only agricultural workers but also artisans and traders, mostly of rural origin. Migration losses are particularly strong from Minho and Tras-os-Montes in the north, the Extramadura in the centre, and the Algarve (Furo district) in the south. In each of these areas of dense settlement and polyculture 'il faut travailler dur pour gagner peu' (Piel, 1966). Outmigration of one form or another has been a result, with, for example, workers and fishermen migrating seasonally to Spain and North Africa (Cavaco, 1971). Interior areas close to the Spanish border initially formed the most important zones of outmigration, which broadened during the course of the 1960s. Areas along the border offer the possibility of clandestine labour migration through Spain to France (Viguier, 1970).

Profound cultural differences underlie Portugal's pattern of migratory loss. The north is a region of fragmented property, with a strongly Roman Catholic population living at high densities and forming a veritable 'human ants' nest' in the Minho area (Poinard, 1972b). By contrast, Moorish domination lasted longer in the south. Religious observance is weaker than in the north and birth rates and population densities are lower. However, properties are large, and many are still worked on the *latifundium* principle by a labouring population having low levels of literacy. Under-employment is rife.

As in Portugal, the origins of Spanish labour migration are to be found in the increased mobility of the country's population which has made geographical migration normal and acceptable. Virtually all parts of southern, western and central Spain are losing population. Galicia, southern Andalusia, and the provinces of Madrid and Valladolid form the only notable exceptions. Only the Mediterranean coast, the Basque country, and the capital emerge as areas of growth and inmigration (Fig. 1.11), with the metropolitan areas of Madrid, Barcelona, Valencia, and Bilbao housing more than one-fifth of the national population. Nevertheless, government schemes for establishing industrial growth poles in the provinces have stimulated population concentration in a number of towns and cities which continue to draw large volumes of labour from the surrounding countryside. Rural management and local industrialization projects have been less successful in fixing population, so that the Spanish interior continues to experience large-scale depopulation to the benefit of Madrid and the relatively privileged coastal areas, especially in the east and north.

As in other countries, different areas send migrants to different destinations. In the past, the majority of labour migrants originated in northern, central, and western Spain. The inhabitants of these areas became more aware of the benefits of migration and had access to more information. Increasingly, migrants from here no longer move to France, as they did traditionally, but to better-paid jobs in West Germany and Switzerland. In the south, where birth rates have been particularly high in recent years, large-scale labour emigration is a recent phenomenon and the majority of migrants from Andalusia and eastern Spain move to France (Sanchez Lopez, 1969).

Unlike the industrial countries of Western Europe (including Italy), neither Spain nor Portugal is well endowed with industrial raw materials and urban-industrial agglomerations are comparatively few. Vast areas of Iberia are agricultural and most have been losing population by emigration (Fig.1.8). In the absence of sufficient attractions at home it was natural for migrants to move abroad. In recent years the deleterious effects of this emigration have become apparent, and, especially in Portugal, there is evidence that the trend towards international migration may have gone too far. Rural depopulation has become almost universal and, more to the point, Portugal's population as a whole declined during the 1960s. At the same time there was evidence of labour shortages in some parts of the two countries suggesting that workers going abroad could usefully be employed at home (Poinard, 1972b; ILO, 1973).

Portugal and Spain illustrate, in fact, one of the major problems faced by supply countries. Labour emigration may be encouraged in the early years by governments wishing to relieve problems of overpopulation and under-employment. But the momentum becomes difficult to check, and severe pressure is put on plans for economic development. This problem has also been faced by Yugoslavia, particularly with respect to the emigration of more qualified workers. The country came into the field as a supplier of labour later than Italy and Iberia, but the outflow of its workers soon achieved massive proportions. As the only communist country heavily involved in Western Europe's labour market, it is of particular interest. Accordingly attention will now be turned to Yugoslavia.

Yugoslavia

Yugoslavia has traditionally been a country of emigration, although the causes have been complicated by cultural and political factors associated with the break up of the Austro-Hungarian and Ottoman empires and the creation of an independent state after World War I. Although much Yugoslav migration has been to areas of European colonization beyond the Continent (especially in North America) significant links have been long established within Europe. For example, migration to Germany for work purposes dates back to the late 19th century, when predominantly unskilled or semi-educated emigrants, especially from Slovenia and Croatia, went to the growing industrial area of the Ruhr. This was followed early in the present century by migration to the industrial areas of northern France and to Paris (Velikonja, 1974).

During the inter-war period, net average emigration was estimated to be 14—20,000 per annum in the 1920s, falling to 4,000 in the 1930s (Kirk, 1946). Most migrants were from the western areas (especially Croatia and Slovenia) and the main country of immigration was the United States. Many immigrants, however, continued to tread the well-established path to industrial Western Europe; for example, the main initial flow to employment in mining and heavy industry in the Maastricht district of the Netherlands and at Liège in Belgium was generated at this time (Velikonja, 1974).

Despite economic improvements in Yugoslavia after the War, the propensity to migrate remained high. Between 1953 and 1961 average annual net emigration was estimated to be 34,500, and 22,500 between 1961 and 1971 (Macura, 1974). In contrast to the inter-war period, and the immediate post-war years, when many Yugoslavs went to Australia, these migrations were chiefly directed towards other European destinations. A higher proportion of the migrants were educated and skilled than hitherto, coming mainly from the cities. Upon this emigration, primarily for settlement abroad, there has been superimposed a legion of temporary labour migrants, variously estimated to number in 1971, 672,000 and 790,500 (Census of Yugoslavia 1971; Baucic, 1974) and in 1973 1,100,000 (Velikonja, 1974). This labour migration is highly significant in the context of Yugoslav emigration history: between 1880 and 1973 there were 600,000 permanent emigrants from Yugoslavia, less than the number of temporary labour migrants since 1960 (Velikonja, 1974). West Germany has been the principal destination, taking 60 per cent of Yugoslav migrants to Europe; Australia has been the second important destination (24 per cent), followed by France (7 per cent) (Baucic, 1974).

The reasons for emigration from Yugoslavia are the familiar ones. An underlying feature has been population growth imposing undue pressure on a predominantly agrarian economy. As in other Mediterranean countries the demographic transition came late, occurring only within the last half-century. Between 1921 and 1971 total population rose from 12,500,000 to 20,500,000 although the rate of growth was not steady. During the inter-war years birth rates fell, from 35 per thousand in 1927 to 26 per thousand in 1939; further falls during the war were followed in the late 1940s and early 1950s by a 'baby boom', with birth rates of up to 30 per thousand in some years (Macura, 1974). After 1957 a steady decline in fertility set in which has continued to the present. Meanwhile, mortality rates have fallen faster and more steadily than fertility rates, to only 9 per thousand in 1971. Rates of natural increase were high, particularly during the post-war baby boom, but over the last two decades they have declined steadily to 9 per thousand in 1971, being influenced strongly by the emigration of so many in the reproductive age groups (Macura, 1974). By the early 1970s, labour migrants represented 5 per cent of the total Yugoslav population (Baucic, 1974).

The country's economic structure has also induced migration. In 1945 much of Yugoslavia—particularly those areas of the south that had been under Ottoman rule—were still at the pre-industrial revolution stage of development. Rapid population growth in the first half of the twentieth century led to serious rural overpopulation. One estimate indicated that in 1953 as much as 30 per cent of the total agricultural population was surplus to demand (Macura, 1974). Thus there was pressure for migration away from rural areas, but Yugoslavia's industrial regions were unable to provide enough non-agricultural employment. Indeed, the urban areas themselves were an early and major source of emigrants, and migration from them increased after the 'reforms' of 1965 reversed economic growth in the economically developed regions. Furthermore, the wages gradient between Yugoslavia and the labour-recruiting countries of north-west Europe greatly encouraged emigration; in 1969 average monthly earnings in Yugoslavia were only $80, compared with $215 for Yugoslavs employed in West Germany (Baucic, 1971).

In the light of the economic situation inherited after 1945, the Yugoslav government decided that if conditions provoked labour migration then it was better for it to be open than illegal. As the streams of migrants in Europe became a flood, after 1960, the Yugoslav government introduced legislation in 1963 permitting Yugoslav workers to move abroad under certain conditions. After the failure of the 1965 reforms, there was complete liberalization of emigration, and recruitment agreements were signed with France (1965), West Germany (1969), and the Netherlands and Luxembourg (1970). One of the

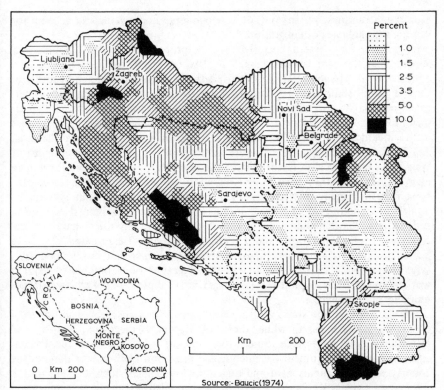

5.2 Yugoslavia: workers temporarily employed abroad as proportion of total commune population, 1971

effects of the liberalization was that instead of the unemployed and under-employed moving abroad, particularly from the south and east, it was the better-educated and trained who left. As a result, measures were introduced in the early 1970s to control more stringently the emigration of better-skilled and educated workers and the most highly qualified were permitted to migrate only in the unlikely event of their being unemployed and unable to find work at home.

Yugoslavia illustrates very well the existence of marked regional variations in the proportion of population emigrating. In some degree these variations reflect levels of economic development, but unlike some other countries, emigration from Yugoslavia tends to be inversely related to underdevelopment, with larger numbers of migrants moving from the more developed areas. To some extent emigration is also related to the cultural and ethnic diversity of a country in which some groups have traditionally emigrated to north-west Europe, but others have not. As a result, differences in natural environment, in socio-economic structures, and in levels of development do not adequately account for varying regional rates of emigration.

In general, the western areas have larger proportions of their populations abroad than those to the east (Fig. 5.2). Two regions in particular have a high emigration rate (Baucic, 1971). One covers the Dalmatian hinterland of southern Croatia and south-western Bosnia—Herzegovina, an economically under-developed karst area, marked by traditional internal and external labour migration, and by permanent emigration of the local population. The second region includes central and western Croatia, Backa, and north-eastern Slovenia, and is characterized by high absolute numbers of emigrants. The main area of emigration in this region forms part of the fertile but overpopulated Pannonian plain. Apart from these two large emigration regions, the urban areas provide most migrants, many of whom are skilled and were originally employed in the domestic economy. At the present time (1975) Croatia, Bosnia—Herzegovina and Slovenia have higher proportions of emigrants than their shares of the country's total population, and Croatia and Bosnia—Herzegovina also have higher proportions of people employed abroad than their shares in the country's total workforce. Croatia has not only the highest absolute number of migrant workers but also the highest rate of emigration (8·2 per cent) of all Yugoslavia's republics and provinces.

The situation is not static and in recent years Croatia's proportion of total emigrants has decreased while those of Bosnia—Herzegovina, Serbia, and Macedonia have increased. Since the conclusion of bilateral recruitment agreements, the government has encouraged migration from poorer parts of the country where unemployment and under-employment are high, but emigration rates low (Kayser, 1972). This policy has succeeded, but while new migration outlets have been created in the east and south, the existing ones in the west and north have not been blocked. Not only is better information about the advantages of migration available in the latter areas, but the economic reforms of 1965 seriously slowed economic growth there. Croatia in particular suffered a loss of employment after 1965 that was not made up until 1971. The result was a fresh spurt of emigration from Croatia, especially after the 1967 recession in West Germany. The Croatian situation was exacerbated by the large numbers of skilled workers among the emigrants; at the end of 1970 they accounted for one-third of all external migrants from Croatia (Baucic, 1971).

Migrants from the different regions of Yugoslavia tend to be attracted to different countries and there is widespread variation, even at the *commune* level. For example, although in 1971 France took only 7 per cent of Yugoslav labour migrants, some *communes*, especially in Serbia, sent over half their migrants to France. West Germany is a much more important destination, taking 60 per cent of the total in 1971. Again there are marked differences between *communes*, even adjacent ones, some of which send over 90 per cent of their emigrants to West Germany. The local situations illustrate how an emigration stream, once established, can become self-reinforcing; migrants flow one way, information flows back to the local area, and more migrants follow the same path of their predecessors—often their relatives and friends.

In general, those parts of Yugoslavia with lower rates of emigration have higher proportions of their labour migrants employed in France (Fig. 5.3). This applies particularly to Serbia, the source of most Yugoslav migrants to France. Partly this reflects traditional ties between Yugoslav regions of emigration and French regions of labour immigration (Friganovic *et al.*, 1972). Partly it is because of France's lack of competitiveness in the foreign labour market, especially with West Germany and Austria, which means that migrants to France have poorer qualifications and are from more remote areas with less information about opportunities elsewhere. It may also result from the bilateral recruitment agreement with France in 1965 after which the Yugoslav government gave greater encouragement to emigration from poorer, less developed areas, such as Serbia, by establishing recruitment offices there.

West Germany is a much more important destination, and in 1973 approximately 500,000 Yugoslavs were working there. The regions sending

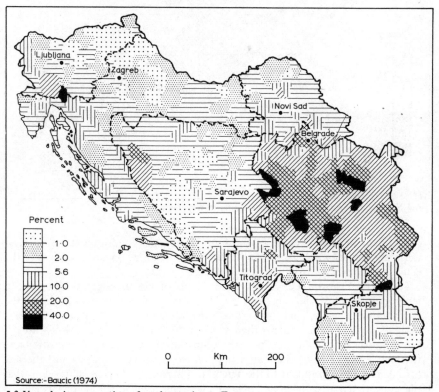

Percent

- 1·0
- 2·0
- 5·6
- 10·0
- 20·0
- 40·0

Ljubljana
Zagreb
Novi Sad
Belgrade
Sarajevo
Titograd
Skopje

0   Km   200

Source:-Baucic (1974)

5.3 Yugoslavia: proportion of workers going to France

workers to West Germany (Fig. 5.4) were the more developed parts of the
country, especially in Croatia and in Bosnia–Herzegovina. However, in recent
years the southern parts of the country, in particular Kosovo and Macedonia,
have become more important sources, especially after the establishment of

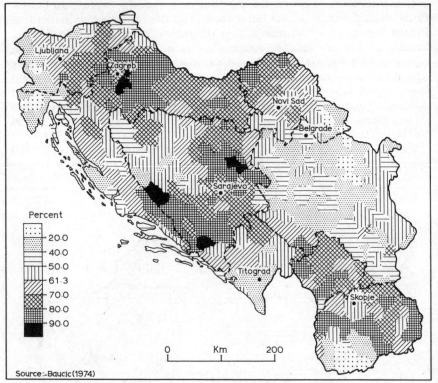

5.4 Yugoslavia: proportion of workers going to West Germany

recruitment offices. Because of the superior pay and conditions it offers, West
Germany has been able to cream off the better Yugoslav migrants, especially the
educated and skilled, from the more developed areas.

The 1971 Yugoslav Census recorded details of labour migrants ('persons in
temporary employment abroad') for the first time. Over two-thirds of the
migrants were male, and over four-fifths aged under 40; women migrants,
however, tended to be younger than men. One of the most distinctive features of
the Yugoslav labour migrants is their comparatively high level of education and
training. This has made them an attraction to recruiting countries, but the loss
has been an embarrassment to the Yugoslav government. In general, it seems that
the educational attainments of migrants is better (Baucic, 1974) or virtually as

good (Nikolic, 1972) as that for the Yugoslav population as a whole. Although the outflow of the highest-educated (university and equivalent) is less than average, those with secondary education, especially those who have attended a school for skilled workers, are more likely to migrate. Workers with vocational training are particularly prone to migration, and of those migrants with vocational training, four-fifths are either 'skilled' or 'highly skilled'. Some occupational types are more likely to migrate than others; for example, the rate of emigration for construction workers is 10 per cent compared with 7 per cent for all migrants (Nikolic, 1972).

There are regional variations in the propensity to migrate of educated workers (secondary school education and school for skilled workers) and of those with vocational training (Nikolic, 1972). For the most part, regional differences in vocational composition between workers employed in Yugoslavia and labour migrants are not very great. The exception is Kosovo, whence fewer vocationally trained people emigrate. But the picture for educated workers is different, and regional ratios correspond more to differences in levels of economic development. The proportions of total numbers of migrants who are educated are highest among those moving from the economically developed republics and provinces, and almost one-third of educated emigrants are from the ten economically most developed centres. The degree of regional concentration increases the higher the educational level; 70 per cent of the highest-educated come from Zagreb and Belgrade. In addition to differences between republics and provinces, there are very pronounced differences between individual *communes* in the propensity of educated workers to migrate. *Communes* with a low proportion of educated among their emigrants are mainly in the economically under-developed areas, but in such areas the outflow of only a few educated people can constitute a serious economic and social problem for the *communes* involved.

Most of the general social and economic effects of labour migration mentioned in the first part of this chapter apply to Yugoslavia. Among the economic consequences for the country, one of the most serious is the 'dilution' of its labour force, arising from the selectivity of migration. One reaction has been government measures in the early 1970s to restrict the flow of skilled, especially highly skilled, workers. Better workers have been lost abroad, and they have been replaced by labour with poorer qualifications. Furthermore, many of the returning workers from abroad are among the less able. For example, a survey of a group of enterprises carried out by the Institute of Geography at the University of Zagreb found that between 1967 and 1972 3,181 employees left their jobs to go abroad but only 406 returned to replace them. Moreover, the qualifications of those who went abroad were much better than the qualifications of those who returned (Baucic, 1974).

Undesirable social effects of emigration have also been noted in Yugoslavia and it has been suggested that emigration breeds 'the emigrating sub-proletariate of tomorrow' (ILO, 1973, p. 98). Yugoslav teachers have reported less motivation to learn in the face of the possibility of easy emigration and an unskilled job abroad with high pay (Anon., 1972b). Migration has probably also been the principal reason for the proportion of illiterates amongst employees in Croatia increasing from 4·5 per cent in 1961 to 6·8 per cent in 1970 (Baucic, 1974).

Thus, in Yugoslavia, emigration has been adopted as a tool of socialist central planning. It has been regarded as desirable because the country's employment structure has been quite unable to provide enough jobs. However, it is clear that the country cannot contemplate with complete equanimity the results of emigration; indeed, it faces a dilemma. On the one hand there are short-term gains because some of the immediate problems of labour surplus have been alleviated and there is more money in circulation. On the other hand, emigration has created problems which threaten, even in a highly controlled political system, the long-term social and economic development of all regions of the country. In these circumstances, balancing the advantages and disadvantages of labour emigration is difficult, especially without the benefit of hindsight. Even if the Yugoslav economy is handled efficiently, it will take some time before its urban-industrial base matches that of north-west European countries. But at least the completion of its demographic transition means that the country is now spared earlier problems of rapid population increase. In other countries, however, demographic pressure remains severe. Attention will now be directed to two areas, the Maghreb states of North Africa and Turkey, where high birth rates have created very substantial 'reservoirs' of migrants, but which also have significant differences in their migration histories.

North Africa

In general terms the reasons for labour migration are similar for all Mediterranean countries, but in the North African case pressure to migrate is particularly strong. Rates of natural increase remain high and the population is also very young, roughly 45 per cent being under 15 years of age (Table 5.1) (Maison, 1973).

Emigration from the Maghreb is not a new phenomenon. Algeria, in particular, has had important but varying types of link with France for more than a century (Augarde and Prevost, 1970). Settlement by the French between 1860 and 1880 involved displacement of native populations. Famine during the 1860s stimulated both internal migration and movement overseas. However, although between 1874 and 1914 travel permits were required for entry to France many North Africans moved there. Some went as traders as early as the 1870s; others went as industrial workers to Marseilles and to Paris where many were involved in building the Métro, for example. From the early years of the twentieth century the mines and factories of the Nord and the Pas de Calais proved an attraction. By 1914 it was estimated that there were 30,000 North Africans in France. Thereafter, Algerians were allowed to enter France in considerable numbers to work in the munitions and transport industries, in agriculture and in road-building. Immediately after World War I, return flows to Algeria increased.

However, the wartime loss of 1,325,000 French soldiers meant that there was still a great need for immigration in the 1920s and 1930s in spite of economic depression. Recruitment schemes were operated by French industrialists working through middlemen in Algeria. Often the policy was to bring over Algerians from distinct regions, villages, or urban quarters and settle them in particular industrial reception areas in order to reduce 'tribal' rivalry in France (Michel, 1956). After World War II France was still critically short of labour and migration flows intensified (Montagne, 1953).

Following Algerian independence in 1962, there was something of a lull in movement. But it was soon clear that in spite of schemes for industrial development the newly independent country could not absorb all its labour force (Augarde and Prevost, 1970). It has been estimated that Algeria would need to create 100,000 jobs in industrial and service activities each year, simply to employ the young workers coming on to its labour market (Moulin, 1970). Such targets have not been met. Industrialization schemes in Tunisia have also been quite inadequate to solve problems of under-employment and unemployment (Simon, 1973). Increasing numbers of young workers have been leaving training centres without finding suitable employment in their home country.

Social and political changes following the independence of all three Maghreb countries have meant that young North Africans have developed higher aspirations which may perhaps be realized only through emigration to a developed economy, in particular to France (Augarde and Prevost, 1970). In addition, destruction of villages and subsequent policies for regrouping settlement by the French during the Algerian war led to 'uprooting' and thus stimulated emigration (Sutton, 1972). Traditional agricultural organization was disrupted in inland regions such as the Grande and Petite Kabylie, the Aurès, and the Ouarsenis, which had received population displaced from the Europeanized plains during the nineteenth and early twentieth centuries. These areas suffered particularly during the Algerian war and in several of them population increased only slightly or even declined between 1954 and 1966 (Maison, 1973).

As was shown in Chapter 4, each newly independent country established agreements for labour migration to the industrial states. Thus, for example, movements from Morocco to France since 1963 have been organized by the Office National d'Immigration. In addition, agreements were signed with Belgium and West Germany in 1964 and with the Netherlands in 1969. Between 1955 and 1963, obstacles were erected by both Tunisia and France to control flows but agreement was then reached and was followed by contracts with Belgium and West Germany in 1969. According to the principle of free circulation between Algeria and France embodied in the Evian Agreement (1962), Algerians could enter France without work permits and live there without residents' permits. Recent years, however, have seen new restrictions imposed on Algerian movement to France.

By 1971, no fewer than 1,000,000 migrants from North Africa were living in France, with much smaller numbers in Belgium (Wallonia, Brussels, Antwerp),

West Germany (the Rhinelands and other urban concentrations), Switzerland, and Sweden. But the essential link has remained with France; by the end of the 1960s, for example, 1 Algerian worker in every 20 was resident in that country. In addition, an estimated 2,000,000 rural Algerians relied for a large part of their subsistence on remittances from overseas (Moulin, 1970). The mass movement of North Africans across the Mediterranean in recent years has led to a build-up of 'racial' intolerance in France. Such feelings have arisen mainly because of the concentration of immigrants from the Maghreb in particular areas of the country and even in selected parts of cities. Events like the killing of a French bus driver at Marseilles by an Algerian migrant have served to spark off anti-North African feelings which, in 1973, led the Algerian government to suspend further migration of its citizens to work in France.

Within the countries of the Maghreb, certain regions stand out as migrant reservoirs. These are not static in distribution and new ones have been added in recent years. High population densities in some areas have led to population pressures which have encouraged outmigration streams. Often in the past, migration was of an internal, rural—rural or rural—urban nature, but the extremes of population increase experienced, the slow growth of indigenous economies, and the existence of employment opportunities overseas have combined to result increasingly in labour migration to north-west Europe. Emigration has undoubtedly eased demographic pressure by removing large numbers of migrants and has also contributed to a reduction in birth rates. For example, in 1971, the net migratory loss from Tunisia was 32,400 persons, equivalent to 20—25 per cent of annual natural increase (Simon, 1973), and in the Algerian Kabylie, emigration has been an important factor in the stagnation and even decline of population in the Tizi Ouzou area (Sutton, 1972).

The diversity of man/land relations in the Maghreb which give rise to conditions especially favourable to emigration from some areas may be illustrated by reference to Algeria. The highest densities (more than 95 persons per km^2) are found between Algiers and Constantine, plus surrounding coastal areas, most notably the Grande and Petite Kabylie. Between Algiers and Oran and around Annaba densities are in the order of 100 per km^2, falling to roughly half that amount in areas south of Constantine and Oran, and diminishing to between 5 and 10 per km^2 on the margins of the Sahara and to even less in the desert. Given such density patterns which apply, in general terms, to each of the Maghreb countries, it is to be expected that most of their migrants coming to north-west Europe will originate from coastal zones where densities are generally above 50 per km^2, and which include such major urban departure points as Algiers, Casablanca, and Tunis (Fig. 5.5). This is indeed the case and the interior of the Maghreb and the Sahara supply few migrants (Simon and Noin, 1972). However, there are some exceptions where population densities have increased as, for example, on the high plains of Constantine, in the Aurès mountains, the Dades valley, and on the Haut-Tell of Tunisia (Simon, 1973). During the 1950s and 1960s, new supply zones developed as general population growth took

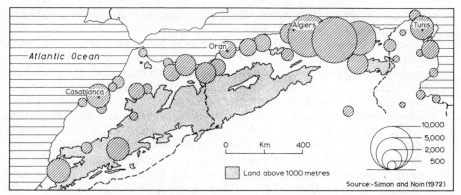

5.5 North Africa: numbers of workers from principal administrative areas going to Western
Europe, 1969–1970

place. Sometimes these were extensions of existing areas but sometimes they
were completely new. As a result, the map of origin areas for migrants to France
in 1969 and 1970 shows that emigration involved virtually all rural areas of the
Maghreb (Fig. 5.6). There were few tribes or groups of population that did not
send some workers to Europe. Hence, emigration has become general from
almost all rural areas of the Maghreb, even the most isolated ones (Simon and
Noin, 1972).

Within the Maghreb, four main areas have long functioned as reservoirs for
emigrants: the Algerian Kabylie; the Pays Chleuhs in south-western Morocco; the
eastern Rif; and the southern parts of Tunisia (Fig. 5.6). Each of these areas has
not only a relatively poor environment for agricultural production, owing to
relief or aridity, but also a high density of population surviving on very limited
resources. From the Kabylie and south-western Morocco, migration was directly
to Europe from early times, but in southern Tunisia and the eastern Rif the

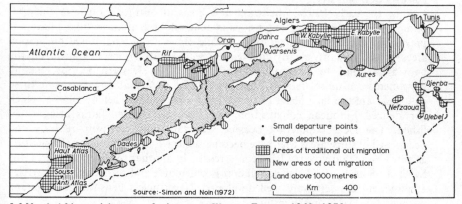

5.6 North Africa: origin areas of migrants to Western Europe, 1969–1970

initial flows were within North Africa, with migration to Europe developing as a second phase.

As noted above, the Kabylie has long been the main reservoir for North African migration to France (Augarde, 1970; Michel, 1956). In 1939, three-quarters of Algerian emigrants to France came from this region. The proportion has declined since then, but the Kabylie is still of great importance as a source of emigrants. The Grande Kabylie is one of the poorest areas of Algeria and it has been estimated that remittances from *émigrés* account for perhaps three-quarters of the region's cash income. With a population of 850,000, the Grande Kabylie contains only 130,000 hectares of agricultural land, with a mere 4,800 hectares under irrigation. In spite of recent progress in arboriculture and the start of a programme for regional development in 1968, emigration is still an absolute necessity. Long-established labour flows mean that important family contacts have been built up in the Paris region, Marseilles, and the Rhône Valley. Migrants prefer to obtain work in manufacturing industry rather than in less stable activities such as building and public works. Migration from the Aurès and Tlemcen areas displays similar characteristics, with workers from the former area being especially established in Lorraine and Marseilles and from the latter in the Nord.

Early migration from the Pays Chleuhs of south-western Morocco took the form of temporary movement to eastern Algeria. Later, this changed to flows to France, with migrants being particularly numerous in manufacturing industries in the Paris region. Similarly, flows from the eastern Rif to neighbouring Algeria began early in the present century and were gradually deflected to France. Parts of southern Tunisia also had long traditions of outmigration, with merchants moving to northern Tunisia and eastern Algeria, seasonal agricultural workers going to the Tell and to the countryside around Sfax, and peasants taking up urban employment in Tunis (Picouet, 1971). Since the mid-1950s, these currents have turned increasingly to France, mainly involving male workers in the construction industry.

Since the early 1960s, important new areas of outmigration have emerged. Some of these are spatial extensions of long-established areas, others have not previously experienced emigration. Unlike flows from established emigration areas, which are fairly clearly directed to specific destinations, migrants from the new areas tend to be more widely dispersed in Western Europe. Family movements are quite frequent, but workers are poorly qualified. Among these new areas are the high plains of Constantine and the Haut-Tell of Tunisia, which experienced European colonization with large mechanized farms being established. The local population became sedentary only relatively recently and occupied hill slope areas that have become subject to serious erosion. Emigration as an escape from poverty has been a result. In another relatively new area, the Sahel de Sousse, the local population is sedentary, and secondary and tertiary employment are relatively well developed. Nevertheless densities are high and outmigration has been the result.

Finally, increasing numbers of migrants are leaving the urban centres of the Maghreb. For example, 30 per cent of Tunisian emigrants are now leaving from Greater Tunis, and the relatively urbanized areas on the coast make up the other main departure zones (Simon, 1973). This situation is reflected in Figure 5.7 which shows that in 1971 the main coastal urban areas received most in

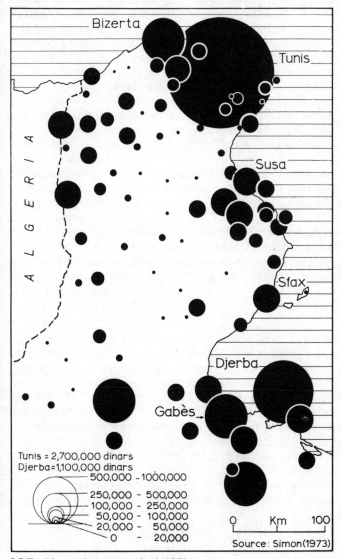

5.7 **Tunisia: remittances received, 1971**

remittances although many interior locations are also well represented. Rural–urban migration in many parts of the Maghreb has inflated city populations, but, as in so many less developed countries, job provision has not kept up with these flows and serious urban unemployment and under-employment have resulted. Emigration to Western Europe is a palliative to this problem which also holds financial attractions for urban workers with some professional training. Hence, whilst the bulk of labour migrants move essentially from rural environments to jobs in construction, manufacturing, and service activities in urban Europe (for example, 28 per cent of the Tunisian emigrants leaving in 1972 moved to jobs in construction, 17 per cent to manufacturing industry, 13 per cent to agriculture, 4 per cent to hotels, and the remainder to a range of jobs), since 1960 there has been a trend for rather more qualified workers to migrate (Simon, 1973; Bousiri and Pradel de Lamaze, 1971).

Conditions within the Maghreb countries have long induced emigration. The present geographical pattern of movement has evolved over a long period of time and contemporary labour migrations reflect the links developed, especially with France, over a century. The former 'colonial' experience has thus been vital in determining the direction of migration flows in recent years. Turkey has had no such links with north-west Europe. Its emigration has grown rapidly, massively, and spontaneously since the early 1960s. But it has many similarities with the Maghreb countries: a high annual rate of population and labour-force increase; a low level of economic development; low average earnings; high unemployment and under-employment; a basically rural population. As with Algerians going to France, most of Turkey's labour migrants have moved to one country—West Germany. Attention will now be turned to this very recent source of migrants whose appearance in such large numbers in north-west Europe has attracted much publicity (Paine, 1975).

Turkey

Unlike other Mediterranean labour sources discussed so far, the country has no tradition of movement to north-west Europe, although as suggested above, the Turkish situation has affinities with the Maghreb. Turkey displays very high rates of natural increase and has experienced a tripling in total population over the past 40 years, rising from 11,500,000 in 1930 to 37,000,000 in 1972—equal to the total for all three Maghreb states. The return of Turks from Bulgaria and Yugoslavia after World War II, together with United States financial aid to the economy, has contributed to the post-war population increase (Esenkova, 1967). The population is youthful, with 44 per cent being under 15 years of age. Crude birth rates, at 40 per thousand in 1975, are a little lower than in the 1950s, with 44 per thousand being recorded between 1955 and 1960. In fact, legislation permitting birth control was introduced in 1965, but the programme is still only in its early stages.

As was the case for the Maghreb states, by far the majority of migrants are men, mainly in their 20s and 30s. For example, in 1971 28 per cent of Turks entering France were aged 21–25, 27 per cent were between 26 and 30, and 21 per cent between 31 and 35. Only 1·5 per cent were women. Over four-fifths of Turkish labour migrants are married, but very few Turkish families have moved. Gokalp (1973) estimated that less than 5 per cent of Turkish workers in France have been joined by their families.

The first examples of contemporary Turkish labour migration date from the mid-1950s, when small numbers of migrants were employed in West Germany and Austria and returned home with favourable reports (Esenkova, 1967). Organized labour migration to north-west Europe began in 1961 and increased in intensity through the decade, so that almost 1,000,000 workers left in 1970. As a result, Turkey became the leading supply country for foreign workers, after having been low on the list until the mid-1960s.

National population increase at 2·5–3 per cent per annum over the past 40 years has affected the regions of the country in varying degrees. The wetter north and west are more densely populated than the interior of Anatolia, with particularly low densities in the east, south, and south-east (Louis, 1972). Between 1935 and 1965, the strongest rates of growth were in the more urbanized provinces, most notably Ankara and Istanbul, where immigration occurred. In addition, very high rates of increase were also achieved in the sparsely-populated provinces to the east beyond Lake Van as mortality fell faster than fertility. When provincial data are regrouped by statistical regions, it is seen that the greatest rates of increase were in the Mediterranean region (increase of 176 per cent), Thrace (109 per cent), and eastern Anatolia (103 per cent). Growth in absolute numbers was highest in central Anatolia, Marmara, and the Aegean and the Black Sea regions.

Environmental conditions in Turkey vary from the Mediterranean climate of the north-west and the humid conditions of the north coast to much harsher conditions in the Anatolian interior. As mentioned in Chapter 2, rural–urban migration has drawn large numbers of country folk to Istanbul and Izmir, and Ankara has grown from 288,000 in 1950 to 1,250,000 in 1970. Squatter settlements have proliferated around these and other cities, housing large numbers of urban unemployed who left the countryside in search of work but were unable to find it. Almost half the population of Izmir (total population 820,000) lives in shanty towns.

These rural–urban migrations have formed the main sources of labour emigrants, with the largest flows being directed from the most densely populated and urbanized parts of north-west Turkey and from central Anatolia. According to Gokalp (1973) almost half the labour migrants to France came from central Anatolia (46 per cent), with important proportions from the more populated north-west (20 per cent) and the north coast (Fig. 5.8). Migration to West Germany is particularly important from the Izmir region, and the city acts as an information centre for the whole of western Turkey (Bartels, 1968). By contrast, eastern, southern, and south-east Turkey have, as yet, dispatched relatively few labour migrants to Western Europe.

Labour emigration from Turkey is thus in its early stages and this is reflected in the geographical pattern of areas of migrant origin. In general it is the more accessible, more urbanized, and more densely peopled areas that have provided most migrants so far. This accords with what has happened elsewhere in the Mediterranean and it is to be expected that future migration from Turkey will increasingly be from the more remote areas. The potential reservoir is great; an estimated 1,000,000 were in the queue for emigration in 1973. Virtual suspension of recruitment by the industrial countries during 1974 will have pent up the mass of potential migrants still further. Inevitably this will create serious difficulties for the Turkish government, which has regarded emigration as a major aid in evening out the disparity between rates of increase in labour supply and in job availability at home.

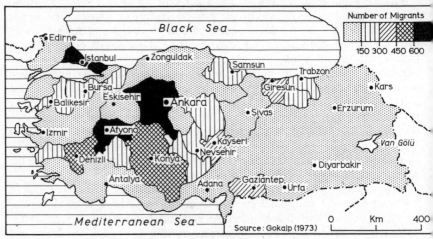

5.8 Turkey: areas supplying migrants to France, 1970

Conclusion

The analysis of individual supply countries suggests that, initially, the main emigration areas are those that are better developed economically and are more urbanized. Such areas are more likely to have access to information about opportunities abroad and to contain people willing to take advantage of these opportunities. Subsequently there is a geographical 'spread' effect of emigration, involving new and increasingly remote areas. Despite the early emergence of more economically developed regions as centres of emigration, contemporary labour migrations seem to be closely related to the rural—urban flows discussed in Chapter 2. The relationship occurs in two ways. In the first case, some migrants decide to leave their rural homelands where conditions will support only a low standard of living. Destinations are usually urban, and opportunities abroad may be perceived as strong enough to overcome the friction of distance and ties to the home country, particularly where the potential migrant has friends or relations already overseas. Hence international labour migration rather than internal rural–urban movement will take place. In the second case, the rural emigrant may first move to an urban area in his own country. He may then conclude that the streets are not paved with gold after all, aspire to better things, and go abroad. In both cases international labour migration may be regarded as an extension of rural–urban movement. In this way the predominant population movement in less developed countries—out of rural areas—has become integrated into the development of a wider European labour market.

It was demonstrated in the last chapter how that market has evolved since the war. In particular its spatial limits have widened as new sources of supply have been progressively drawn into the system. If, as is likely, the industrial countries continue to need migrant workers when the current economic crisis is over, those spatial limits may well be widened further. One of the consequences of the net loss of labour from the supply countries has been evidence of some labour shortages there in recent years. By 1970 Italy, traditionally a labour-exporting country, contained between 30,000 and 40,000 foreign workers. The majority were white-collar employees, although in recent years several thousand Tunisians have migrated to Sicily to take up low-status jobs there. Spain has an estimated 100,000 foreign workers, about 40 per cent being Moroccans and Algerians. An OECD (1972) report on Greece noted that complaints of labour shortage were voiced in some regions and that some African workers had recently been recruited for employment there. In 1973 it was estimated that about 30,000 Egyptians, Sudanese, Ethiopians, and Somalis were working in Greece, especially in mining, hotels, and catering (ILO, 1973). Migration from Portugal and Yugoslavia has also been taking its toll. Migrants from the Cap Verde Islands have been moving to the Portuguese mainland, especially to Lisbon, to replace Portuguese emigrants to France (Poinard, 1972b). In Yugoslavia, workers from Czechoslovakia and Poland have been brought in to make up for labour shortages in the tourist industry (Baucic, 1971).

What seems to have been happening therefore is the emergence of a second stage in the evolution of European labour migration. In some regions and sectors of their economies certain of the industrially more developed supply countries have themselves experienced similar partial labour shortages to those faced by the main destination countries in the 1950s. Although the reasons for shortages are different, a consequence has again been recruitment of foreign workers. It is much too soon to suggest that today's supply countries will be among the major destinations for migrant workers tomorrow; as things are at present this seems most unlikely. None the less, that these replacement flows have occurred suggests that mass emigration has created regional and sectoral imbalances in labour supply and demand in the supply countries. To some extent such imbalances may reflect the immobility of the indigenous population. More probably they reflect changing aspirations as standards of living improve; if a menial occupation has to be performed, then why not do it abroad for a greater monetary reward?

The construction of this great web of international migration has occurred within a fairly permissive political situation, including the attitude of Yugoslavia. Indeed, all of the migration essays so far have concentrated on Western European (and North African) situations. It is often assumed that the conditions for migration are different in Eastern Europe, owing to greater political control over the population. Hence, for purposes of comparison, the final chapter will review post-war trends in migration on the other side of the Iron Curtain.

References

Abadan, N. (1972) 'Problems concerning cyclically determined flows of Turkish workers from Germany', summarized in Kayser, B. (1972).

Anon. (1971) 'La Population du Portugal depuis un siècle', *Population*, 26, 1157—60.

Anon. (1972a) 'L'Émigration espagnole au XXe siècle', *Population*, 27, 301—5.

Anon. (1972b) Report quoting Zagreb newspaper *'Vus'*, *Der Spiegel*, 44.

Anon. (1974) 'Le SOPEMI, un système d'observation permanente des migrations', *Options mediterranéennes*, 22, 42—9.

Arles, J. F. (1966) 'Manpower mobilization and economic growth: an assessment of Moroccan and Tunisian experience', *International Labour Review*, 94.

Augarde, J. and Prevost, G. (1970) 'La Migration algérienne', *Hommes et migrations: Etudes*, 116, 1—150.

Bartels, D. (1968) 'Türkische Gastarbeiter aus der Region Izmir', *Erdkunde*, 22, 313—24.

Battesti, L. M. (1966) 'Une Main-d'oeuvre temporaire en voie de disparition', *Information géographique*, 30, 218—23.

Battesti, L. M. (1968) 'L'Émigration portugaise vers l'Europe en 1966', *Information géographique*, 32, 167—76.

Baucic, I. (1971) *The Effects of Emigration from Yugoslavia and the Problems of Returning Emigrant Workers*, OECD Manpower and Social Affairs Directorate, Paris.

Baucic, I. (1974) 'Yugoslavia as a country of emigration', paper read at First International Slavic Conference, Banff, September 1974.

Böhning, W. R. (1972) *The Migration of Workers in the United Kingdom and the European Community*, Oxford University Press, London.

Bouscaren, A. T. (1969) *European Economic Community Migrations*, Martinus Nijhoff, The Hague.

Bousiri, A. and Pradel de Lamaze, F. (1971) 'La Population d'Algérie d'après le recensement de 1966,' *Population*, 26, 25—46.

Braun, R. (1970) *Sozio-kulturelle probleme der Eingliederung italienischer Arbeitskräfte in der Schweiz*, Eugen Rentsch Verlag, Erlenbach-Zürich.

Bundesanstalt für Arbeit (1973) *Repräsentatur-untersuchung 1972, Beschäftigung Ausländischer Arbeitnehmer*, Bundesanstalt für Arbeit, Nuremberg.

Castles, S. and Kosack, G. (1973) *Immigrant Workers and Class Structure in Western Europe*, Oxford University Press, London.

Cavaco, C. (1971) 'Migracoes internacionais de trabalhadores de Sotavento do Algarve', *Finisterra*, 6, 41—83.

Censis, (1968) *Enquiries on the Economic Aspects of Migration: Labour Mobility and the Labour Market in the Bari-Brindisi-Taranto Area*, OECD Working Party on Migration, Paris.

Courtot, R. (1971) 'Quelques enseignements du dernier recensement de la population espagnole', *Bulletin de la Société Languedocienne de Géographie*, 24, 337–46.

Daumas, M. (1971) 'Où en est le remembrement rural en Espagne? *Revue Géographique des Pyrénées et du Sud-Ouest* 42, 213–27.

Dewdney, J. C. (1972) 'Turkey: recent population trends', in Clarke, J. I., and Fisher, W. B. (eds.), *Populations of the Middle East and North Africa*, Athlone Press, London.

Dubois, P. (1959) 'Aspects économiques des problémes de l'emploi au Maroc', *Bulletin économique et social du Maroc*, 22(80), 489–500.

Esenkova, E. (1967) 'Connaissance des Turcs et de la Turquie', *Hommes et migrations*, 108, 1–139.

European Economic Commission (1966) *The Free Movement of Workers and the Labour Market in the EEC*, Brussels.

European Economic Commission (1971) *The Free Movement of Workers and the Labour Market in the EEC*, Brussels.

Friganovic, M., Morokvasic, M., and Baucic, I. (1972) *Les Travailleurs Yougoslaves en France*, Institut de Géographie, Université de Zagreb.

Garnier, J. P. (1971) 'Tendances récentes de l'émigration portugaise', *Annales de démographie historique*, 73–75.

Gokalp, C. (1973) 'L'Émigration turque en Europe et particulièrement en France', *Population*, 28, 335–60.

Haut-Commissariat à la Jeunesse et aux Sports, Maroc (1962) 'Regards sur l'emploi et le chômage au Maroc, Guide des animateurs de cercles économiques', *Cahier d'éducation populaire*, 2.

Hume, I. M. (1973) 'Migrant workers in Europe', *Finance and Development*, 10, 2–6.

Istituto Centrale di Statistica (1972) *Annuario Statistico Italiano*, Rome.

International Labour Office (1963) *Technical Meeting on Productivity and Employment in Public Works in African Countries, Lagos, December 1963, Conclusions and Papers*, ILO, Geneva.

International Labour Office (1973) *Some Growing Employment Problems in Europe*, ILO, Geneva.

International Labour Office (1974) *International Yearbook of Statistics*, ILO, Geneva.

Kayser, B. (1971) *Manpower Movements and Labour Markets*, Manpower and Social Affairs Committee, OECD, Paris.

Kayser, B. (1972) *Cyclically Determined Homeward Flows of Migrant Workers and the Effects of Emigration*, OECD, Paris.

Kirk, D. (1946) *Europe's Population in the Interwar Years*, Gordon & Breach, New York.

Kuhne, H. (1971) *Bericht über die hage der Gastarbeiter in Ludwigshafen am Rhein*, Amt für Grundlagenforschung und Stadtentwicklung, Stadt Ludwigshafen.

Leloup, Y. (1972) 'L'Émigration portugaise dans le monde et ses conséquences pour le Portugal', *Revue de géographie de Lyon*, 47, 59–76.

Louis, H. (1972) 'Die Bevölkerungsverteilung in der Türkei 1965 und ihre Entwicklung seit 1935', *Erdkunde*, 26, 161–77.

Macura, M. (1974) 'Employment problems under declining population growth rates and structural change: the case of Yugoslavia', *International Labour Review*, 109, 487–501.

Maison, D. (1973) 'La Population de l'Algérie', *Population*, 28, 1079–1107.

Michel, A. (1956) *Les Travailleurs algériens en France*, Centre National de la Recherche Scientifique, Paris.

Montagne, R. (1953) 'L'Émigration des Musulmans d'Algérie en France', *L'Afrique et l'Asie*, 22, 5–20.

Monticelli, G. L. (1967) 'Italian emigration: basic characteristics and trends with special reference to the last twenty years', *International Migration Review*, 1, 10–24.

Moulin, J. (1970) 'Algériens en France: une étude du Club Jean Moulin', *Hommes et migrations*, 115, 79–89.

Nikolic, M. (1972) 'Yugoslav skilled labour temporarily employed abroad', *Yugoslav Survey*, 13, 51–72.

Nikolinakos, M. (1971) 'Zur Frage der Auswanderungseffekte in den Emigrations ländern, *Das Argument*, 13, 782–99.

Organisation for Economic Co-operation and Development (1972) *Economic Surveys: Greece*, OECD, Paris.

Paine, S. (1975) *Exporting Workers: the Turkish Case*, Cambridge University Press.

Perotti, A. (1967) 'Italian emigration in the next fifteen years: 1966–1980', *International Migration Review*, 1, 75–95.

Picouet, M. (1971) 'Aperçu des migrations interieures en Tunisie', *Population*, 26, 125–148.

Piel, E. (1966) 'L'Immigration portugaise', *Hommes et migrations*, 105, 1–204.

Poinard, M. (1971) 'L'Émigration portugaise de 1960 à 1969', *Revue géographique des Pyrénées et du Sud-Ouest*, 42, 293–304.

Poinard, M. (1972a) 'Les portugais dans le département du Rhône entre 1960 et 1970', *Revue de géographie de Lyon*, 47, 35–58.

Poinard, M. (1972b) 'La Stagnation de la population portugaise 1960–1970', *Revue géographique des Pyrénées et du Sud-Ouest*, 43, 427–44.

Rodgers, A. (1970) 'Migration and industrial development: the southern Italian experience', *Economic Geography*, 46, 111–35.

Roux, M. (1972) 'Contemporary emigration of Yugoslav manpower', summarized in Kayser, B. (1972).

Russo, G. (1964) *Quinze Millions d'italiens déracinés*, Éditions Ouvrières, Paris.

Sanchez Lopez, F. (1969) *Emigración española a Europa*, Confederación Espanola de Cajas de Ahorros, Madrid.

Silberzahn, C. (1964) *L'Emploi en Tunisie en 1961 et 1971*, Sécretariat d'Etat au Plan et aux Finances, Tunis.

Simon, G. and Noin, D. (1972) 'La Migration maghrébine vers l'Europe', *Cahiers d'outre-mer*, 25, 241–76.

Simon, G. (1973) 'L'Émigration tunisienne en 1972', *Méditerranée*, 4, 95–109.

Sutton, K. (1972) 'Algeria: Changes in population distribution, 1954–1966', in Clarke, J. I., and Fisher, W. B. (eds.), *Populations of the Middle East and North Africa*, University of London Press, pp. 372–403.

Tiano, A. (1963) *La Politique économique et financière du Maroc Indépendant*, Institut d'Étude du Développement Economique et Social, Études Tiers Monde, Paris.

Time (1973) 'Europe's other energy source', *Time*, 3 December, 12–19.

Trebous, M. (1970) *Migrations et développement: le cas de l'Algérie*, OECD, Paris.

Velikonja (1974) 'Yugoslavia: emigration', paper read at First International Slavic Conference, Banff, Sept., prepared as chapter 3 in Grothusen, K. D. (ed.), *Emigration*, Vandenhoek & Ruprecht Verlag, Göttingen (forthcoming).

Vigorelli (1969) 'Returning migrants re-employed in Italian industry', *Migration News*, 2.

Viguier, M. C. (1970) *Les Travailleurs portugais dans la région toulousaine*, Centre de Sociologie de la Main-d'oeuvre, Université de Toulouse.

Zingaro, R. (1969) 'Re-integration of returnees in Andria', *Migration News*, 2.

6. MIGRATION IN EASTERN EUROPE

PAUL COMPTON

Introduction

During the post-war period the countries of Eastern Europe have undergone extensive economic, social, and political transformation. From being orientated towards agriculture their economies have been reshaped; manufacturing and, more recently, the tertiary sector have expanded rapidly. The converse of this process has been a relative and absolute decline in the importance of agriculture, although it remains more significant than in the economies of Western Europe. Growth of manufacturing and services has been accompanied by a massive socio-economic restratification of population. The proportion occupied in farming has dropped rapidly and is still falling because of rising productivity and widespread mechanization. Labour released from the land has been absorbed readily in non-agricultural employment. It is against this background that recent migration in Eastern Europe must be set, since change in the socio-economic character of the population has been accompanied by high geographic mobility.

Economic management in Eastern Europe is accomplished through central planning. The balance between central control and local initiative on the part of state enterprises has varied from country to country over the years, but one common feature has been central determination of major investment decisions and, through this, strict control of industrial location. Within such a system it is unnecessary to operate explicit control over migration to achieve a balance between population, resources, and employment opportunities, contrary to the impression that is sometimes created. Central control of major locational decisions means implicit control over the main directions of population movement. Administrative regulation of migration is thus rare, and where it does occur is invariably a restriction of movement to cities, usually capitals, where previous inmigration has placed undue strain on housing, transport, and general services. Eastern European migration is thus similar to that in Western Europe and North America. The individual is essentially free to make his own migration decisions within a framework provided by economic and social policy—such as siting of new towns, provision of housing, agricultural policy, and so on. The obvious difference is that whereas in Eastern Europe this framework is controlled by the state, in Western Europe and North America it is more loosely developed and is provided by both state and private institutions and organizations.

The emphasis is on internal rather than international migration in this chapter which is concerned mainly with migration in Bulgaria, Czechoslavakia, East Germany, Hungary, and Poland. Romania and Yugoslavia receive less attention because their migration statistics are not collected on the same basis as in the other countries, are less complete, and are thus not strictly comparable. The chapter falls into a number of sections. The availability of migration statistics is briefly examined, leading into an evaluation of the role of migration in the context of population change. This is followed by a description and inter-pretation of geographical patterns of movement and finally by a consideration of the implications of migration for natural increase, ethnic composition, and regional policy.

Migration data in Eastern Europe

The census and registration of change of residence are the main sources of internal migration data throughout Eastern Europe. The latter records are particularly complete in most instances although comprehensiveness of published data varies from country to country. Where migration is registered continuously the census becomes a subsidiary rather than a major source of statistics and this is beginning to apply to Eastern Europe. Yugoslavia and Romania are exceptions. Yugoslavia collects no data on a continuous basis and reliance must consequently be placed on the census. The situation for Romania is difficult to assess. Migration dates are not available from the 1966 census and although change of residence is recorded on a continuous basis the statistics have only appeared for the first time in the latest demographic yearbook; they were too late to be incorporated in this chapter.

Migration data derived from the continuous registration of change of residence are published (generally annually) in the demographic yearbooks of the countries concerned.[1] Although there is no standardization of information published, data on more important aspects of migration are usually given for rural and urban districts and for areas of 'county' status which include larger cities. In this regard not only are numbers of in-, out-, and net movers recorded but also cross-tabulations of flows between geographical areas. Each national yearbook has its own strengths and weaknesses in the field of migration statistics but on balance the most comprehensive information is published for Hungary.

Although a wealth of migration data exists for these five countries, one is confronted with certain handling problems. Firstly, the years of data availability vary from country to country. Statistics for Bulgaria have been published since 1947, for Czechoslovakia since 1950, for Poland since 1951, for East Germany since 1953, and for Hungary since 1955. In addition, very restricted data for Romania, apparently based on the registration of change of residence, were published in scientific papers for 1955–64. There is, then, virtually a continuous run of annual migration statistics since the mid-1950s. Unfortunately the content and format have tended to vary from year to year. Secondly, the recognition of various categories of migrant, depending on the type of boundary traversed, can lead to difficulties of interpretation. For instance, in East Germany some tabulations are produced for migration across commune boundaries (*Gemeindegrenzen*), district boundaries (*Kreisgrenzen*), and county boundaries (*Bezirksgrenzen*). Similar distinctions are made in Czechoslovakia.

Since the number of apparent migrations varies inversely with scale, caution must be exercised when using these data for inter-country comparisons. Finally the definition of what constitutes a 'migrant' is not standardized throughout the area.

In Eastern Europe, as elsewhere, migration information from the census is derived from place of birth and from place of residence statistics for given years—usually 1, 5, or 10 years prior to the census. For migration during the 1960s census sources are at present generally inadequate because information from the latest enumerations of 1970 or 1971 is not yet fully published. This applies to Czechoslovakia, East Germany, Hungary, Poland, and Yugoslavia for all of which the most recent comprehensive census surveys of migration date from the early 1960s. The last full census of Bulgaria was held in 1965 when gathering of very full migration data was part of the enumeration programme, but now the results are dated. The lack of census information on migration in Romania has been noted already.

The role of migration in the growth of population

According to the mid-1972 estimate, the population of the seven countries of Eastern Europe numbered 125,000,000 which is 8,500,000 or 7 per cent more than in 1962. The increase was highest in Yugoslavia and Romania, where growth exceeded 10 per cent, and lowest in Hungary, where the increase was just over 3 per cent. In East Germany the population decreased by 1 per cent. Rates of growth were considerably lower than during the 1950s, primarily attributable to falling birth rates, stable or slightly rising crude death rates, and declining rates of natural increase. International migration has played a significant role in the development of the population only in East Germany where the falling rate of natural increase was reinforced by important net emigration during the 1950s and early 1960s.

Declining birth rates have been welcome in Poland and Yugoslavia, since age structures derived from the very high birth rates of the 1950s and earlier have conferred on their populations a considerable inbuilt momentum favouring growth, but the fertility fall poses severe problems for the other countries. Reproduction rates have been below replacement level in Hungary since 1958, and in Romania between 1962 and 1966, and have hovered around replacement level in Czechoslovakia, Bulgaria, and East Germany (where deaths have exceeded births since 1969). The effects of this are now beginning to be felt in the economic field. The main source of concern is shortage of labour involving many sectors of the economy. Vacant jobs can no longer be filled by surplus manpower from agriculture since in some countries this reservoir has now been absorbed more or less completely by industry. The reaction to the recent course of demographic evolution has been formulation and introduction of measures designed to stimulate the number of births and to generate more 'favourable' rates of natural increase. In Romania this involved the virtual rescinding, in 1966, of a very liberal abortion provision; in Hungary it has meant the introduction of housing subsidies for families with children, of generous maternity and child allowances, and of guarantees of job security to mothers (Berelson, 1974). Partly as a result of such measures the decline in the number of births has been halted and the early 1970s have witnessed a small upturn in birth rates, although this may prove to be only a temporary phenomenon.

It is against this background that migration must be viewed. As observed in chapter one, one of the effects of the fall in birth rates has been to narrow former geographical disparities in rates of natural increase. In consequence, internal migration is becoming an increasingly important factor in determining regional and rural/urban variations in rates of population change throughout Eastern Europe. Moreover, there is strong evidence that movement of population from high fertility rural areas to low fertility urban and industrial areas has itself had a bearing on the fall in birth rates because migrants usually adopt the fertility characteristics of the population of their new settlements. A further feature is that the decline in birth rates and in rates of natural increase has been paralleled by a fall in the incidence of internal migration.

The declining rate of natural increase has reduced the enormous pressure of population in backward areas which was formerly relieved by outmigration. This in turn is linked with changes in spatial patterns of mobility as short-distance, local moves increasingly displace the longer-distance inter-regional migration so characteristic of the 1950s and early 1960s.

As in many other parts of the world the most significant change in population distribution throughout Eastern Europe has been the growing dominance of urban centres (Dziewonski, 1964; Lettrich, 1965; Velcea, 1972; Kosiński, 1974). Initially this was purely a relative phenomenon as urban populations increased at faster rates than their rural counterparts, but latterly rural populations throughout the area have declined absolutely. It is difficult to measure accurately the extent of urbanization because of varying national definitions of 'urban' settlements. The picture presented in Table 6.1 does not therefore precisely reflect numerical differences in levels of urbanization. However, the data suggest that East Germany is the most urbanized country of Eastern Europe—this is certainly true in terms of the proportion living in cities with 100,000 or more inhabitants—although the German definition of 'urban' overstates the degree of urbanization in comparison with most of the other countries.[2] At the opposite end of the scale, Romania and Yugoslavia are least urbanized while Czechoslovakia, Hungary, Bulgaria, and Poland occupy inter-mediate positions with around 50 per cent of their populations living in urban settlements. Precise levels of urbanization are open to argument, but the steep rise since the Second World War in the 'urban' population in all the countries is undeniable. Much of this increase has, of course, been the product of net population movements from rural to urban areas, although incorporation of former villages into urban settlements and changes of designation should not be ignored. Bulgaria, Romania, and Yugoslavia have witnessed the largest pro-portionate increases in urban population since the war, although they

TABLE 6.1 *Urbanization in Eastern Europe*

	Total population (thousands)	Urban %		Total population (millions)	Urban %
	Bulgaria			*East Germany*	
1934	6,078	21·4	1939	16,745	72·2
1946	7,029	24·7	1946	17,180	65·4
1956	7,614	33·6	1950	17,199	68·8
1965	8,228	46·5	1964	17,012	72·9
1972(E)	8,579	55·2	1971	17,068	73·8
	Poland			*Romania*	
1931	29,892	36·8	1930	14,281	21·4
1946	23,625	31·4	1941	16,126	23·6
1950	24,614	39·0	1948	15,873	23·4
1960	28,799	47·2	1956	17,489	31·3
1970	32,589	52·3	1966	19,103	39·1
1972(E)	33,068	52·9	1971(E)	20,470	41·1
	Czechoslovakia			*Hungary*	
1930	14,730	46·8	1941	9,316	36·2
1947	12,164	48·8	1949	9,205	34·5
1950	12,338	51·2	1960	9,961	39·7
1961	13,746	47·6	1970	10,354	45·2
	Yugoslavia				
1948	15,772	16·2			
1953	16,991	18·5			
1961	18,549	28·4			
1971	20,523	38·6			

E = Estimated

Source: U.N. and national demographic yearbooks.

commenced from a low base, while Poland has seen the largest advance in terms of absolute numbers. Urban growth in Czechoslovakia, East Germany, and Hungary has been more moderate.

The main feature of territorial distribution of population in Eastern Europe is high concentration and rapid growth in developing industrial areas and in major urban agglomerations in each country. Using data for 1969–71 it is possible to characterize the present pattern of population dynamics in Eastern Europe (excluding Yugoslavia) in terms of combinations of natural increase or decrease and migration gain or loss. For this purpose the area has been subdivided into 78 regions of approximately equal population size based on administrative regions or aggregates of administrative regions. The results are portrayed in Fig. 6.1 and are similar to those described by Kosiński (1968) for 1961–5. Naturally the pattern that is produced is in part a reflection of the scale selected for the analysis, and in this instance the influence of urban settlements, with the exception of capital cities, is largely hidden because they are grouped with

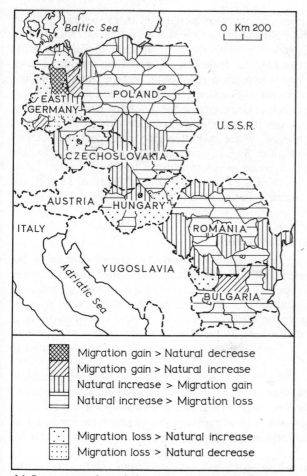

6.1 Components of population change in Eastern Europe, 1969–1971

surrounding rural areas. The scale, therefore, is such that the effect of essentially short- and medium-distance migration is omitted.

With this proviso in mind the pattern that emerges is reasonably clear. Perhaps the most significant feature is that natural increase is the dominant component of population change in 58 of the 78 regions. These contain over three-quarters of the total population of the area although the proportion varies from country to country. Thus the dominance of natural increase is very high in Poland and Romania, and rather low in Hungary and East Germany. These variations point to the simple truism that where natural increase is high, as in Poland and Romania, it will tend to override migration in accounting for population change, and vice versa where natural increase is low.[3]

Migration is the dominant component of population change in only 20 of the 78 regions. In ten of these population loss through migration exceeded natural increase and this type tended to dominate in rural areas of East Germany, Hungary, and north-eastern Bulgaria. These areas differed from the other regions of net population outflow not so much in terms of intensity of outmigration but in terms of low natural increase. Elsewhere, where migration dominated, net population inflow was the rule. These comprise the six capital cities (East Berlin, Budapest, and Prague, where net inmigration exceeded natural decrease; and Bucharest, Sofia, and Warsaw, where migration gain was larger than natural increase) and four regions—three in East Germany and one in Bulgaria. In only 13 regions did population decrease, which in addition to the rural areas of East Germany and Hungary included the industrial regions of Dresden, Leipzig, and Karl Marx Stadt where migration loss aggravated natural decrease.

Intensity of migration in Eastern Europe

The system of migration data collection means that annual changes in the number of internal migrations can be readily ascertained for the period beginning in the late 1950s. It is also possible to compare intensity of internal migration among the countries of Eastern Europe, although caution must be exercised in interpreting the statistics because of variations in defining a 'migrant' and because of the scale factor. The only country for which annual data are not available is Yugoslavia, while data for Romania are limited to 1956—64.

In 1970, a grand total of 2,100,000 people migrated between settlements in Bulgaria, Czechoslovakia, East Germany, Hungary, and Poland, which amounted to approximately 2·5 per cent of the combined populations of these countries. Fifteen years earlier, however, in 1955, migration within the same five countries involved just under 4,000,000 people. Clearly a marked decline in mobility has occurred.

These summary figures hide significant variations from country to country (Fig. 6.2). Thus in Czechoslovakia, East Germany, and Poland the rates and absolute numbers of migrations were highest during the early and mid-1950s. This was a time of intense change throughout Eastern Europe and the high rate of movement relates to extensive sectoral and spatial transformations that the economies of these countries were undergoing. During this phase up to 10 per cent of the population of East Germany were migrating annually, and although rates in Czechoslovakia and Poland were lower they still represented very high mobility levels, which lasted for a few years only. By the late 1950s rates in Czechoslovakia had fallen by 50 per cent from the peak values, and they have remained at about the same level ever since, while similar changes have occurred in Poland although the period of declining rates extended into the early 1960s. East Germany is somewhat different in that migration rates have declined more steeply and practically continuously to the present.

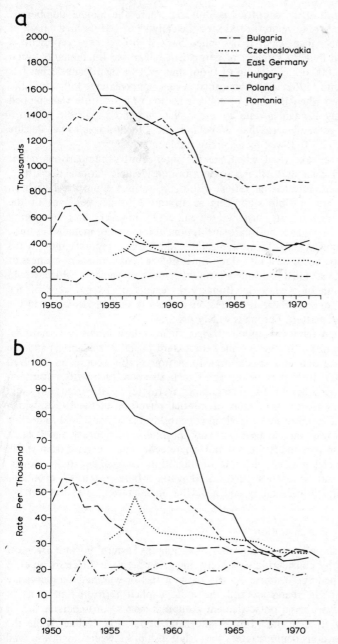

6.2 Intensity of migration in Eastern Europe; (a) number; (b) rates per 1,000 population

Contrasting with these countries is Bulgaria where the annual number of migrations tended to move upwards during the early years and reached a peak of 185,000 in 1965, since when it has fallen back slightly. Hungary presents a similar pattern in that the number of permanent migrations fluctuated between 31 and 35 per 1,000 population up to 1966, since when a significant decline has set in. 1957 and 1958 were abnormal years immediately following the counter-revolution when the pace of collectivization of agriculture was stepped up. Unfortunately Romanian data are incomplete but those available suggest a pattern of change similar to that in Poland and Czechoslovakia, i.e. decline during the late 1950s followed by generally stable rates.

Caution must be exercised when making inter-country comparisons but it seems reasonably clear that, from a pattern of considerable national disparities, rates of permanent internal migration within the various countries have been converging and are possibly stabilizing at around 2 to 2·5 per cent of the population per annum. It must be remembered, however, that temporary migrations which could seriously affect this conclusion are not included in these data. If the Hungarian statistics are typical it is likely that temporary movements in Eastern Europe occur at a rate three times higher than permanent changes of residence. To these must be added intra-settlement movements which would suggest a total mobility rate in Hungary in excess of 10 per cent of the population per annum. There is no reason to believe that the situation in the other countries of Eastern Europe is widely dissimilar.

One explanation relates temporal changes in migration intensity to national levels of development (in this instance the extent of industrialization) and the extent of the sectoral and spatial transformation of the economies involved (Pivovarov, 1972). In East Germany and Czechoslovakia, each with a considerable industrial base before 1939, economic restructuring occurred early and stimulated the extremely high rates of internal migration of the 1950s, which subsequently fell to more stable levels in Czechoslovakia or continued to decline although at a slower rate in East Germany. Secondly, in Hungary and Poland, which are only in part industrialized and where economic reorganization is still proceeding in many regions, the rate of migration has declined more slowly. Thirdly, there are countries such as Bulgaria where extensive economic reorganization is still continuing and a decline in migration rates has not yet been observed.

Geographical types of migration

The geographical patterns of internal migration in Eastern Europe are most clearly depicted by considering separately migration between different types of settlement, defined for instance on the basis of size or whether the places are 'rural' or 'urban' in character, and the more explicit territorial patterns of movement. Analysis based on settlement groupings assists our understanding of the role of migration in urbanization and rural population decline, while the territorial dimension demonstrates the relationship between migration and regional changes in population distribution. It is of course in the strict sense artificial to make this division, because many inter-settlement moves are at the same time inter-regional moves, but it does clarify the complexity of the spatial process.

Migration between settlement types—rural and urban migration

In Eastern Europe it has generally been the case that rates of natural increase are higher in rural than in urban areas. It therefore follows that, apart from changes in the administrative status of places, the mechanism primarily responsible for broad advance in urban populations has been migration from villages to towns. The dramatic nature of this process with all its social, economic, political, cultural, and planning implications has meant that attention has been focused on this aspect of migration so that analysis of flows in other directions among urban and rural settlements has been neglected. Thus, although there is an understanding of the significance of migration in the context of urban population growth, the full detail of migration among rural and urban settlements is not always fully appreciated. This section will therefore describe the role of migration in urbanization and then relate this to other migration flows among rural and urban settlements.

In assessing the magnitude of the recent movement of population from rural to urban areas in Eastern Europe the post-war era may be divided into two parts. During the decade 1951—60, especially in the early years, mobility was intense. Pivovarov (1972) has estimated that this phase witnessed the movement of over 11,000,000 people (about 10 per cent of the total population) from village to town. Although a portion of these may have represented multiple moves of highly mobile individuals the period saw a revolutionary change in population distribution within a short period of time. Unfortunately, consistent migration statistics do not exist for each country of the region for the pre-1960 period but those that are available are set out in Table 6.2. These data, although influenced by variations in definition of 'rural' and 'urban', suggest that the countries fall into two groups. Bulgaria and Poland belong to the first group, where annual rates of movement from village to town exceeded 125 per 1,000 population. Yugoslavia also should probably be placed here since its migration values are based on census information which notoriously underestimates the volume of gross movements. Into the second group fall Czechoslovakia, Hungary, and Romania where rates of rural to urban migration were significantly lower. It must be stressed immediately, however, that part of the difference between values may be statistical rather than a reflection of real differences. Thus data for the second group all relate to the latter half of the 1950s when migration rates were probably lower than in earlier years. Moreover, in the case of Czechoslovakia the designation of 'villages' (i.e. settlements of fewer than 2,000 persons), has the effect of establishing a smaller rural population total than would the definitions used in the other countries, which reduces the apparent size of the rural—urban migration stream still further.

TABLE 6.2 *Rural–urban migration in Eastern Europe (gross flows)*

	Time interval	Rural–urban migrants	Annual average	Rate per 1,000 population	Time interval	Rural–urban migrants	Annual average	Rate per 1,000 population
Bulgaria	1951–60	950	95	125	1961–70	826	83	100
Czechoslovakia	1955–59	565	113	84	1961–70	1,050	105	73
East Germany	–	–	–	–	1961–70	1,450	145	85
Hungary	1956–60	517	103	104	1961–70	888	89	87
Yugoslavia	1951–60	1970	197	113	–	–	–	–
Poland	1946–60	5,000	333	127	1961–70	2,573	257	82
Romania	1958–60	543	181	99	–	–	–	–

Source: National demographic yearbooks and Pivovarov (1972).

Since 1960 there has been a practically continuous coverage of migration on an annual basis for Bulgaria, Czechoslovakia, Hungary, East Germany, and Poland which permits an accurate statement of the magnitude of rural—urban flows for these countries. The data in Table 6.2 indicate a decline in the annual number and rates of such migration in all five countries as compared with the pre-1960 period. After estimating the number of rural—urban moves for Yugoslavia and Romania one may conclude that over the decade 1961—70 the total flow from villages to towns throughout Eastern Europe fell from 11,000,000 to less than 9,000,000 persons. Although the magnitude of the stream of migrants from rural to urban areas may now be tailing off, its impact nevertheless has been so great that in many of the towns and cities of the region up to 50 per cent of the population is composed of people who have only recently left the countryside, together with their children (Kowalewski, 1970).

While it is the volume of rural outmigration that so strongly affects the composition of the population of urban areas—age and sex composition are but two examples—it is the net component of this stream that is significant as regards the absolute and proportionate increase in the size of urban populations. Viewed in this way, the number of rural to urban migrants is considerably lower. The example of Hungary demonstrates this point well. Between 1961 and 1970,

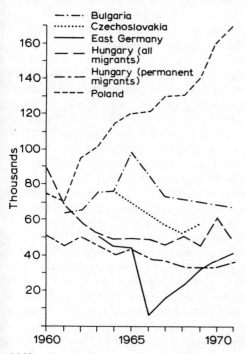

6.3 Net migration from rural to urban areas, 1960—1970

while an estimated 888,000 people moved from village to town, the net increment to the urban population was under 400,000, i.e. less than half the gross movement. The figure for Poland over the same period was 2,573,000 gross moves from rural areas, which produced an urban population increment through migration of 1,275,000, again approximately half the volume of gross movement.

Net rural—urban flows during the 1960s can be examined for Bulgaria, East Germany, Hungary, Poland, and in part for Czechoslovakia on a year to year basis (Fig. 6.3). These data clearly demonstrate that, far from being uniform in trend, the net movement of population to urban areas displays considerable variability from one country to another. Thus while the net flow from village to town fell rather steadily in Hungary during the 1960s—quite rapidly when temporary movements are also included—numbers were rising steeply in Poland with the result that the net growth of urban places through migration was 100,000 more in 1970 than in 1960. In Bulgaria movement to towns reached a peak in 1965 and has since declined, which contrasts with East Germany where minimum values were achieved in 1966. These varying trends are a product of the differing social and economic backgrounds of the countries concerned. In Poland agriculture is still largely in private hands but the pace of modernization and consolidation is accelerating, especially with the implementation in 1963 of a law forbidding subdivision of holdings. This has had the effect of raising the net outflow of population from the countryside (Kostrowicki and Szczesny, 1974). In Hungary stabilization and even slight growth in movement to the towns since the late 1960s would seem to be related in part at least to the new economic mechanism, which has laid great stress on raising productivity, and to the severe shortage of labour in manufacturing industry.

It remains necessary to place rural to urban migration in the context of over-all population movements. Again data coverage is incomplete and relationships may only be described for Hungary, Bulgaria, and Poland (Table 6.3), but if the patterns displayed may be taken as representative they clearly suggest considerable variability in the directional emphasis of flows in Eastern Europe. Thus in Bulgaria rural—urban migration is the dominant type, where it comprises more than half the total number of permanent migrations, but is less important in Hungary and Poland. However, rates of movement to towns as opposed to relative numbers are similar in all three countries and it is clearly the incidence of migration in other directions that accounts for differences in the relative significance of rural—urban flows. Thus the counter-flow from town to village and inter-village moves are weakly developed in Bulgaria compared with Hungary or Poland. On the other hand, inter-urban migration is most significant in Poland. There is also a suggestion that the directional bias of flows is changing through time, although again there is no consistency of pattern. In Hungary and Poland rates of migration in all directions are declining, but this is particularly marked in the cases of urban—rural and inter-urban moves. By contrast, in Bulgaria rates of movement in these directions have increased.

TABLE 6.3 *Migration flows among rural and urban areas in Hungary, Poland, and Bulgaria*

	1956–60			1961–5			1966–70		
	Number	%	Rate	Number	%	Rate	Number	%	Rate
Hungary									
Rural–Urban	517	27·4	17·2	475	29·0	16·2	413	28·2	14·6
Urban–Rural	285	15·1	14·4	252	15·4	12·9	237	16·2	10·4
Rural–Rural	885	47·0	29·4	757	46·2	25·8	670	45·8	23·6
Urban–Urban	196	10·4	10·0	155	9·5	7·4	143	9·8	6·2
Net Rural–Urban	232	—	—	223	—	—	176	—	—
Poland									
Rural–Urban	1,645	24·3	21·3	1,303	25·9	16·9	1,270	29·6	16·1
Urban–Rural	1,170	17·3	17·0	801	15·9	10·6	550	12·8	6·7
Rural–Rural	2,385	35·2	30·8	1,797	35·7	23·1	1,515	35·4	19·2
Urban–Urban	1,570	23·2	22·8	1,129	22·5	15·2	950	22·2	11·5
Net Rural–Urban	475	—	—	502	—	—	720	—	—
Bulgaria									
Rural–Urban	—	—		411	51·4	17·7	415	53·8	19·4
Urban–Rural	—	—		34	4·3	2·0	64	8·3	4·1
Rural–Rural	—	—		242	30·3	10·4	110	14·2	5·2
Urban–Urban	—	—		112	14·0	6·6	183	23·7	8·9
Net Rural–Urban	—	—		377	—	—	351	—	—

Source: National demographic yearbooks.

It has been demonstrated already that net movement of population is generally much less than gross flow of population from rural to urban areas; when compared with the total number of migrations in a country it becomes relatively insignificant. For instance, net movement to urban areas averaged just over 15 per cent of total permanent migrations in Hungary, just under 15 per cent in Poland, and even lower proportions are observed in Czechoslovakia and East Germany. Bulgaria is again an exception in that the net rural–urban migration component comprises more than two-fifths of total movement. However, the most interesting feature that emerges is that variations described in the rates of net rural–urban migration are not so much a product of changes in the over-all incidence of movement to the towns but rather a function of differences in counter-flows to the villages. Thus in Poland the rising net movement to urban areas during the 1960s was not a result of an increase in the over-all rate of migration to the towns—indeed it actually fell—but rather a product of a very steep decline in return movements to the countryside. Similarly the fall in the growth rate of towns of Bulgaria through migration since 1965 has not been a function of declining over-all migration to the towns—the reverse actually occurred—but rather of an even greater rate of increase in counter-moves to the villages, especially those in the vicinity of towns.

Migration and settlement size

The simple rural/urban division used in the discussion so far masks important details of the spatial pattern of migration. These are revealed by a finer grouping of settlements—in this instance defined on the basis of population size. As before, data coverage is incomplete, but the consistency of findings for Czechoslovakia, East Germany, Hungary, and Poland suggests that similar relationships probably apply throughout Eastern Europe. The relationship between migration and population growth will be examined first and then flow patterns will be analysed. Two types of information are available for this purpose. For Hungary, data are derived from the 1970 census of population, apply to a ten-year period, and are useful as an illustration of the medium-term population growth implications of internal migration. They are also valuable in that separate breakdowns are available for villages and towns. Data for the other three countries are derived from the change of residence statistics and are used here primarily to examine flows of migrants by settlement size.

The Hungarian situation displays a number of interesting features. Firstly, regardless of size, rural settlements, on balance, lost population while urban settlements gained population through migration, although there were exceptions to this general rule. Secondly, there was a consistent inverse relationship between the rate of net migration and population size, i.e. the larger the rural settlement the lower the rate of net population outflow, the larger the urban centre the higher the rate of net inflow. Thirdly, net migration was the dominant component of population change for all size groups with the exception of villages whose populations exceeded 10,000. It is also of note that the rate of natural increase was directly and strongly related to settlement size, which itself is an indirect consequence of migration. Although data are less detailed and for a shorter period, similar patterns emerge for Czechoslovakia, East Germany, and Poland. Rates of net migration are inversely related to settlement size, and are invariably more important than natural increase as a component of population change.

Regarding migration flows between settlement size groups, the most recent data for Czechoslovakia and East Germany reveal similar patterns which may again be suggestive of a degree of uniformity throughout Eastern Europe. For instance, the rate of migration, whether of in- or outmigration flows, tends to fall as the size of settlement increases. Thus the rate of inmigration regardless of origin is, surprisingly, higher to settlements of less than 2,000 population than to cities with populations exceeding 100,000. However, rates standardized on the basis of the product of population sizes of origins and destinations, while reinforcing the finding that the incidence of outmigration diminishes with increasing population size, suggest that places of intermediate size are most attractive to inmigrants. In other words, the array of standardized inmigration flows assumes the form of a humped distribution, and maximum values are attained for settlements in the 10,000–100,000 size range.

Evidence on net migration flows for Czechoslovakia and East Germany is similar. Settlements in various size categories gain migrants on balance from settlements of smaller size but lose people to larger places. There is thus a net transfer of people from small settlements (populations not exceeding 2,000) to larger settlements, and it is clear that these flows comprise the most fundamental element of the process of population redistribution. Furthermore, the largest towns and cities attract population from all smaller settlement groups, although (as the net migration flow indices show) transfer of population in a relative sense is not predominantly towards these places. Thus net outflows from the smallest settlements are directed mainly towards places of small and medium size, while inhabitants of settlements in the 5,000–10,000 category are most likely to be attracted to towns of between 20,000 and 50,000 population and so on. These findings are suggestive of a multi-step pattern of movement whereby individuals leaving the village migrate first to a small local town and move on later in a series of migrations to places of increasing size and importance.

Inter-regional patterns of migration

The size of Eastern Europe makes it difficult to summarize the territorial features of internal migration. The question of scale, on which the configuration of migration patterns is so dependent, is the crucial factor and is not easy to resolve. Also bearing on the problem is the comparability of various national migration statistics, for although data may be available for apparently identical regional levels, the similarity may be superficial since individual areas are found to differ greatly in area and population size. This can therefore invalidate direct comparison. Disparities in quality and availability of territorial data pose further difficulties.

A striking aspect of the regional patterns of migration is that, as elsewhere, the vast majority of moves within Eastern Europe occur over short distances. For instance, as a proportion of all moves, migrations between settlements in the same county or its equivalent rarely comprise less than 50 per cent of the total. Naturally this proportion tends to vary directly with the size of counties and is consequently relatively low in Hungary and Bulgaria, where counties tend to be small, but relatively high in Poland.[5] The effect of short-distance moves is very localized and usually involves progressive concentration of population in larger villages and nearby urban centres. Short-distance moves are thus of significance in altering the proportion of population between rural and urban areas, but, unlike long-distance moves, have little influence on the regional distribution and composition of population. Longer-distance moves will be examined in detail here.

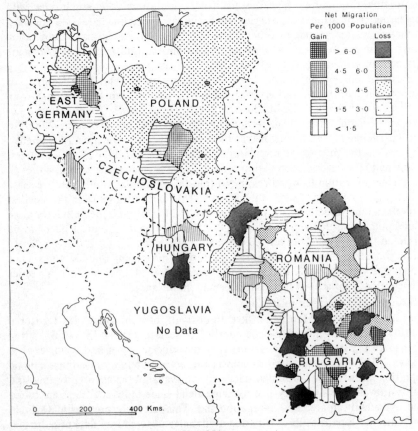

6.4 Net migration, annual average, 1969–1971

It has already been stressed that predominantly agricultural regions are the main source areas of outmigrants, and that developing industrial regions and major urban agglomerations are main reception areas. This has been a consistent migration theme throughout post-war Eastern Europe and, although tending to break down, is still evident in the net migration pattern for the late 1960s and early 1970s (Fig. 6.4). Thus the vast majority of areas within the region remain agricultural and are still losing population, despite the growth of local centres of non-agricultural employment. The scale of Fig. 6.4 is rather coarse and variations in the rates of outmigration are difficult to depict, but the Great Hungarian Plain, much of north-east and central Poland, and northern regions of East Germany are highlighted as areas of above average outflow. In the cases of Hungary and Bulgaria it is also possible to detect a higher rate of out-movement from peripheral border zones. These tend to be the least developed and most rural areas of the region. Movement of population is to large urban agglomerations, particularly to capital cities and their surroundings. It is also directed towards major industrial regions, the Silesian area straddling the Czechoslovak—Polish border providing a good example. The characteristics of inter-regional migration will now be examined in each country of Eastern Europe.

Poland

Three phases of internal migration have been identified in post-war Poland (Iwanicka-Lyra, 1972). The first, lasting until 1950, was a period of national reconstruction and resettlement of the western territories ceded to Poland at the end of World War II. Migration during this phase was consequently dominated by the western *voivoidships*. Some 4,500,000 people were resettled in this region between 1945 and 1948, under the guidance of the State Repatriation Board. An important proportion comprised Polish population repatriated from the former eastern provinces who expected to find an equivalent for their homes and trades abandoned in the east. By far the larger group, however, were migrants from central regions of the country enticed to new lands by gross overpopulation in their home areas (Ziolkowski, 1974). In addition there was intense mobility in other parts of the country. Much of this was short-distance movement as people flooded from the countryside to large- and medium-sized towns, thus transforming the composition of the urban population. For instance, 41 per cent of the population of Wroclaw in 1947 was composed of recent inmigrants from rural areas. However, despite the scale of movement, only Warsaw and Krakow (Nowa Huta) attracted migrants from all parts of Poland.

The second phase, lasting up to 1960, was a period of reduced migration intensity and consequently of greater residential stability. Yet although inter-regional movement was considerable, and approximately half the migrants moved between settlements in different *voivoidships*, it was still only Warsaw and Krakow that attracted migrants nationwide. The spheres of attraction of other large centres remained local. Thus Gdansk was the focus for migrants from northern *voivoidships*, while Katowice attracted people in southern Poland.

Regionally the regained territories remained an important area of population inflow up to about 1955.

Increasingly, however, shorter-distance and multi-step movements have grown in frequency and have tended to dominate the third phase since 1960. Short-distance migrants move to nearby towns and cities within the same *voivoidship* and much of the present net transfer of population to Poznan, Wroclaw, Lodz, Krakow, and Warsaw is of this type (Fig. 6.5). The main source

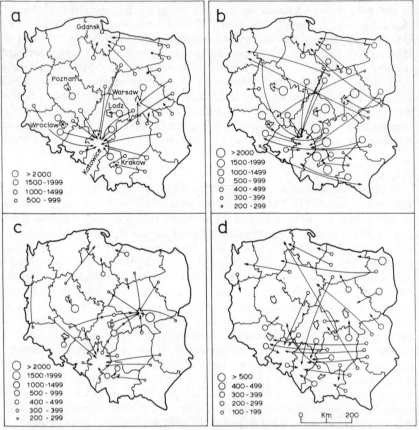

6.5 Poland: (a) net migration flows, 1971; (b) rural—urban net migration flows, 1971; (c) inter-urban net migration flows, 1971; (d) inter-village net migration flows, 1971

areas of current medium- and long-distance migration comprise eastern *voivoidships*, the central provinces of Lodz and Kielce, and Wroclaw in the south-west. Main areas of attraction are (i) the *voivoidship* of Katowice, the industrial hub of Silesia, which during the four years 1968—71 was the net recipient of at least 500 migrants annually from most provinces; (ii) Warsaw,

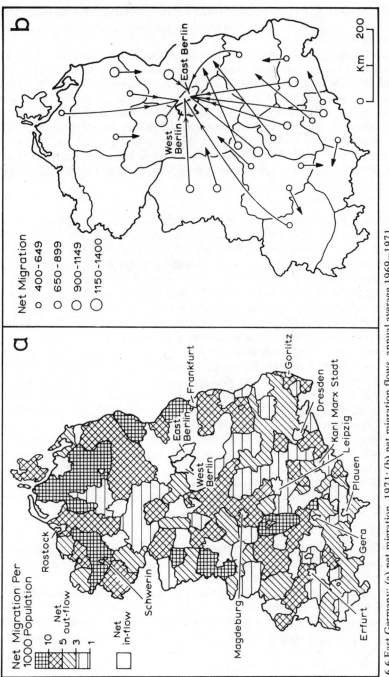

6.6 East Germany: (a) net migration, 1971; (b) net migration flows, annual average 1969–1971

whose sphere of attraction is now reduced compared with previous years; and (iii) Gdansk and Krakow which receive short-distance movers from their own immediate vicinity.

Migration data for Poland also allow rural and urban flows to be tied to *voivoidships* of origin and destination. The more important of these relationships for 1968–71 are mapped in Fig. 6.5. The territorial pattern of net rural to urban migration is very similar to that of all moves. But in addition to Krakow and Gdansk, urban areas in Szczetin and Wroclaw *voivoidships* now stand out as centres attracting population from rural areas of eastern Poland (Latuch, 1973). With regard to inter-urban movements Warsaw especially and the towns of Katowice remain the main centres of attraction. Gdansk and Krakow attract urban population from neighbouring regions, but Poznan, Wroclaw, and Lodz are purely local centres of attraction.

East Germany

In East Germany the regions of Neubrandenburg, Rostock, Schwerin, and Magdeburg, where agriculture on sandy soils of the North German Plain is difficult, have remained leading source areas for outmigration. Net outflow from many parts of this general region still exceeds 1 per cent of the total population per annum (Fig. 6.6a). While most people involved move to local cities and towns, such as Wismar, Rostock, and Magdeburg, a significant proportion migrate further afield to Berlin and the nearby regions of Potsdam, Frankfurt, and Cottbus (Fig. 6.6b). However, an important change that has recently occurred in the pattern of migration is the emergence of the industrially developed region of the south as an area of general outmigration, which as late as 1960 absorbed 76 per cent of internal migrants annually (Benderman, 1964). The net loss of population from this area is almost entirely a consequence of movement to Berlin and neighbouring regions. Yet the outflow is rather small in comparison with considerable redistribution in the region as a result of short-distance movements to Karl Marx Stadt, Leipzig, Dresden, Zwickau, and Gera. Bose (1970) relates the strong inflow to the Berlin, Frankfurt, Potsdam, Cottbus region to the vast construction projects taking place in such towns as Eisenhüttenstadt and Schwelt. The pattern of movement in East Germany is one to local towns and cities, especially regional capitals, and to their commuter zones, upon which regional net transfers of population to Berlin and surrounding areas are superimposed.

Hungary

In Hungary, rural areas have persistently lost population through migration since World War II. An important exception involves settlements surrounding Budapest which have been transformed into dormitory settlements (Fig. 6.7a). A similar process, but not for precisely the same reasons, has generated migration growth in villages in the immediate vicinities of other main urban centres. Territorially the Great Hungarian Plain and the border zones have suffered the highest rates of population loss (Compton, 1971). By contrast, and with the

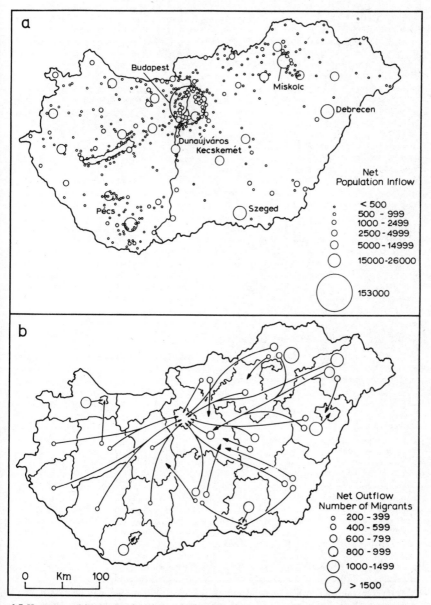

6.7 Hungary: (a) net inmigration 1960–1970 by communes, urban districts, county boroughs, and Budapest; (b) net outmigration flows, annual average 1969–1972

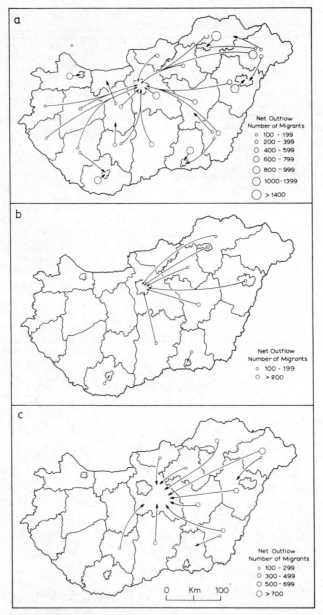

6.8 Hungary: (a) rural—urban net migration flows; (b) inter-urban net migration flows; (c) inter-village net migration flows (Each map represents annual average 1969–1972; only flows exceeding 100 migrants are shown)

exception of some market towns of the Great Plain, the urban centres of Hungary have been the main destinations. Budapest has experienced by far the largest absolute inflow of population, in many years exceeding that of all other towns combined, although rates of inmigration have been higher to main provincial cities and to new socialist towns (Dunaujvaros, Leninvaros, and Kazincbarcika) (Dávid and Pesti, 1971). Geographically population gain has been mainly restricted to the major industrial and energy axis of the country which pivots on the capital in a south-west to north-east direction. The pattern of net migration flows is strikingly simple (Fig. 6.7b) and is dominated by Budapest, which attracts migrants from all areas of the country but especially from north-eastern parts of the Great Plain. Compared with Budapest, the spheres of influence of main provincial centres are purely local. With the exception of very short-distance migration, other significant movements of population occur between neighbouring counties. As with the Polish statistics we are able to break down rural and urban migration flows by region of origin and destination (Fig. 6.8), but these only serve to emphasize the pull of greater Budapest. Indeed

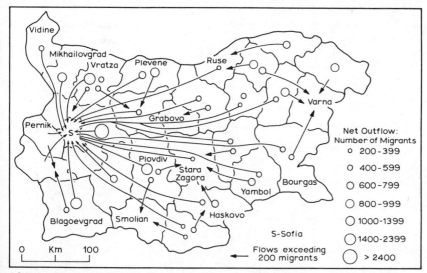

6.9 Bulgaria: net outmigration flows, annual average 1969–1971

the only significant regional implication of inter-village movement is a net shift of population to Pest country—presumably to the capital's dormitory settlements.

Bulgaria

The geographical features of internal migration in Bulgaria conform to the general pattern identified. On the one hand are relatively short-distance movements to local urban centres with the result that practically all towns and

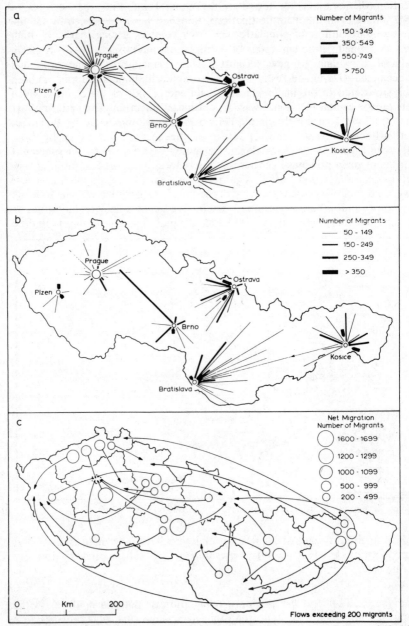

6.10 Czechoslovakia: (a) inmigration, 1969; (b) net migration to major cities, 1969; (c) net migration flows, 1969

cities are net recipients of migrants, and with county seats experiencing the highest inflows (Popov, 1969). Notable exceptions are smaller towns in the counties of Plovdiv, Mikhailovgrad, Haskovo, Tolboukhine, and Burgas whose populations are attracted to larger centres in the vicinity, and the city of Pernik immediately west of Sofia. The latter is the centre of a declining brown coalfield and this, coupled with the pull of the nearby capital, provides an explanation for population loss.

Medium- and long-distance migration is dominated by Sofia (Fig. 6.9). It attracts people from all parts of the country and over the last few years has experienced a net influx of approximately 15,000 people annually. The other regions to attract longer-distance migrants are undergoing rapid economic expansion and most migrants go to the dominant cities in each. Their migration catchment areas are essentially local, however, and most inter-regional movers come from neighbouring counties. It is notable that Plovdiv county, with the second largest city in Bulgaria, is an area of net outflow, with population moving to Stara Zagora, Smolian, and the capital. The city of Plovdiv itself continues to grow through migration, however, although the rate of net inflow is small when compared with more dynamic places such as Varna and Ruse.

Czechoslovakia

Migration in Czechoslovakia, unlike that in Bulgaria or Hungary, is not dominated by the capital. Each important regional centre has its own local migration catchment area (Fig. 6.10a and b). Inter-regional migration exhibits a number of interesting features. Firstly, the number of inter-regional migrations as a proportion of total number of movements has been declining as shorter-distance moves to local growth centres increase in significance (Table 6.4). The late 1950s and early 1960s marks a watershed in this process.

TABLE 6.4 *Czechoslovakia: percentage distribution of local and inter-regional migration, 1950–1972*

	1950–4	1955–9	1960–4	1965–9	1970–2
Inter-commune migration within same district	24·6	27·1	41·0	42·5	45·5
Inter-district migration within same region	33·4	33·4	29·3	28·3	26·7
Inter-regional migration	42·0	39·5	29·7	29·2	27·8
Total	100·0	100·0	100·0	100·0	100·0

Secondly, despite the fact that the Czech lands are much more developed economically than Slovakia, there is relatively little movement of population between the two. However, the balance of gross flows favours the Czech lands and Slovakia has in the last few years been losing population at a rate of approximately 5,000 people per annum. Thirdly, while most inter-regional moves in Bohemia occur between neighbouring regions, longer-distance moves are more common in Slovakia (Fig. 6.10c). The most important factors generating these movements are the agglomerating characteristics of Prague and Bratislava, rapid expansion of medium-sized cities (such as Kosice and Gottwaldov), and development of main industrial regions, notably Ostrava–Karvina (Andrle and Pojer, 1968; Blažek, 1971; Haufler, 1966; Novaková, 1973).

Yugoslavia

In 1961, according to census information, 63 per cent of the population of Yugoslavia were living in the settlement in which they were born. Although not conclusive, this would appear to suggest a high level of long-term residential stability, despite the intensive migration of population during the post-war era. Of those not living at their place of birth in 1961, 29 per cent were resident in another settlement in the same county, 45 per cent in a different county but in the same republic, and 24 per cent in a different republic, while 2 per cent were born abroad. The trans-republic movements are most significant from the view point of population distribution, and data indicate that of the six republics only Serbia had experienced a net inflow of lifetime migrants, while net outflow has been greatest from Bosnia–Herzegovina and Montenegro (Table 6.5).

TABLE 6.5 *Yugoslav lifetime migrants according to the 1961 census of population (in 000s)*

	In-movement	Out-movement	Balance
Bosnia and Herzegovina	109	369	−257
Montenegro	24	99	− 75
Croatia	256	301	− 45
Macedonia	66	71	− 4
Slovenia	66	67	− 1
Serbia	568	183	385

Flows of lifetime migrants are mapped in Fig. 6.11. These findings appear to conflict with the economic explanation of migration, in that differences in levels of development would lead one to expect net in-movement to the most advanced republics, Slovenia and Croatia. However, three qualifying factors must be mentioned. Firstly, Belgrade, the capital of the Federal Republic, which has been the most important destination of internal migrants, is located in Serbia. Secondly, the autonomous region of the Vojvodina, also within Serbia, has exerted a strong pull on the population of other regions because of superior organization of agriculture, its low rate of natural increase and, in the immediate

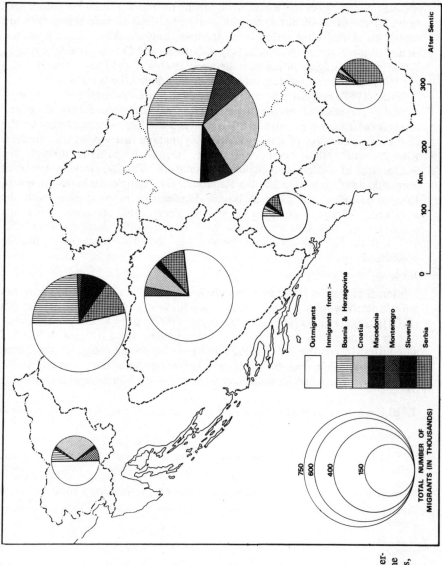

6.11 Yugoslavia: inter-republic lifetime migration flows, 1961

post-war period, areas left vacant by departing Germans. Thirdly, migration data derived from place of birth statistics cannot be fixed in time unless they are related to similar information from previous censuses. When this is done the picture changes, for in addition to Serbia, Slovenia and Croatia are now shown as having positive migration balances between 1948 and 1953 and between 1953 and 1961. Macedonia also falls into this category during the latter period.

Sentić (1968) suggests that four factors should be considered in formulating a general explanation of inter-republic migration in Yugoslavia. Firstly, the ethnic heterogeneity of the country is important and can have a large bearing on the choice of destination of migrants. Secondly, natural increase, which correlates strongly with ethnic group, influences migration patterns through the mechanism of differential population pressure. Thirdly, varying levels of economic development among the Republics, for example the backwardness of Kosovo—Metohija and parts of Bosnia—Herzegovina in comparison with the advanced economy of Croatia and Slovenia, are important migration determinants. This view is strongly supported by other workers (Klemenčič, 1972). Fourthly, climate, topography, and soil differences must also be considered.

Romania

Internal migration statistics have only just become available for Romania and unfortunately were too late to be analysed in detail in this study. However, Biji (1964), Grigorescu (1966), and Measnicov (1969) provide a reasonably clear picture of migration for 1948—64, although their work is based on the old administrative regions. Industrialized and more urbanized zones, i.e. the Banat, Brasov, Hunedoara, and the Bucharest agglomeration, attract migrants at the expense of other areas. As is demonstrated in Table 6.6 these regions exceed the

TABLE 6.6 *Internal migration, urbanization, and economic level in Romania in 1964 (after Grigorescu)*

	Net migration coefficient	Urban population (%)	Industrial output	Agricultural output	Investment	Retail sales
Romania	–	33·4	100·0	100·0	100·0	100·0
Group I regions	6·61	63·3	211·8	83·9	134·1	162·4
Group II regions	−0·37	31·7	97·2	96·7	105·0	95·2
Group III regions	−2·85	20·5	49·9	109·2	81·5	73·8

Group I regions: Banat, Brasov, Hunedoara, Bucharest.
Group II regions: Bacu, Galati, Maramures, Ploiesti.
Group III regions: Arges, Cluj, Crisana, Dobrogea, Lasi, Oltenia, Suceava.
Source: Grigorescu, 1966.

national average in the spheres of investment, industrial output, and retail sales but are of below average dependence on agriculture. These findings are confirmed by Pecican's (1973) factorial analysis of inter-district migration. Continued industrialization of backward areas means that regional disparities are narrowing, and this is affecting patterns of spatial mobility. For instance, while in 1956 the Banat, Hunedoara, Ploiesti, and Bucharest were the destinations of one-third of all inter-regional migrants, this proportion had fallen to one quarter by 1963. By contrast Bacu, which before 1948 was an area of labour surplus, has been transformed into a region of population inflow because of economic advancement, and between 1956 and 1963 attracted a net increment of over 10,000 people. Similarly there has been a marked reduction in net out-movement of population from Oltenia relating to new employment created by the Craiova natural gas complex and the Iron Gorge project. Such developments throughout the country have had the effect of reducing the extent of inter-regional migration and increasing the significance of short-distance moves to local growth centres.

Interpretation of migration patterns

Spatial mobility is characteristic of all societies regardless of development level, but during periods of rapid transformation migration increases in both frequency and intensity. At present Eastern Europe is passing through such a phase—during which disparities between areas and places in terms of economic structure, investment, job opportunities, wages, housing provision, etc. have widened. The consequence of this has been large-scale migration of population which may, therefore, be viewed as a mechanism to restore the equilibrium between

TABLE 6.7 *Employment structure by branches of industry (% economically active in each branch)*

	Industry and construction	Agriculture		Industry and construction	Agriculture
	Bulgaria			*Hungary*	
1950	11·4	79·5	1950	23·3	50·6
1960	27·1	55·5	1960	34·0	38·9
1971	39·8	33·9	1971	43·1	37·4
	Czechoslovakia			*Poland*	
1950	36·3	38·6	1950	26·2	54·0
1960	45·6	25·9	1960	32·2	44·2
1971	46·4	17·9	1971	37·4	35·2
	East Germany			*Romania*	
1950	43·7	27·3	1950	14·2	74·3
1960	48·3	17·3	1960	20·0	65·6
1971	49·8	12·6	1971	32·8	46·6

Source: Council for Mutual Economic Assistance (COMECON), *Yearbook*, 1973.

population distribution, resources, and opportunities. Despite the simplicity of this explanatory model causes of internal migration in Eastern Europe are nevertheless complex and vary according to directions of movement (Losonci, 1969). Thus, for instance, rural—urban migration has been generated mainly by modernization of agriculture and industrialization of larger towns and cities. But these factors do not explain adequately either the considerable inter-urban movement or return migration from urban to rural areas.

Factors generating rural—urban migration will now be considered in greater detail. Agricultural modernization has achieved significant advances in productivity which has brought about a rapid and continuing decline in demand for workers on the land in all the Eastern European countries (Sárfalvi, 1965; Hajek, 1971; Vielrose, 1973). Parallel with this has been the development of heavy and light manufacturing industry—and latterly of the tertiary sector—in urban areas, with the result that the distribution of labour demand has moved decisively away from the countryside (Herma, 1968; Klemenčič, 1970; Wendl, 1970). This process is reflected in the changing structure of employment throughout Eastern Europe which shows a marked rise in the proportion of jobs in industry and construction at the expense of agriculture (Table 6.7). Rural to urban migration thus reflects wider socio-economic changes (Sárfalvi, 1965).

In short, in recent decades Eastern Europe has been experiencing industrial and agricultural 'revolutions' which more advanced countries of Western Europe largely completed much earlier. One essential difference, however, is that while in Western Europe the process affected the various countries at different times and was unplanned, in Eastern Europe the process is occurring simultaneously in each country (East Germany is the important exception) and is under strict government control. It is thus deliberate policy to encourage movement of population from the land into industry and the whole process of industrialization has been constructed around a surplus of agricultural workers that can be absorbed easily into labour-intensive industry. At first it was those who were representative of persistent structural unemployment and under-employment of the pre-war period who moved to towns—in many instances workers in the middle age range—but increasingly it has become cityward migration of school leavers, students, and young workers and their dependents. Although data are not complete, evidence to hand suggests that higher wage rates in non-agricultural employment form an important contributory factor in this process. In both Poland and Bulgaria wage rates in agriculture are still at least 10 per cent below the national average and were much lower in earlier years. Only in Hungary, where one of the objectives of the 1968 reform of the economy was to redress the balance between agricultural and non-agricultural income levels, are farm wages at the national average and indeed slightly above those in industry.

Initially throughout Eastern Europe industrial development was restricted to larger cities and towns and to areas with raw material endowments. The consequence of this locational concentration has been widespread inter-regional migration from poorer agricultural regions in each country to centres of growing industrial employment. However, as rural infrastructures have been improved and manufacturing decentralized, non-farming employment has sprung up in small towns and larger villages in regions traditionally dependent on agriculture with the result that not only is the total number of migrations per annum now falling but the balance between long-distance inter-regional and short-distance local migration is changing in favour of the latter. The consequence of this is increasingly that socio-economic restratification is taking place locally and whereas rural to urban migration was accompanied initially by widening disparities in levels of territorial development and occupational structure this process is now going into reverse.

It should be stressed that as well as moves on a permanent basis, temporary migration and commuting form essential components of the rural to urban migration process. Temporary migration is naturally associated with particular branches of the economy, for instance with the construction industry and in the past with agriculture, but both it and commuting are more importantly a response to the rapidity of change throughout Eastern Europe and represent an intermediate stage between rural and urban living. In a word, both may broadly be viewed as a response to growing separation of labour availability and employment opportunities during the 1950s and 1960s (Bence and Tajti, 1972; Macka, 1969).

The precise causal factors are, of course, more specific than this, as will be demonstrated by the following two examples. In some instances commuting or temporary migration is forced on individuals either because of housing shortages in large industrial centres or because of restrictions on movement to such places—although, as exemplified by Budapest and Warsaw, residential restriction is a function of past heavy inmigration which has placed intolerable strain on urban infrastructure. The potential migrant responds to this in one of two ways: either he moves in the vicinity of the large city to an unrestricted village or town which is consequently slowly transformed into a commuter settlement; or he retains his permanent dwelling and migrates on a weekly, monthly, or even longer-term basis to his city job. In this way labour surplus areas become source regions not only of heavy permanent outmigration but also of heavy out-movement on a temporary basis. Large-scale temporary migration from backward regions of the Great Hungarian Plain to Budapest and other expanding settlements of the Central Industrial Region is a notable example. These movements are composed almost entirely of labour migrants whose dependants remain at the permanent residence. In many cases, particularly when the individual is migrating to Budapest, he will have a specific job to which to go and will be housed in a workers' dormitory. Otherwise it can mean renting a room in a private dwelling for which high rents are charged.

In other instances, commuting and temporary migration may be a consequence of insufficient earnings from agriculture, which gives rise to a transitional peasant-worker type who retains his links with the land. Moves for this reason are common where agriculture still remains in private hands, as in

Poland and Yugoslavia, although they are not unknown in areas where agriculture has been collectivized (Friganović, 1970; Vresk, 1971/2).

The dominant factors generating movement from the countryside to the towns do not provide an adequate explanation for migration in other directions. Indeed, in many respects the explanation of inter-urban, inter-village, and urban—rural migration in Eastern Europe is governed by factors similar to those operative in Western Europe. Economic motivation is of obvious significance, and factors such as job satisfaction, wage levels, and promotion, as elsewhere, generate migration. In addition, social factors such as marriage and education stimulate a large degree of spatial mobility. These are also factors, of course, accounting for movement from the countryside to the town but the difference lies in the fact that, whereas rural to urban migration operates explicitly within the framework of agricultural modernization and industrialization, movements in other directions cannot be tied to one dominant process. Nevertheless industrialization and modernization have also played a role in movements from urban areas. For example, the improvement of rural services has encouraged migration of trained and professional people from towns and cities to the countryside. Mechanization and reorganization of agriculture, by creating demand in the co-operative and state farms for skilled managers, agricultural engineers, veterinary surgeons, and so on, have generated similar movements. In addition, a proportion of inter-urban movements has been a direct consequence of disparities in employment opportunity among towns and cities as a result of differential industrialization.

One consequence of this is that the occupational, educational, and age composition of migrants can be expected to vary according to the origins and destinations of migrants. For instance, Hungarian statistics suggest that migrants from rural to urban areas are on average younger and less qualified educationally and occupationally than their counterparts moving in the reverse direction. Dobrowolska and Herma (1968) have demonstrated that significant compositional disparities are exhibited by migrants in Poland according to the nature of destinations. Those moving to mining and heavy industrial regions are largely unskilled and of primary school attainment, contrasting with the technical education and skilled trades of migrants to engineering centres. Moreover, development of high technology industry has resulted in migration of qualified workers and trained apprentices between industrial regions, while Latuch (1973) has shown that the educational and occupational status of inmigrants rises according to the rank of urban centres, and is highest in the case of Warsaw.

The 1965 census data for Bulgaria enable one to examine in considerable detail the factors that motivated migration during the years 1956 to 1965 and to exemplify some of the general points made above. These data are particularly useful because as well as summarizing the general situation they are disaggregated by direction of movement. Table 6.8 clearly shows that migration is initiated by a wide range of factors. Migration for work reasons—including lack

TABLE 6.8 *Bulgaria: the causes of migration by number of previous moves and sex 1956–1965*

	All moves	First moves	Second moves	Subsequent moves	For first moves Males	For first moves Females	For subsequent moves Males	For subsequent moves Females
Change of employment all reasons	21·5	19·8	28·2	32·7	34·6	6·7	45·7	10·1
for more pay	11·8	11·0	15·5	16·0	19·1	3·7	24·5	5·4
for more skilled work	2·8	2·7	3·3	3·5	5·0	0·7	5·2	1·2
work unsuitable in previous settlement	2·1	2·0	2·3	2·7	3·3	0·8	3·7	0·9
other reasons	4·8	4·1	6·9	10·4	6·8	1·4	12·4	2·6
Lack of work at place of residence	5·1	5·7	2·4	1·1	4·7	6·5	1·5	2·7
Commencement of work	2·0	1·9	2·4	2·7	2·7	1·2	3·3	1·6
End of education and commencement of work	5·2	4·4	8·5	11·5	5·3	3·5	9·7	8·9
Accompanying spouse	14·0	14·0	14·2	12·8	1·9	24·9	1·4	28·2
Marriage	12·1	13·2	7·6	4·3	3·7	21·8	2·3	11·9
Beginning or continuation of education	19·2	19·4	18·4	17·2	21·2	17·8	17·0	19·5
Leaving parental home	14·1	14·3	13·0	13·0	15·9	12·8	12·4	13·7
Other	6·8	7·3	5·5	4·7	10·0	4·8	6·7	3·4
Total	100·0	100·0	100·0	100·0	100·0	100·0	100·0	100·0
Total number of moves	1,405,635	1,164,811	176,231	64,593	552 757	612,054	129,374	111,450

Source: 1965 Census of Bulgaria.

of work, change of employment (within which low pay was the most important reason), and entering the labour force for the first time—accounted for approximately one-third of all moves. In other words, even if one assumes that all migration for work reasons was the direct effect of modernization and industrialization, most moves appear to have been caused by other factors. However, there were clear differences between the sexes in this respect for, whereas migration for work reasons comprised approximately one half of total moves by males, the corresponding proportion for females was less than 20 per cent. Other factors, each motivating more than 10 per cent of migrants, were marriage, commencement or continuation of education, leaving the parental home, and accompanying a spouse.

As might be expected there were differences in this mix between first and subsequent moves; thus the higher the number of previous moves by an individual the greater the significance of change of employment and the lower the importance of marriage as generators of migration. In addition to migration primarily motivated by work considerations, other important differences between the sexes in reasons for moving relate to marriage, accompanying a spouse (more significant in the case of females), and commencement or continuation of education and leaving the parental home (more significant among males).

TABLE 6.9 *Bulgaria: the causes of migration by geographical type of movement (% deviations from national average)*

	Inter-urban	Inter-village	Urban to rural	Rural to urban
Change of employment all reasons	4·3	−8·3	10·9	1·7
for more pay	−30·4	−11·9	4·7	3·0
for more skilled employment	43·4	−58·0	−24·3	18·8
unsuitable employment at old residence	−23·2	−11·6	10·8	12·2
other reasons	83·9	−28·0	50·7	−18·0
Lack of employment	−10·2	−37·5	−47·6	27·9
Commencement of employment	0·0	−52·1	−17·9	28·9
End of education and commencement of employment	80·5	−57·4	155·0	−13·4
Accompanying spouse	6·8	−7·1	−4·9	2·0
Marriage	−29·7	90·6	10·8	−38·5
Beginning or continuation of education	3:5	−42·3	−50·2	26·3
Leaving parental home	1·7	9·9	−18·4	−3·6
Percentage distribution of all moves	16·4	26·5	5·7	51·4

Source: 1965 Census of Bulgaria.

The motivation structure of first movers, recorded in Table 6.9 as a percentage deviation from the national average, supports the contention that reasons for migration vary according to rural and urban origins and destinations. When compared with the mean number of moves attributable to each factor, migration from rural to urban areas is more likely to be a function of inability to find employment in the countryside and to be related to change of employment—notably because of unsuitable work or difficulty in obtaining work commensurate with skills offered. Additionally, rural dwellers are more likely to move to towns when seeking their first job, or when beginning or continuing full-time education. On the other hand they are less likely so to move because of marriage.

By contrast, counter-movements from towns to countryside, although also more likely to be generated by change of employment, are in other respects motivated differently. They are less likely to be a consequence of lack of employment in urban areas or to occur when beginning or continuing full-time education, but are more likely to be a consequence of marriage. Inter-village movement also shows a higher probability of being a result of marriage, but is less likely to be generated by most of the other factors—and is very much less likely to occur because of low pay, seeking a first job, or when beginning or continuing full-time education.

The balance of factors is different once again in the case of inter-urban migration. Compared with the average, such moves are very much more likely to occur on completing full-time education or to be a function of a lack of suitably skilled work at the former residence. On the other hand they are less likely to be generated by low pay, lack of work, and marriage. In summary, compared with the average position:

(i) only inter-village movements are less likely to be a function of migration for work reasons;

(ii) migration to the towns is more likely to be a product of lack of work in the countryside;

(iii) urban destinations are more likely to be selected for educational reasons;

(iv) village destinations are more popular among migrants motivated by marriage.

A similar analysis, based on the division of Bulgaria into mountain, hill, and plain areas, also supports the contention that factors generating migration vary according to types of origin and destination. For example, a person migrating because of marriage is more likely to move to a settlement within the same type of geographical area than to a different area (Table 6.10). On the other hand, lack of suitable work is more likely to generate migration to a different region, while no work induces movement to the plains. Migration to a mountain or hill destination is more likely to be for better pay or for a first job than are moves to the plains. Against this, mountain and hill destinations are less likely to attract individuals for reasons of education.

A full understanding of the associations discussed would require a thorough analysis of Bulgarian conditions, which is not possible here. A question of some

TABLE 6.10 *Bulgaria: the causes of migration by geographical type of movement (% deviation from national average)*

	Mountains to mountains	Mountains to hills	Mountains to plains	Hills to mountains	Hills to hills	Hills to plains	Plains to mountains	Plains to hills	Plains to plains
Change of employment all reasons	−18·1	39·0	15·8	6·0	3·9	8·8	22·2	25·1	−4·4
for more pay	3·6	72·7	12·6	14·4	22·1	−4·5	47·7	32·0	−8·9
for more skilled employment	60·2	31·8	−17·0	−42·3	4·2	1·5	−37·1	64·7	5·7
unsuitable employment at old residence	−39·8	29·1	34·8	−12·5	−24·0	18·8	−6·8	9·3	−3·4
other reasons	−38·7	−42·7	36·4	2·0	−27·9	6·6	8·1	−9·1	0·4
Leaving parental home	−56·9	−29·1	10·9	−42·3	−5·9	6·0	−49·7	−19·9	8·9
Lack of employment	−49·0	−23·6	−26·8	49·0	97·5	6·1	43·5	124·8	−9·4
Commencement of employment	−58·8	−46·4	−56·6	25·0	−2·2	−21·5	94·2	97·0	7·1
End of education and commencement of employment	−15·1	−12·7	18·6	−26·9	−9·2	3·0	−3·9	−17·5	1·1
Accompanying spouse	48·2	−16·4	−32·2	−19·2	14·5	−17·2	−28·7	−14·5	4·9
Marriage	2·8	−26·4	−64·3	8·6	−6·7	−3·3	22·3	−4·0	5·7
Beginning or continuation of education	14·5	19·1	45·7	−15·4	−11·5	10·4	−25·5	−29·0	−6·0
Percentage distribution of all moves	6·4	1·1	8·5	1·0	3·6	11·4	3·1	4·3	60·6

Source: 1965 Census of Bulgaria

importance, however, is the extent to which general findings for Bulgaria apply to other countries in Eastern Europe. This is difficult to assess because, apart from Bulgaria, motivation data are only available for Czechoslovakia and Hungary. Unfortunately these are not directly comparable either with each other or with the Bulgarian statistics as regards level of aggregation or causal factors. Nevertheless, the finding that motivation varies according to types of origin and destination is broadly substantiated (Compton, 1971; Srb, 1970). For example, in both Hungary and Czechoslovakia movements relating to village origins or destinations are more likely to involve marriage and dependents. On the other hand, migration to urban areas is more probably for reasons of education or to be closer to the place of employment, although the balance of generating factors varies strongly from town to town. In addition, the differentials are even more strongly developed in the case of temporary migration.

Causes of internal migration in Eastern Europe are complex. Although rural to urban migration can be satisfactorily explained at the macro-level as a response to agricultural modernization and industrialization, the Bulgarian data demonstrate that a whole range of additional factors must be brought into play. This applies even more forcibly to the explanation of migration in other geographical directions. Contemporary migration within Eastern Europe is therefore a multi-faceted rather than single-cause phenomenon.

Some consequences of migration

The consequences on internal migration are not only a function of numbers but also of the selectiveness of migrants by age, sex, education, ethnic group, etc. Age selectiveness in particular has important demographic and socio-economic consequences. As elsewhere, migration throughout Eastern Europe is a phenomenon mainly affecting young adults; approximately 50 per cent of all permanent movers fall within the 15–29 age range, and on the basis of the limited information available, this percentage probably rises to over two-thirds in the case of temporary migration (Fig. 6.12). The consequence, especially when migration rates are accelerating, is a rise of both young and old-age dependency in the populations of areas suffering from outmigration, and a reduction of dependency in main reception areas.

Thus areas of out-movement progressively lose that section of population which is most productive demographically and the result is a fall in crude birth rates even under constant fertility conditions. At the same time because of the increasing proportion of elderly people crude death rates tend to rise, and the combined effect is a marked fall in the rate of natural increase. By similar reasoning, areas of inmigration experience climbing birth rates, falling death rates, and rising rates of natural increase under constant conditions.

Throughout Eastern Europe rural areas are losing population and urban areas are gaining through migration. Traditionally fertility has been higher in rural areas and still remains so, but the impact of migration has progressively reduced the birth rate disparity between the two. For example, there is now virtually no

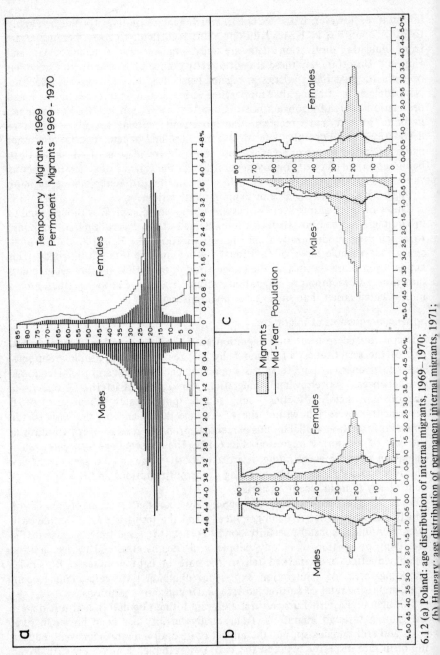

6.12 (a) Poland: age distribution of internal migrants, 1969–1970;
(b) Hungary: age distribution of permanent internal migrants, 1971;

differential between rural and urban birth rates in Hungary, while in Bulgaria urban birth rates are actually higher. In both countries the traditional differential between town and country as regards natural increase has been reversed. Moreover, where outmigration has been intense over many decades, as has occurred in certain isolated regions, the unbalancing of age structures can bring about population decline and eventual demographic non-viability because of excess of deaths over births, even though fertility rates remain high. Rural populations in more difficult parts of Eastern Europe exhibit such characteristics. The same process has tended to reduce spatial disparities in rates of natural increase as traditional areas of high natural growth have also been those subject to the largest population outflows, while regions of low growth have been main reception areas.

The age selectiveness of migrants thus has significant implications as regards natural increase. But in addition, because individuals tend to emulate the fertility behaviour of the general population of the area in which they reside, migration of population from high fertility rural areas to low fertility urban centres has been an important auxiliary mechanism bringing about the recent decline in fertility in Eastern Europe (Acsádi, Klinger and Szabady, 1970). Migration, therefore, has·a threefold effect on population growth: first, there are the direct numerical effects of individuals changing residence; second, migration influences growth through its indirect bearing on natural increase, the link being through age structure; and third is the effect upon fertility itself.

Economic consequences of migration are many-sided and are closely related to the question of regional planning. The size and quality of the local labour force will in large degree be a function of previous migration. Manpower planning, which forms an integral component of state planning throughout Eastern Europe, is carried out at both national and regional level. At the regional scale planning does not entail the direction of labour, but is rather a tailoring of plans to projected populations, taking into account both quantitative and qualitative aspects (Bartke *et al.*, 1972). Within the planning context, problems thrown up by migration are similar to those confronting the countries of Western Europe. On the one hand are problems associated with depopulation and on the other those related to congestion.

Since about 1950, outmigration from rural areas has been beneficial in that overpopulation and attendant under-employment and unemployment have been largely eliminated at least in official figures. At the same time it has been an implicit assumption of planning in socialist countries that each separate region should develop a balanced economy, and industry is now being installed in local growth centres throughout the countryside. However, although depopulation rarely approaches the levels common in certain parts of the British Isles, some regions of Yugoslavia excepting, where the process has bitten deeply into the fabric of a region it is difficult to reverse. It is, therefore, problematical whether industry can be brought successfully to regions not only of sparse habitation but also with elderly and poorly trained populations. Nevertheless, in spite of the existence of problem areas, the size of the local rural population is generally not the greatest constraint on development. Lack of infrastructure is a more pressing question although it also relates to migration in that provision becomes increasingly questioned on economic grounds as rural populations decline.

A different set of problems is presented by rural settlements where populations have been transformed from dependence on agriculture to a semi-industrial state either because of the introduction of industry or because of evolution into commuter settlements. Both processes generate inmigration, and the primary concern is the provision of adequate services—piped water, sewerage, paved roads, retail outlets, schools, and health centres. Rapidly expanding small and medium-size urban centres face similar difficulties. Different yet again are the problems of large cities—involving pressure on housing and public transport in addition to inadequate provision of services (Viszkei, 1972). Decentralization of industrial establishments and employment from such centres is part of planning policy in most countries, and Budapest, from which 200 industrial plants have been removed to the provinces since 1967, well exemplifies this planning trend (Bora, 1976).

A cultural consequence of migration that deserves mention is its impact on the ethnic structure of individual countries. Population exchange, expulsion, and voluntary migration at the end of the World War II certainly reduced ethnic heterogeneity, which is now minimal in Hungary and Poland. However, Czechoslovakia, Romania, and Yugoslavia remain ethnically diverse and the political structures of Czechoslovakia and Yugoslavia recognize this reality. This is not the case in Romania and, contrary to the trend elsewhere for giving greater recognition to the aspirations of ethnic minorities, the Hungarian Autonomous Region was abolished in 1967.

In these three countries ethnic groups have traditionally been highly concentrated geographically, but in view of the high rate of contemporary migration one might expect this to be now breaking down. As an adjunct one might also expect migration away from their main geographical centres to be an important facet of the process of assimilation of minorities. The evidence in these regards is conflicting. Of the titular populations in Yugoslavia, the Montenegrans and Serbs have been the most mobile groups, with inter-republic lifetime migration rates in 1961 of 134 and 61 per 1,000 population respectively. Other groups have experienced even lower rates and it is clear that where dispersal is going on it is occurring at a very slow pace. Examination of geographical patterns of lifetime migrants supports this view (Table 6.11). Outflows of Croats and Slovenes from their home republics have been largely balanced by return movements, while the evidence of a net inflow of Serbs to Serbia suggests greater rather than lesser concentration. Minority populations appear to have behaved in a similar fashion. Slow dispersal of Hungarians and Albanians from main ethnic centres is indicated, but balancing this is the apparent increased spatial cohesiveness of the Turks in Macedonia. The dominance of Slovenes in Slovenia (95 per cent of the population in 1961), of

TABLE 6.11 *Yugoslavia: Lifetime migration by ethnic group (per 1,000 poula population)*

	Total inter-regional life time migration rate	For titular republic or republic/autonomous region where most numerous		
		Inmigration	Outmigration	Net migration
Serbs	61	57	15	42
Croats	40	18	25	− 7
Slovenes	43	18	21	− 3
Macedonians	38	12	25	−13
Montenegrans	134	35	120	−85
Albanians	37	11	30	−19
Hungarians	37	12	22	−10
Turks	74	83	9	74

Source: Sentic, 1968.

Serbs in Serbia (90 per cent of the population), of Croats in Croatia (85 per cent of the population), and Montenegrans (80 per cent of the population) has ᴊhus been little affected.

In Czechoslovakia, there is evidence of a net inmigration of Slovaks to the Czech lands at a current rate of approximately 3,000 persons per annum. However, the reverse flow of Czechs to Slovakia is largely in balance and the net effect of these movements on the geographical distribution of the titular groups is slight. The position of the Hungarian minority, along the Hungarian border in Slovakia where it comprises 12 per cent of the population, is of more interest. During the 1950s various factors induced a considerable migration of Hungarians to the industrial areas of Ostrava−Karvina. Many of these later returned to their own ethnic areas, and the most recent statistics suggest that this process is still continuing. Hungarians also form the largest ethnic minority in Romania, where they make up one-third of the population of Transylvania. But here again, although data are limited, the geographical cohesiveness of the group appears little affected by migration, and in 1966 only 2 per cent of ethnic Hungarians were recorded as living outside their traditional areas.

Contemporary internal migration thus appears to have had little impact on the distribution of ethnic groups in Czechoslovakia, Romania, and Yugoslavia. Nor would it appear to be an important mechanism in the assimilation of minority communities. Although hard statistical evidence is lacking, one is left with the distinct impression that migration between ethnically disparate regions is lower than would be expected on the basis of normal criteria, such as differences of economic level and geographical distance.

International migration

The policy of the governments of Eastern Europe towards international migration for settlement is that permission to emigrate or immigrate is given whenever the reasons are considered to be well founded. In practice there is now little movement of population either between the countries of Eastern Europe or between Eastern Europe and the rest of the world (except migration for work reasons from Yugoslavia), which contrasts markedly with heavy emigration from the region prior to World War II (Kirk, 1946). Immigration is now uniformly low, mainly involving return migrants. Emigration is somewhat higher but only attains sizeable numbers from Poland, where the outflow of population during the decade 1960–9 was just under a quarter of a million. Nevertheless the post-war era has been marked by a number of migration waves. Enormous movements of population during the mid- and late 1940s, generated by hostilities and their aftermath (chapter one), have simplified the ethnic map of Eastern Europe. Two hundred thousand people are estimated to have left Hungary as a result of the counter-revolution of 1956, although many have since returned to their country of birth. Romanian policy has been to allow Jews and Germans to emigrate, which has greatly reduced the size of those communities. Between 1970 and 1972 a special agreement with Turkey provided for the voluntary emigration of 35,000 Turks from Bulgaria.

International migration for permanent settlement is complemented by the temporary movement of workers across international frontiers. In Eastern Europe, the most notable example of the latter is the migration of Yugoslav workers to West Germany, described elsewhere in this book. The migration of labour from the other countries of the region to Western Europe is minimal and stems from contracts between individual firms and enterprises rather than from agreements between countries (ILO, 1973). Co-operative construction projects, for instance between West Germany on the one hand, and Poland and Romania on the other, generate this type of movement, as do agreements to manufacture under licence, and sub-contracting work. Falling into the same general category is the temporary migration of skilled personnel—technicians, engineers, etc.—to selected countries of the Third World (notably to the Arab states) in order to provide technical assistance in a wide range of projects. In the other direction, Egyptian workers are employed in construction in Bulgaria and Czechoslovakia.

Bilateral agreements within the framework of the Council for Mutual Economic Assistance regulate the movement of workers among the socialist countries themselves. These are regarded as short-term migrations and do not lead to permanent settlement. East Germany is evolving into the main labour-importing country of the area and in 1974 offered employment to 12,000 Hungarian and 2,000 Czech workers. To these should be added a few thousand Russian specialists and a number of Romanians. Agreements between East Germany and Hungary have proved successful and it was planned to increase the number of Hungarians involved to 20,000 by 1975. Initially the agreement envisaged the employment of young Hungarians in the engineering industry for the improvement of their skills but is now being placed on a firmer reciprocal basis. Also within the framework of the CMEA is growing co-operation with the U.S.S.R. Some 12,000 Bulgarian workers are employed in forestry and construction in the U.S.S.R. while Hungary is co-operating in building a new aluminium-producing combine in the Ukraine.

Continuing a long tradition are the movements of frontier workers. These are presently being strengthened between Hungary and Czechoslovakia as a result of an agreement for a common border zone development programme. Poles also continue to find employment in the border regions of both East Germany and Czechoslovakia.

As to the future, the ILO suggests that growing labour-market imbalances may lead to an increased migration of workers. East Germany, Czechoslovakia, and Hungary will face growing labour deficits, Bulgaria will probably be in balance, while Poland and Romania are likely to have a labour surplus in the range of 2,500,000 to 4,000,000 workers by 1980. Such striking differences must lead to greater manpower co-ordination in Eastern Europe.

Conclusion

The socialist countries of Eastern Europe have generally experienced a high rate of internal migration since the war. Although there are serious questions concerning data comparability, wide national disparities in the incidence of over-all movement apparent during the 1950s have since narrowed and rates of permanent migration appear to be stabilizing everywhere at around 20 per 1,000 population per annum. However, it is similarities rather than differences between countries that are prominent. On the one hand is the common process of urbanization and concomitant local and regional population concentration, which is a consequence of net transfer of population through migration. On the other hand are similarities in migration flow patterns. Thus, throughout the area long-distance inter-regional migration is being displaced by short-distance local movements, while migration among the components of a settlement hierarchy defined on the basis of size takes on the same shape, regardless of country. Naturally, rates of net movement and the size of migration streams vary from state to state, but these reflect differences of degree rather than of underlying principles.

Internal migration, because of its selectiveness, contains implications for natural increase, and heavy out-movement promotes falling birth rates and rising dependency ratios. Although some initial economic benefit is to be derived from this process, when it results in excessive depopulation the situation is difficult to retrieve. Heavy inmigration, on the other hand, creates problems that are almost as intractable.

Geographical patterns of migration have been generated by similar causal chains. Agricultural modernization and industrialization have been the dominant factors accounting for movement of population from the countryside to the cities and for the regional pattern of net migration. Spatial mobility and the socio-economic restratification of the population have thus been closely related, and in the intensity of these processes internal migration in Eastern Europe differs from that in Western Europe. Both processes, however, are specific to a particular stage of economic development and may be expected to wane as industrial transformation progresses towards completion. Apart from agricultural modernization and industrialization there is a complete set of additional migration generating factors that are not necessarily specific to any stage of economic development or to any particular type of society. Factors such as pay, promotion, job satisfaction, educational considerations, and marriage fall into this category. As elsewhere, evidence suggests that these are the factors that account for most internal migration in Eastern Europe, particularly for the considerable movement of population between villages, between towns, and from towns to the countryside. One may thus envisage a two-tier causal structure of migration. At the lower level are non-specific causal factors; upon these has been superimposed a set of factors associated with a specific stage of development, which in Europe is unique to the socialist countries.

Notes

[1] In the case of Bulgaria, *Naselenie Narodna Republica Bulgaria*; Czechoslovakia, *Pohyb Obyvatelstva*. East Germany, *Bevolkerungsstatistisches Jahrbuch der DDR*; Hungary, *Demografiai Evkonyv* and Poland, *Rocznik Demograficzny*.

[2] In East Germany settlements with 2,000 or more inhabitants are classed as urban. This was also the definition used in Czechoslovakia until 1960 since when the lower limit has been raised to 5,000. In the other countries legal-administrative definitions are used.

[3] Scale, however, is also an important factor as demonstrated by the example of Hungary; an identical analysis at the level of individual settlements reveals natural increase as the dominant component of population change in one-fifth of the cases containing approximately 17 per cent of the population of the country compared with an area containing 40 per cent of the inhabitants suggested by the present regional analysis.

[4] Even higher rates of mobility occurred during the immediate post-war years as a result of population exchange and resettlement. The tail-end effects of these traumatic upheavals may partly account for the high mobility during the early 1950s in both East Germany and Poland.

[5] The Czechoslovakia data provide a vivid example of the effect of scale on the apparent number of moves. In 1969 40 per cent of all moves occurred between settlements in the same district (*okres*), 66 per cent within the same county or province (*kraj*) and only 6 per cent between the Czech lands and the Slovak lands.

References

Acsáid, Gy, Klinger, A., and Szabady, E. (1970) *Family Planning in Hungary. Main Results of the 1966 Fertility and Family Planning (TCS) Study*, Publications of the Hungarian Demographic Research Institute, Budapest.

Andrle, A., and Pojer, M. (1968) 'K některým otázkam bydlení a potenciální migrační mobility mladých zemedelských pracovníků' (Habitation and potential migration mobility of young agricultural workers), *Demografie*, 10, 201–12.

Bartke, I., Kóródi, J., Kulcsár, V., and Szabó, K. (1972) *Teruleti tervezés, tanácsi tervezés (Regional and Council Planning)*, Közgazdasági és Jogi Könyvkiadó, Budapest (especially pp. 95–6).

Bence, I., and Tajti, E. (1972) *Budapest, an Industrial-geographical Approach*, Akadémiai Kiadó, Budapest (especially pp. 101–63).

Benderman, G. (1964) 'Regionale Besonderheiten der Bevolkerungs bewegung in DDR. Dargestellt am Beispiel des Jahres 1960', *Petermanns Geographische Mitteilungen*, 108, 221–27.

Berelson, B. (ed.) (1974) *Population Policy in Developed Countries*, McGraw-Hill, New York.

Biji, M. (1964) 'The development of Rumania's regions and its influence on the population's structure', *Revue roumaine des sciences sociales*, serie de sciences économiques, 11, 33–44.

Blažek, M. (1971) Les Perspectives de l'urbanisation en Tchecoslovaquie,' *Geografický Ústav Brno*, 91–7.

Bora, Gy (1976) Effects of changes in the spatial structure of Hungarian industry on the factors of industrial location', in *Proceedings of the first British-Hungarian Geographic Seminar*, Akadémiai Kiadó, Budapest.

Borejko, W. (1968) 'Migracje ludności w wojewodztwie zielonogórskim w latach 1953-62' (Population migration in the voivoidship of Zielona Góra 1953–62), *Lubuskie Tow. Nauk., Zielona Góra*, 150.

Bose, G. (1970) 'Entwicklungstendenzen der Binnenwanderung in der DDR im Zeitraum 1953 bis 1965', *Petermanns Geographische Mitteilungen*, 114, 117–31.

Compton, P. (1971) *Some Aspects of the Internal Migration of Population in Hungary since 1957*, Publications of the Hungarian Demographic Research Institute, Budapest.

Dávid, V., and Pesti, L. (1971) 'A vándorlások szerepe a föváros népesség-fejlödesében' (The role of migration in the population growth of the capital), *Területi Statisztika*, 21, 646–63.

Dobrowolska, M., and Herma, J. (1968) 'Migration of manpower in Southern Poland as a factor of changes in regional structures', *Geographia Polonica*, 14, 321–9.

Dziewonski, K. (1964) 'Urbanization in contemporary Poland', *Geographia Polonica*, 3, 38.

Friganović, M. (1970) 'Commuting in Croatia as an index of the socio-economic mobility of the population', *Geographical Papers, Zagreb*, 1, 95–103.

Grigorescu, C. (1966) 'Rolul utilizarii fortei de munca in repartizarea teritoriala a industriei' (The role of the utilization of the labour force in the territorial division of industry), *Probleme Economie*, 19, 35–53.

Hajek, Z. (1971) 'Les Sources de travail et la migration selective de la population du point de vue régionale', *Geograficky Ustav Brno*, 101–7.

Haufler, V. (1966) *Changes in the Geographical Distribution of Population in Czechoslovakia*, Rozpravy Československé Akademie Věd, Prague.

Herma, J. (1968) 'Napływ ludności do miast regionu siarkowego jako współczynnik procesow urbanizacji przemystu siarkowego' (The influx of population into the towns of the sulphur-mining district as a coefficient of urbanization processes), *Zesz. Bad. Rejon. Uprzem*, 29, 139–76.

International Labour Office (1973) *Some growing employment problems in Europe*, ILO, Geneva, 106–10.

Iwanicka-Lyra, E. (1972) 'Changes in the character of migration movements from rural to urban areas in Poland', *Geographia Polonica*, 24, 71–80.

Kirk, D. (1946) *Europe's Population in the Interwar Years*, Gordon and Breach, New York.

Klemenčič, V. (1970) 'The migration of population and the industrialization of Slovenia', in Sárfalvi, B. (ed.) *Recent Population Movements in the East European Countries*, Akadémiai Kiadó, Budapest.

Klemenčič, V. (1972) 'Geografija prebivalstva Slovenije' (The population geography of Slovenia), *Geografski Vestnik, Ljubljaha*, 133–57.

Kosiński, L. (1968) 'Population growth in East-central Europe in the years 1961–5', *Geographia Polonica*, 14, 297–304.

Kosiński, L. (1974) 'Urbanization in East-central Europe after World War II, *Eastern European Quarterly*, 8, 130–53.

Kostrowicki, J. and Szczesny, R. (1974) *Polish Agriculture: Characteristics, Types and Regions*, Akademiai Kiado, Budapest (especially pp. 9–16).

Kowalewski, J. (1970) 'Niektore konsekwencje demograficzne migracji ludnośći wiejskiej do miast w europejskich krajach socjalistycznych 1950–1965' (Certain demographic consequences of the migration of population from villages to towns in the socialist countries of Europe), *Studia Demograficzne*, 31, 39–57.

Latuch, M. (1973) 'The role of internal migration in contemporary population growth in big cities in Poland', *Studia Demograficzne*, 34, 35–47.

Lettrich, E. (1965) *Urbanizálódás Magyarországon (Urbanization in Hungary)*, Geographical Monographno. 5, Akademiai Kiado, Budapest.

Losonci, K. (1969) 'A népesség mozgásának okai' (The reasons for population mobility), *Területi Statisztika*. 439–53.

Macka, M. (1969) 'Typologie vyjíždkových oblastí' (Typology of regions of commuting), *Studia Geographica, Brno*, 1, 117–20.

Measnicov, I. (1969) 'Contributii la studiul migratiei interne in Romania. Migratia interna in perioado 1948–56' (Contributions to the study of internal migration in Romania. Internal migration during the years 1948–56), *Revista de Statistica*, 18, 22–32.

Novaková, B. (1973) 'Migrační zázemí měst ČSR' (Migration regions of towns in ČSR), *Demografie*, 15, 35–9.

Pecican, E. (1973) 'Probleme ale migratiei interjudetene' (Problems concerning inter-district migration), *Revista de Statistica*, 22, 60–5.

Pivovarov, V. (1972) 'A népesség váriosiasodása és vándorlása az európai szocialista országokban (a Szovjetunió nélkül)' (The urbanization and migration of population in the socialist countries of Europe (excluding the Soviet Union)), *Földrajzi Értesitö*, 21, 227–36.

Popov, P. (1969) 'Statistika migrace a migračních procesu v Bulharsku' (Migration statistics and processes in Bulgaria), *Demografie*, 11, 137–47.

Sárfalvi, B. (1965) *A mezögazdasági népesség csökkenése Magyarországon (The Decline of Agricultural Population in Hungary)*, Akadémiai Kiadó, Budapest.

Sárfalvi, B. (1970) 'Historical and geographical types of socioeconomic restratification in Europe', in Sáfalvi, B. (ed.) *Recent Population Movements in the East European Countries*, Akadémiai Kiadó, Budapest, 77–92.

Sentić, M. (1968) 'Some aspects of migration movements in the Yugoslav population', in Szabady, E. (ed,), *World Views of Population Problems*. Akadémiai Kiadó, Budapest, 321–8.

Srb, V. (1970) 'Důvodý vnitřního stěhovaní v Československu v roce 1966 a 1967' (Reasons for internal migration in Czechoslovakia in 1966 and 1967), *Demografie*, 12, 1−12.

Velcea, I. (1972) 'The urbanisation process of the rural settlements of Romania', *Revue roumaine de géologie, géophysique et géographie, serie de géographie*, 16, 93−101.

Viszkei, M. (1972) 'A budapesti agglomeráció kialakulása, helyzete és fejlesztési problémái' (The evolution, situation and developmental problems of Greater Budapest), *Területi Statisztika*, 22, 515−22.

Vielrose, E. (1973) 'Changes in the percentage of agricultural population in Poland', *Studia Demograficzne*, 34, 49−60.

Vresk, M. (1971−2) 'Social fallow and other forms of abandonment of agrarian activities due to the emigration and restructurisation of the population', *Geografski Glasnik, Zagreb*, 33−4, 79−90.

Wendl, J. (1970) 'Résultats des recherches relatives aux causes du mouvement mecanique de la population en Bohème de Sud,' *Demografie*, 12, 37−47.

Ziolkowski, J. (1974), 'Poland', in Berelson, B. (ed.), op. cit., 451−5.

CONCLUSION

The essays in this book provide a record of the evolution of selected components of Europe's complicated system of human migration. Each chapter presents its own conclusions which will not be repeated here. However, four main points are worthy of further comment, being related to migration as a social process and to the changing nature of European economy and society in the second half of the twentieth century.

First, it has been shown that Europe's migration system is maintained by a wide range of migrants who display a great diversity of detailed motivations. Flows of population in contemporary Europe reflect social and economic conditions that are found not only in the continent but also beyond its periphery. For many people migration offers a means of 'escape' from the hard grind of poverty and unemployment. In the 1970s this is particularly true of many international labour migrants. However, much of the great tide of rural—urban movement that has taken place in every European country since 1945 has undoubtedly been motivated by a desire to leave areas that offered neither adequate rewards nor sufficient opportunities for advancement. Of course, it may be argued that almost all migrants are attempting to 'escape' from something. But in contemporary Europe a growing share of migration—especially inter-regional movement—involves people who are already living in urban areas, and such flows may best be understood in terms of an ascent of a socio-economic 'ladder' rather than an 'escape' from poor living conditions. The lower rungs of the 'ladder' are supplemented by various forms of welfare aid—unemployment relief, health insurance, and so on—which reduce the absolute necessity of migration to keep body and soul together. In these circumstances, geographical mobility is closely associated with social mobility. Migration may be viewed by many people as the best way of advancing their career and improving their status. Thus migration has become customary normal behaviour for some groups in society.

Second, despite this emphasis on migration as a means of improvement, it is clearly not a panacea for *all* the problems of the people involved or of the regions experiencing demographic pressure, economic stagnation, or labour shortage. One must agree that most migrants believe their moves to have been worthwhile—even though they may rationalize their actions after the event. For example, many international labour migrants return again and again to reception countries in Western Europe and seem willing to tolerate inadequate housing and poor social conditions for the economic gain they receive and the chance of advancement that they expect when they finally return home. Some, indeed, abandon their ideas of going home and choose to bring their families to settle in the host country. Similarly, relatively few rural—urban migrants return to their farms or villages, except, perhaps, when they retire. For most of them the move from a rural to an urban environment is a one-way trip. Likewise most inter-urban migrants pronounce themselves satisfied with the results of moving and consider that their lives have been improved. Of course, there are some migrants who are disappointed but decide to stay in their new found location rather than return home to face the stigma of being 'failures'. But there are others—among internal and foreign migrants alike—who feel this disappointment more keenly, and find their new environments truly 'alien' and hard to fit into. Many foreign workers, in particular, experience living conditions in Western Europe that may be little better than those they left behind—or perhaps even worse. Misery, illness, despair, and sometimes violence are features of many 'immigrant quarters' in Western European cities. In a comparable way, not all internal migrants in industrial countries find that their situation has improved after the move. Many are unhappy and either return to familiar ground or move on elsewhere as soon as possible. Others only gradually become accustomed to new people and to new areas, adapting to new situations slowly and reluctantly.

In addition to its significance for the human beings involved, in both Western and Eastern Europe migration has also been regarded as a means of striking a more satisfactory balance between population and resources in specific areas. Undoubtedly it does ease some problems but also creates others. The selective nature of the migration process has led not only to depopulation but also to distorted age structures in areas of outmigration. In addition the 'quality' of population may suffer since it is usually the young, skilled, educated, and energetic who leave. What is more, even in the few countries where emigration has been encouraged by government, evidence shows that many hopes have not been fulfilled. Reception areas have also experienced their share of problems. On the one hand, urban destinations of internal migrants in the less developed parts of Europe and especially North Africa have frequently failed to provide the necessary jobs and housing required by an increasingly mobile and demanding population. On the other hand, in the more developed countries international labour migration has not proved to be a short-term expedient and host countries have incurred unexpected social and economic costs. The presence of foreign workers has compounded problems such as inadequate housing and social services that are already experienced by internal migrants.

Third, Europe's post-war migration patterns have been extremely dynamic. This is in response to political, economic, and social situations that have been anything but static. Within the continent there is still a wealth of diversity in patterns of living. However, few would deny that, on the whole, there is now greater parity in levels of economic development than existed in the late 1940s. As Europe has become more urbanized there has been a tendency for greater uniformity in human environments. Of course, drawing the Iron Curtain has produced two different approaches to social organization, but in East and West alike a crucial political tendency has been towards greater co-operation and integration between countries. This has paralleled a reduction of area differentials in levels of living. Increasingly, and as the continent becomes more urbanized, European migration should be thought of as a series of exchanges of population between similar types of area rather as one-way flows. This is particularly true of inter-regional movements since most migrants in the industrialized societies of north-west Europe, at least, now move between urban regions. It is only in the poorer and more remote areas that the traditional type of rural—urban migration, emphasizing spatial differentials in explaining migrant motivations, now predominates. Indeed, it is apparent that what now passes as movement from country to town in Western Europe frequently involves people who are already engaged in dispersed forms of urban life before they leave 'the countryside'. A further blurring of the rural—urban distinction in migration results from the development of strong flows back to 'the countryside' of long-distance urban commuters, second homers, and people retiring either by virtue of their age or in search of the peace and quiet that city life fails to provide.

It is on this changing pattern of internal movement that international labour migration has been superimposed. In many respects, however, this is a spatial extension of rural—urban movement, often via an urban 'stepping stone' in the country of emigration. It developed in response to strikingly different manpower conditions in demand and supply countries and has modified its form as time has passed. It is particularly prone to trade fluctuations, and economic events have produced quite violent changes in flows. For example, the recession of 1967—8 brought a sudden reduction in movement, while the 'crisis' of 1974—5 threatens even more profound consequences for foreign workers. In short, the changing geography of all long-distance migration in post-war Europe reflects the march of improved standards of living across the continent. In north-west Europe movement between urban areas has ousted rural—urban flow as the dominant type of migration, just as in the nineteenth and early twentieth centuries rural—urban movement overtook flows between rural areas. By contrast, in less developed eastern and southern Europe rural—urban flows of population are still important. In this respect the European continent and its southern neighbours exhibit the characteristics of Zelinsky's (1971) 'mobility transition' in which parallel stages in the processes of economic development and of human migration may be identified.

Finally, it should be stressed that most migration in Europe is spontaneous in character. This is especially true of internal flows. Few governments wish or attempt to channel or otherwise control the movements of their own citizens in their own country. Even where strong policies for regional development have been adopted, as in the United Kingdom, comparatively little has been done to stimulate or to direct population movement. As a result, migration remains related to regional policies in only an indirect way. Such policies have tended to react to migration rather than to initiate or suppress it. As far as international movements are concerned, Eastern and Western Europe must be treated separately. Movement between states to the east of the Iron Curtain is allowed only in certain cases and migration between East and West is very strictly controlled. Only Yugoslavia, of all the Communist countries, has allowed relatively free access for its citizens to Western Europe. In the West frontier policies have been much less restrictive and movement between states has been easier. Governments in neither departure nor reception countries have been very concerned with defining which areas should supply migrants and which should receive them. Thus, with respect to international as well as internal migrants, policies have not been developed to channel migrants either from particular origins or to specific destinations in accordance with regional strategies and other planning objectives. In making this point we are not suggesting that it is desirable to restrict the movement of migrants in their choice of where to live. However, we would stress that the spontaneity of movement and its continuing evolution emphasize the need to monitor carefully European migration behaviour in the final quarter of the twentieth century.

References

Zelinsky, W. (1971) 'The hypothesis of the mobility transition', *Geographical Review*, 61, 219–49.

POSTSCRIPT

As the ramifications of the oil crisis of Autumn 1973 unfolded, it became obvious that in the new recessionary conditions the industrial countries of north-west Europe would modify their demands for immigrant labour. As a consequence, during late 1973 and 1974 various steps were taken to stem immigration from the south. The degree of restriction that was imposed varied from country to country. Luxembourg alone took no special restrictive measures. In contrast, West Germany imposed a ban on recruitment in November 1973, France in July 1974, and Belgium in August 1974. Other measures were also taken. In April 1975 West Germany decided to try to limit the size of the migrant labour concentration in any area to 12 per cent of that area's total labour force. France adopted a policy of no longer allowing illegal immigrants to regularize their positions; those caught by the authorities would be deported. Other countries tightened up their existing legislation; the Swiss government resolved in August 1974 to stabilize its immigrant population numbers by the end of the decade; the Netherlands, from 1974, has interpreted its immigration rules more strictly; in Denmark the general ban on immigration of 1970 had been eased in the summer of 1973 but was re-imposed the following November.

These measures had the effect of severely curtailing new entries, although immigration did not cease. Yugoslavia's State Employment Office estimated that demand from north-west Europe for workers fell by 90 per cent between 1973 and 1974, with an average of 650 job placements abroad per month during 1974 compared with 7,000 in 1973. In France, numbers of newly-entering foreign workers in 1974 were only half the total for 1973 but 53,000 still arrived. For some types of labour, notably highly skilled and professional workers, demand remained buoyant.

While new entry was curbed in the months following the oil crisis there has been little evidence of a vast tide of migrants moving home, although lack of hard statistical evidence makes accurate quantification impossible. Certainly, numbers returning have been nearer a trickle than a flood. One estimate for 1974 was a fall of about 120,000 foreign workers living in West Germany, while another, after 18 months of recession, suggested that numbers were down by only 300,000 from the 1973 peak of 2,500,000. There is no reason to think that declines of a similar order had not taken place in other countries.

By no means all of the migrant workers who remained in host countries stayed in employment. By the end of May 1975 the West German Federal Labour Office reported that numbers of unemployed aliens had risen at twice the rate for indigenous workers. Between the summer of 1974 and that of 1975 the number of unemployed Frenchmen went up by 88 per cent but the rise for foreign workers was 167 per cent. By autumn 1975 one in ten of France's 1,000,000 unemployed were aliens.

The main reason why so many unemployed foreign workers have not returned home has been their entitlement to unemployment benefit, which has made many of them financially better-off than they would have been by returning to uncertain job prospects at home. In these circumstances some countries have resorted to 'golden handshakes' to encourage foreign workers to go home. France has recently been preparing a scheme to give a lump sum of several months' unemployment pay to unemployed migrant workers who were prepared to pack up and go home, with a target of 15,000 assisted repatriations during 1976. In autumn 1975 a Bill was presented to the West German Parliament for a similar scheme following a pilot operation in parts of Baden-Württemberg during 1975.

While the downturn in demand has drastically curtailed numbers of newly-entering foreign workers, immigration of family members seems to have remained at a higher level. For example, although numbers of immigrant workers coming to France in 1974 were half those in 1973, the numbers of family members arriving hardly changed. Similarly, in West Germany during 1974, total numbers of aliens (including family members) continued to increase although the foreign workforce was falling. In part this situation appears related to fears among migrants that if they left the host country they might not be allowed back in. A natural reaction was thus to view the migration as more permanent, with the family being brought in to make it so. In West Germany this reaction has been complemented by new regulations affecting child allowances. Until January 1975 allowances were paid regardless of whether the children concerned were with parents in West Germany or back home in Turkey, Yugoslavia or elsewhere. The new higher allowances are paid in full only in respect of children actually resident in West Germany; hence many workers have brought their children into the country.

For countries of emigration, the problems associated with cut-backs in recruitment have been concerned more with damming-up of labour in over-populated areas, with consequent rises in unemployment and under-employment, than with the need to resettle in homes and jobs large numbers of returning migrants. In some cases foreign migration streams have been diverted to internal destinations. In Yugoslavia, for example, many migrants from the poor areas of the south have travelled north to Slovenia where about 25 per cent of the labour force is now composed of internal migrants. These southern migrants have often taken the poorest jobs, such as sweeping streets and emptying dustbins, where labour shortages have occurred in recent years owing to Slovenian migration to other countries.

Other problems for supply countries have been financial. With fewer migrants abroad, and with more unemployment and less overtime being worked in the industrial countries, receipts from remittances have fallen. For example, in 1973 remittances ranged from 12 per cent of Italy's trade deficit to 150 per cent of that of Turkey, but in 1974 the figures were 8 per cent and 68 per cent respectively. If these reductions last for long, and particularly if migrants start returning in greater numbers, then the economies of the supply countries will suffer long-term damage to their investment programmes.

The recession since 1974 has undoubtedly had a dramatic effect on the pattern of labour migration but it does seem that during 1974 and 1975 the worst fears—of wholesale returns home—have not been borne out. Indeed, it may yet be shown that during the recession fewer migrants than usual have returned, the rest preferring to sit tight and wait for things to improve. Falls in total migrant numbers have probably occurred mainly because of cuts in numbers of new entrants. North-west Europe's economies have become too dependent on immigrant workers for their release from employment and subsequent re-patriation to be a reasonable proposition except in a much longer and deeper recession than the present one is expected to be. Perhaps the most significant feature emerging from the last two years has been the tightening-up of entry-requirement procedures by the host countries. The 1960s and early 1970s witnessed something of a free-for-all in the immigration of non-EEC nationals. Even before the recession, concern about social tensions and inadequate infrastructures for immigrant communities indicated that the host countries could not long maintain their *laissez-faire* migration policies. When the barriers against recruitment are again lifted it is likely that some at least of the restrictions on entry will be maintained.

February 1976

INDEX